TRENDS IN LIBRARY AND INFORMATION SCIENCE

TRENDS IN LIBRARY
and
INFORMATION SCIENCE

(Essays in Honour of Professor G.D. Bhargava)

Editors
SURENDRA SINGH
SONAL SINGH

GYAN

GYAN PUBLISHING HOUSE
New Delhi-110002

TRENDS IN LIBRARY AND INFORMATION SCIENCE
[*Library and Information Science, Education, Library Management*]

ISBN: 81-212-0676-6

Published in 2000 in India by
Gyan Publishing House
5, Ansari Road
New Delhi 110 002

Laser Typeset at Alphabet, Delhi
Printed at Mehra Offset Press, New Delhi.

In Honour of

Professor G.D. Bhargava

Contents

Foreword

I am really glad to write this Foreward to the book *Trends in Library & Information Science* being brought out as a Festschrift volume in honour of Dr G.D. Bhargava, retired Professor and former Head, Department of Library and Information Science. Vikram University, Ujjain. The very fact that a group of dedicated library professionals have decided to honour him by publishing this volume, clearly reflects the high esteem in which Dr Bhargava is held by his colleagues in the country. I have myself personally known Dr Bhargava for almost three decades and have always admired him as a friend, a teacher and a great human being.

Information, whether in the form of empirical data, or, in the developed form called knowledge is rightly being regarded today as a vital national resource, as essential to the nation's well-being and security as any natural resource, such as water, and minerals. Beyond the boundaries of a country, it provides an important basis for international relations, peace, prosperity and overall development of the world. The wealth of popular, intellectual, scholarly and research resources, in libraries, information centres and information systems of a country is therefore one of the greatest strengths of that nation. This information resource is infinite and evergrowing. But like several natural resources, information or knowledge resources if unsupported and uncoordinated in growth and usage, would certainly be in danger of being wasted and inefficiently utilized.

Historically speaking, a substantial part of the human culture has been handed down to generations in the form of recorded knowledge. This resource consists of documents such as clay tablets, books, journals and other categories of texts: of audio and visual materials; and, of other units of information or data that can be processed and organized by a computer. In recent years, these records have become increasingly varied, through technological extensions of written words, pictures and sounds. For example, a significant part of a country's information resource is today on films, magnetic tapes, videocassettes, CD-ROMs and in computer files. As the nation's knowledge grows and the number of these records increases, our dependence upon them also increases proportionately and the need to gain access to them becomes more essential and even crucial. It has been rightly said that, "no society can advance beyond a certain point without effective access to its collective memory of records, or, conversely, an advanced society that loses control of the record will regress".

Libraries, information systems, and other information facilities are thus the custodians of this part of our cultural heritage which is recorded. They must be adequately equipped, organized, financed and interconnected if their resources are to be made available to all the people in every country. This can be possible only with the active support of the governments, related public and private agencies and institutions.

It hardly needs to be emphasised here that, ready access to this information and knowledge is indispensable to individuals advancement as well as to national growth. The right information provided, when it is needed, where it is needed and in the form in which it is needed; improves the ability of an individual, a business, a government agency, or various other organisations to take informed decisions and achieve targeted goals. Undoubtedly, library and information needs are felt at all levels of society, regardless of an individual's location, social condition, or level of intellectual achievement. While library and information needs are usually not the same in all parts of the country, and they generally vary widely among people by age, sex, religion, physical handicap (if any), educational achievement, work assignment, and several other factors; most people certainly have dependence on the availability of accurate and useful information.

This nation's future capability to handle information effectively and efficiently, depends to a great extent on how well and how rapidly we are able to integrate new information technological methods and devices into the mainstream of our library and information systems and services. In today's world among the several developments in IT, the ones which are directly affecting library and information services, mention may be made of: computers, reprographics, micrographics and developments in storage media; telecommunications which have made it possible to have connectivity and networking, and, audiovisual media. The use of computers and other gadgets of IT has now greatly changed the face of library & information systems and services in the country. They are being actively used in many libraries and information centres not only for housekeeping functions but also for recording, analysing and retrieving of information, and also for their networking. The use of reprographics, micrographics and other media of information storage has been increasing at a fast speed. Documents on media such as magnetic tapes, microforms and CD-ROMs have changed the whole complexion of publishing world, libraries and information services. These developments undoubtedly offer considerable potential for space and cost savings and represent a new era in information transfer. Libraries and information centres these days are quite active in acquiring audio-visual materials such as films, audio-cassettes, video-cassettes and video tapes which are being found to be useful in their services. Development in telecommunications have now brought the world within the format of an information village and these provide immense potentials for services to be provided by the libraries and information centres within the country and the world at large. Frankly speaking, establishment of the National Information Infrastructure (NII) and Global Information Infrastructure (GII) has become a necessity for the development of this country and the world as a whole.

Because of these developments and needs, the present day society has rightly been given different names such as 'information society', 'information age', 'knowledge society', and even 'post industrial society'. Such a society can be defined as one in which the quality of life as well as prospects for social change and economic development depend increasingly on information and its positive exploitation. In such a society, living standards, pattern of work and leisure, the educational system, R&D activities, and market places are all influenced markedly by advances in information and knowledge. This is evidenced today by an increasing array of information intensive products and services, produced and communicated through a wide range of media, many of them electronic in nature.

In such a society the information and library professional is expected to function as an intermediary between information sources, information systems and information seekers. This role has been gaining prominence since the 1970s primarily because of the application of information technology in library and information services. Developments such as On-line Public Access Catalogue (OPAC), access to databases, whether online or through a network on CD-ROMs, access to information through global networks such as Internet and ERNet, use of A.V. media, and several others, emphasise the need for a different breed of information professionals with the required background, motivation and expertise. Library & Information schools would certainly have to play a vital role in this vastly changing information world by educating the future L & IS professionals with proper perspective and understanding.

In view of the vast interests of Dr Bhargava in this profession, this volume has rightly included contributions dealing with different facets of library and information services and systems. I am quite certain that these would be found useful by library practitioners, teachers and others interested in this field.

August, 1999

Prof. P.B. Mangla
Ex Head. Dept. of
Library & Information Science;
Dean, Faculty of Arts,
University of Delhi;
Former President,
Inddian Library Association &
Vice President, IFLA.

Preface

Professor Gopal Das Bhargava - an excellent and impressive teacher, an accomplished author, a research guide and an able administrator all rolled into one, is an affectionate and a lovable personality. He is a renowned figure in the field of Library and Information Science, who has always earned appreciation and good comments for his efficiency, potentiality, punctuality and straight forwardness. He is a brilliant, energetic, enthusiastic and mobile person who possesses an intellectual personality.

We happen to know him personally and closely right from our student life. On many occasions, social gatherings and professional meetings from time to time, we observed that Prof. Bhargava has some rare good qualities, sense of humour, excellent nature, infectious enthusiasm, dynamic and manifested personality and capability of testing the candidates very sharply and promptly. It is not only a matter of great pleasure but, infact, it has greatly honoured us to bring out Festschrift volume in honour of Prof. G.D. Bhargava.

With high respect and regards we dedicate this volume to Prof. Gopal Das Bhargava on completion of his seventy three years of age and wish him a long, happy, healthy and prosperous life.

The present volume is a collection of Thirty One essays. The authors represent a cross-section of India. Although the articles vary in scope and nature but the unifying theme is Library and Information Science. The material gives a wide coverage ranging from the magnetic personality of Prof. G.D. Bhargava to the field of Library and Information Science Education; Library Management; Resource Sharing; Academic, Public and Apecial Libraries; Classification; Net-working, Research in Library and Information Science, Computerisation and Marketing of Library and Information Science Services.

Dr Surendra Singh
Dr Sonal Singh

Preface

Contributors

1. B. Bhagwati Sudha
   No.12, 'D' Block
   Government Staff Quarters
   Shenoy Nagar,
   Chennai - 600032
2. Bardol A.K. (Dr.)
   Professor & Chairman
   Department of Library and Information Science
   Mangalore University,
   Mangalagangotri -
   Dharwad, Karnataka - 574 199
3. Chand, B.B.
   Department of Library & Information Science
   Sambalpur University,
   Jyotivihar
   (Orissa) - 768019
4. Chaudhry B.K. (Dr.)
   Department of Library & Information Science
   Sambalpur University,
   Jyotivihar
   (Orissa) - 768019
5. Chopra, H.R. (Dr.)
   Reader,
   Department of Library & Information Science
   Punjab University,
   Chandigarh - 160014
6. Chopra Y.L.
   University Librarian
   Rani Durgavati University,
   Jabalpur. (M.P.)

7. Desh Bandhu
Asst. Librarian
University of Jammu,
Jammu (J&K)

8. Dabas, K.C.
Assistant Librarian
M.D. University Library
Rohtak, (Haryana) - 124001

9. Dilly K.T.
Librarian
Loyala College
Chennai
(TN) - 600034

10. Gautam, J.N. (Dr.)
Reader & Head
School of Studies in Library and Information Science
Jiwari University
Gwalior (M.P.)

11. Hiremath, C.V.
Librarian
U.T.I. Institute of Capital Markets,
Plot No. 82, Sector 17, Vashi,
Navi Mumbai (Maharashtra) - 400703

12. Ijari, S.R. (Dr.)
Professor & Chairman
Department of Library and Information Science
Karnataka University,
Dharwad (Karnataka)

13. Karisiddappa, C.R. (Dr.)
Professor
Department of Library and Information Science
Karnatak University
Dharwad (Karnataka) - 580003

14. Lattoo, A.R.
Iqbal Library,
The University of Kashmir,
Srinagar (J&K) - 190006

15. Mukherjee, Bhaskar
Assistant Librarian
Rani Durgavati University,
Jabalpur (M.P.)

16. Pai, Rekha, D.
Assistant Librarian
Manipal Institute of Technology,
Manipal - 576 119

17. Raina Roshan
Librarian
Indian Institute of Management,
Lucknow,
(U.P.) - 226013

18. Rajya Lakshmi, D.
Information Officer
Distributed Information Sub-Centre
Neeri, Nagpur
(Maharashtra)

19. Reddy, J. Yadagiri (Dr.)
Reader and Head
Department of Library and Information Science
Osmania University,
Hyderabad
(AP) - 500007

20. Sahni, Neera (Mrs.) (Dr.)
Librarian
Dev Samaj College of Education
Sector 36-B, Chandigarh (Punjab)

21. Sethi, A.R.
University Librarian
Punjab University,
Chandigarh, (Punjab)

22. Sewa Singh (Dr.)
Department of Library & Information Science
Guru Nanak Dev University,
Amritsar
(Punjab) - 143 005

23. Shukla B.B. (Dr.)
Reader and Head,
Department of Library & Information Science
and Editor,
Indian Journal of Information, Library and Society,
Professorpara
Cuttack (Orissa) - 753 003

24. Singh, Mahaveer (Dr.)
DOC Assistant
National Social Science Documentation Centre
ICSSR,
New Delhi

25. Singh, Sonal (Dr.)
Lecturer & Head
School of Studies in Library and Information Science
Vikram University,
Ujjain (M.P.) - 456010

26. Singh, Surendra (Dr.)
Librarian & Head
Department of Library and Information Science
Sandipani P.G. College
Ujjain (M.P.) - 456010

27. Sood, Sudesh Kumar
Librarian
State Central Library,
Solan (H.P.) - 173212

28. Upadhyaya, Padma V. (Mrs.)
Addl. Librarian
M.I.T.
Manipal

29. Venugopal, S.
Bharathidasan University Library,
Tiruchirapalli (Tamil Nadu) - 620024

30. Vijay Kumar, M.
Library,
National Aerospace Laboratory,
P.B. No. 1779
Bangalore (Karnataka) - 560017

31. Zabeen Ahmed
Deputy Librarian
Cotton College,
Guwahati (Assam) - 781001

One

Felicitations to Prof. G.D. Bhargava

1.1 Professor G.D. Bhargava: A Biographical Analysis

DR SURENDRA SINGH

Introduction

Professor G.D.Bhargava is a renowned personality in the field of Library and Information Science. He is an excellent professional and a dedicated and sincere teacher in the field. An embodiment of simplicity, honesty and deep scholarship, he has endeared himself to the academics, students and Library and Information Science professionals. Throughout his entire career, he has maintained high professional standards based on ethical values. He is a simple man, an early riser, with controlled eating habits and regular time table. Even after his formal retirement, he has close associations with the library professionals owing to his several qualities of head and heart. It is really gratifying and a matter of pride and honour to write in honour of Professor Bhargava.

Family Background

Being the eldest of all the brothers and sisters, Shri Gopal Das Bhargava had an ability to bring all of them together and to take firm and desired decisions, agreeable to all.

On December 13, 1946, he was married to Prabha. His family life is moving very happily and smoothly. He has an ability to face every tension boldly without exposing it to other family members. Mrs Prabha Bhargava is purely a housewife, devoted to domestic affairs. She has been a source of inspiration and never interfered in the professional life of Professor Bhargava. She is a dutiful, alert and affectionate mother and always cares for her family. The Bhargava couple is blessed with four daughters (all happily married) and two sons, and four grand children.

Education

Professor Bhargava is an aluminus of Agra, Rajasthan and Vikram Universities. He had his early education, graduation as well as postgraduation from Kota.

After completing postgraduation in political science he became lecturer of Political Science. After teaching political science for seven years, his life slanted towards the field of Library Science and he did his Dip. Lib. Sc. in first division from Vikram University, Ujjain in 1958-59. He was the most loving student of Dr S.R. Ranganathan. He also did his M.Lib. Sc. from Vikram University, Ujjain in 1976.

Positions Held

He served as lecturer in political science from 1952-57. Then he was appointed as the first full time lecturer in Madhya Pradesh in the Department of Library Science, Vikram University, Ujjain. In 1967, he became the first full time Professor of Library Science in Madhya Pradesh and served as head of the Department till his retirement, (1967-1987). After his formal retirement, he was appointed as UGC visiting Professor at S.P. University, Vallabh Vidyanagar, and served there for two years (1987-1989). He served as Professor of Library Science at Makhanlal Chaturvedi National University, Bhopal for two years (1993-1995). Presently he is working as Honorary Director, Department of Library Science, Sandipani Post Graduate College, (Vikram University), Ujjain.

Research Guidance

Professor Bhargava is a registered guide for Ph.D. in Library Science from Vikram University, Ujjain; Jiwaji University, Gwalior and Kota Open University, Kota. Scholars who have obtained Ph.D. degrees in Library and Information Science under his valuable supervision are (1) S.M. Charan, 'Library Legislation in MP & Gujarat' from S.P. University, Vallabh Vidyanagar (2) V.K.

Thomas, 'Financing of Public Libraries of India' from Bhagalpur University, Bhagalpur and (3) Subhash Jain, 'Library Services in Defence Establishments of Madhya Pradesh' from Vikram University, Ujjain.

Presently six research scholars are working for Ph.D. degree under his guidance in various universities.

Visits Abroad

Professor Bhargava was a lone recipient of UNESCO Fellowship from India for UNESCO Seminar for Teachers of Librarianship held at Copenhagen (Denmark) from August 1 to December 30, 1968. He toured UK, France, West Germany, Holland, Denmark, Sweden, Norway and Finland and studied Library Services of these countries. He also delivered lectures in the Library Schools of London and Copenhagen.

Professional Writings

Professor Bhargava has authored two, co-authored three and edited two books. In addition to the field of Library and Information Science, he has also contributed one book, in the field of Political Science. His publications are as under:

1. *Adhunic Rajnitik Samvidhan* (Political Sc.) in collaboration with H.E. Gurmukh Nihal Singh: (Mcmillan & Co. Ltd., Bombay. 1957.)
2. *Colon Classification* (Theory & Practice): Bhargava, GD and Sood, SP, 1972.
3. *Granthalaya Vargikaran*
   (M.P. Hindi Granth Academy, Bhopal, 1972)
4. *Librarianship in India and Abroad*
   (Metropolitan Book Co. Ltd., Delhi. 1977)
5. *Granthalaya Vargikaran Ki Bhumika*
   (M.P. Hindi Granth Academy, Bhopal, 1984)
6. *Dimensions in Library & Information Science* - 1986.
7. *Granthalaya Vargikaran & Suchikaran ke-Siddhanta*: Bhargava, GD and Sood, SP (RBSA, Jaipur, 1989)

Besides writing books, he has more than sixty research papers and radio talks to his credit. He has equal fluency both in hindi and english. His book *Granthalaya Vargikaran* is most widely used by Library Science students of different universities in Hindi Speaking States of India.

Honours

Professor Bhargava is widely known in the field for his hyperactive nature, excellent teaching and intellectual thinking. He has been honoured by different associations for his valuable contributions in the field of Library and Information Science. He was honoured with a scroll, shawl and cash award for his Hindi Book *Granthalaya Vargikaran* by Madhya Pradesh Hindi Granth Academy, Bhopal, 1985. He was also presented with citation and scroll for distinguished services in the field of Library Education by ILA, IASLIC and IATLIS in 1987. He also received ILA Felicitation with citation, momento and shawl at 40th ILA Conference held at Goa, 1995. Recently he was honoured by a momento, citation, and shawl at the Sixth Convention of Medical Libraries Association of India (MLAI) - Lucknow in November 1997.

Professional Activities

Professor Bhargava's outstanding contribution in the field of Library and Information Science is very well known. He is a life member of ILA, IATLIS and IASLIC. He served as Vice-President of ILA (1984-86) (1992-1994) and EC Member; ILA (1994-1996). He was President of Madhya Pradesh Library Association (1976-86). He is an active participant in professional seminars and other deliberations.

Retired Life

After his formal retirement, Professor Bhargava is leading a healthy and happy life. He has settled at Ujjain, at Ram Bhawan, C-8/2, Rishi Nagar, Ujjain - 456010. (Res. Tel: [0734] 510019).

He is simplest of all, greatest of all and youngest of all. May the God Almighty grant him a long and healthy life to serve the profession for many years to come.

1.2 Professor G.D. Bhargava: An Untiring Personality

DR SONAL SINGH

Prologue

Professor Bhargava has been a person of national fame, born to enlighten the field of Library Science with his distinguished activities, qualitative teaching, impressive and lucid lectures, valuable guidance and esteemed publications. I feel greatly honoured that he was my teacher and still he directs me at the right path in my professional journey. His untiring personality, infectious enthusiasm, ability to work efficiently, authoritative voice, clearcut instructions and specifications, loving, affectionate and bold behaviour, have been impressing me all these years to follow his path and enrich the field of library and information science.

Childhood

Professor Gopal Das Bhargava was born on 18th January 1926 at Kota. He was the eldest and most brilliant son of his father. During his childhood he was keenly interested in arranging his things, toys, books, etc., in a systematic manner. He was studious, active and laborious child of his times.

Education and Inclination Towards Library Science

After completing school education from Kota, he did B.A. from Herbert College, Kota. Young Gopal Das was a self confident, brilliant and most sincere student of his time. He completed his

Postgraduation in Political Science and joined Government College, Kota (Rajasthan), as Lecturer in Political Science in July 1952. In November 1995, he was transferred to Government College, Sri Ganganagar (Rajasthan). As was the practice in those days, he was nominated Professor-in-Charge, College Library, by the Principal. It was during this assignment, while taking stock of the reading material available in the library he laid his hands on a book on Library Science - *Five Laws of Library Science* - lying unused since its acquisition in the year 1951. He read this book and got himself acquainted with the basic concepts of libraries and its three constituent elements i.e. reading material, readers and library staff. Having gone through this book he realised that library service is perhaps the most impersonal service. It is actually humanism in practice. It is a service rendered with devotion, irrespective of cast, creed, sex or religion. Library is a social service institution, the doors of which are open to all without taking into consideration, the status of the people. The philosophy of library profession discussed in this monumental book illuminated him and consequently he could develop a feeling that library profession was something worth adopting. Until this time he was unaware of any institution providing formal library science training course. But, the Lord Almighty lead Shri Gopal Das Bhargava to the field of Library Science in the most mysterious way. In October 1957, Sardar Gurmukh Nihal Singh, the then Governor of Rajasthan, planned an official visit to Shri Ganganagar. Professor Bhargava had known Sardar Sahib since 1953, as he prepared a book written in his collaboration *Adhunik Rajnitik Samvidhan*, published by M/s Macmillan & Co. Ltd., Bombay, in July 1957. He sought an interview with Sardar Sahib during his visit to Sri Ganganagar and expressed his desire to take up the Library Science training. Sardar Gurumukh Nihal Singh reviewed the pros and cons of Shri Bhargava's present assignment. After a detailed discussion he was pleased to approve his proposal especially in the context that the professional training might be instrumental in providing Bhargava, a permanent assignment in the discipline of Library Science at some university and he would also be spared from being shunted as lecturer from one college to another throughout Rajasthan.

Incidentally, Shri Bhargava could secure information from

his relations at Ujjain - Shri S.P. Bhargava (Senior Advocate and Legal Advisor to the newly established Vikram University), that Vikram University had started Diploma in Library Science course from July 1957 with S.R. Ranganathan as a visiting Professor of Library Science.

Sardar Gurumukh Nihal Singh (the then governor of Rajasthan) was the ardent admirer of S.R. Ranganathan and had personally known him since 1949. Shri Bhargava informed Sardar Sahib about Ranganathan's association with Vikram University for arranging Library Science programme. Sardar Sahib immediately permitted Shri Bhargava to go ahead. Ultimately Shri Bhargava applied for admission to the course in July 1958. Having secured admission, he joined Library Science course at Ujjain on 5th August 1958. Finally he was on the right track towards giving a concrete shape to his deep intention and great desire. He worked hard and secured First division in Dip. Lib. Sc. in 1959. He was selected as a lecturer in the Department of Library Science, started by U.G.C. in July 1959. It was indeed a great achievement for G.D. Bhargava to join Library Science to materialize his dreams. Incidentally it was an achievement for the field of Library Science as well to have such a great personality in its fold. Shri Bhargava was appointed as first full time Professor in Library Science and served as Head of the Department of Library Science, Vikram University, Ujjain for nearly two decades (1969-1986).

Teacher-Taught Relation

As a student of Library Science Course (1979-1981) at Vikram University, Ujjain. I had an opportunity of closely watching him as a teacher and his teacher-taught relations. His ability to explain even the complex concept of library classification in the most explanatory manner is highly appreciable. An embodiment of simplicity, discipline, clear thinking, intellectual honesty and deep scholarship, Professor Bhargava has endeared himself to the academics, students and Library and Information Science Professionals. A stickler to principles, Professor Bhargava has strived, throughout his entire career to maintain high professional standards based on ethical values. He is a first rate guide, Guru, teacher and philosopher who dedicated his life for the upliftment of library profession and for the spread of library movement in India, and particularly in the State of Madhya Pradesh. He has a strong faith in academic pursuits and he continues enlighting the future generations of library professionals even after retirement. He is retired but not tired. By his work efficiency he is the youngest library professional. Even after formal retirement, he is rendering distinguished services to the cause of Library and Information Science education in particular and Library and Information Science profession in general in various capacities during the last three decades.

Contribution to Library Science

Professor Bhargava's contribution to Library and Information Science literature has been prolific. He has authored seven books (three after retirement). He has also contributed sixty research papers to various national and international professional journals both in Hindi and English. He has guided about half a dozen candidates for the Ph. D. Degree in Library Science, especially during the post superannuation period.

Professor Bhargava is a life member of ILA, ITALIS and IASLIC. He served as Vice-President, ILA (1984-86) (1992-1994) and EC Member, ILA (1994-96). He was President of M.P. Library Association (1976-86). He was presented with a citation and scroll for distinguished services in the field of Library Education by ILA, IASLIC and IATLIS-1987. He received ILA Felicitation with citation, memento and shawl at ILA Conference held at Goa in 1995. He was honoured with a scroll, shawl and cash award for the highest sale of Hindi Book (*Granthalaya Vargikaran*) by Madhya Pradesh Hindi Granth Academy, Bhopal in 1985.

Message to Library and Information Science Professionals

Library Science being a service oriented discipline, it is imperative on the part of the library professionals to inculcate the habit of sincerity, integrity and devotion to the profession in providing the desired and effective Library services to the readers. India, today, has the unique distinction of imparting teaching in Library Science and providing library services to the enlightened citizens. To maintain and invigorate this distinction, there is need for the library professionals, especially the young entrants to the profession, to work with indefatigable energy, tremendous power of concentration and sustained enthusiasm.

I am confident that the professionals will not leave any stone unturned to maintain and enhance the reputation of our mother-land in the field of library professions.

Professor G.D.Bhargava is a living legend of Library and Information Science. A glance at his multidimensional intellectual personality compels me to conclude that he is the personification of Library and Information Science itself. May the Lord Almighty shower his blessings upon all of us in the field of Library and Information Science and grant a very very long and healthy life to Professor G.D.Bhargava so that his untiring personality, keeps on guiding us on the right path for ever.

1.3 Professor G.D. Bhargava: Three Decades of My Association

Y.L. CHOPRA

It was winter of December 1964 when I left my hometown, Delhi, by rail to Ujjain to join Department of Library & Information Science, Vikram University, Ujjain for training in Certificate in Library and Information Science. Even today it looks as if it was just yesterday when I was there. Later I also did my B.Lib. Sc. and M.Lib. Sc. and M.A. from Vikram University, Ujjain. In 1964 for the first time I was introduced to the discipline of Library Science and Prof. G.D. Bhargava. There were other good teachers on the staff too, but there was something distinct and special about Prof. Bhargava which attracted every student of the Department towards him. It was his lively approach towards the subject which made lectures easy to follow and thus pursue the discipline, completely new to the students.

It was his eagerness to help, lively nature and ability to mix with students which made him a tall figure among the teachers of Library and Information Science. Prof. Bhargava has been instrumental in moulding many young people in the discipline of Library Science. I feel, grateful to him since I am also one of them.

Prof. G.D. Bhargava has been the seniormost Information Scientist being the first full time lecturer and Professor of Library Science in Madhya Pradesh. He has edited and authored number of books and contributed a large number of papers which have been published in various journals. His contributions in teaching of Library Science and his efforts to shape the Library Movement in Madhya Pradesh has been acknowledged by all. He has to his credit building the Department of Library and Information Science, Vikram University, Ujjain and making it compatable to any other department in India. He has also visited many foreign countries as a lone recipient of UNESCO Fellowship from India during the year 1968.

Prof. Bhargava has been President of Library Association of Madhya Pradesh and Vice-President Indian Library Association, having held both these offices with distinction and making significant contribution to the cause of Librarianship in India.

There is hardly any committee constituted by MP Govt. and Universities for professional matters with which Prof. Bhargava is not associated. He has been member of large number of Selection Committees for the various levels of Library Science faculty members and Librarians in the country and specially in Madhya Pradesh. He has, in a way, helped number of young people in holding responsible positions in libraries and Departments of Library Science. It is his clarity of thoughts and openness in approach which has made his position tall in the profession.

Prof. Bhargava has always shown deep regards for his senior professionals and love for the juniors. That is why he has always been treated with very high regards by his students and juniors. It will not be out of place to mention here that if Prof. S.R. Ranganathan was father of Library Science in India then Prof. Bhargava is truly the Father of Library Science in Madhya Pradesh.

I wish Prof. Bhargava a happy, healthy and long prosperous life.

1.4 My Guru Prof. Bhargava: A Living Legend

DESH BANDHU

Every body's life is full of events and eventualities, chained together by boredom. It seems to me, that boredom is forgotten and some events and eventualities always remain in memory. Some of these occurrences seem trivial to other people, but to me they are unforgettable and inalien part of my life.

I am not going to comprehend all the memories that are in my faculty of remembering. I am only trying to recall some of them that involve some personalities who have influenced my life most.

It is more than two decades ago, I was undergoing my B.Lib. Sc. degree from Kashmir University, Srinagar, and residing in the University Boys Hostel and was an alien there. I met Bashir Ahmed Nengroo, a local from the valley. He was a law student and I was also doing my professional degree B.Lib. Sc. We were room-mates. Our acquaintance soon ripened into a friendship. He is now the Minister of State for Transport in Jammu and Kashmir State. I am presently, Assistant librarian in the University of Jammu. But our friendship continues to be alive. Recalling the past, I nostalgically remember all the happenings that played a significant role in making me what I am today. Nengroo was interested in my professional growth and desired that I may complete my M.Lib. Sc. I promised him that I will. Later, I fulfilled his desire at Ujjain.

Before I left Srinagar to rejoin my duty at the University of Jammu on 17th of December, 1977, I called on Prof Noor-ul- Hassan Khan the then HOD of Library Science Department, Kashmir

University, at his residence. He was sprawling over a small chair in his flat exactly as he had sprawled in his office chair in his chamber in the Department of Library and Information Science. A spell of kindness and sympathy came from him, that was almost palpable. It was as though you could stretch your arm out and feel it from the air around him. He was very worried about my future. "Pandit ji", Prof. Khan addressed me in his usual way, "it is better if you do your M.Lib. Sc. soon after your B.Lib. Sc. without any gap". "Yes Sir," I replied and lost in my thoughts. "You know," he advised me, "it is in the nature of studies that if discontinued for some time, it has the tendency to remain incomplete." As there was no M.Lib. Sc. Course at Srinagar, I asked, "Where should I go for my M.Lib. Sc?" "Anywhere, wherever you can get admission. But it will be better if you join Vikram University, Ujjain. I have a friend there at Ujjain, Prof. Bhargava." The name struck my memory.

Back in Jammu, I thought of the promise I had made to Mr Nengroo and Prof. Khan's words rang inside my ears reminding me that "It is in the nature of studies that if discontinued for some time, it has the tendency to remain incomplete."

In May 1978, I applied for M.Lib. Sc. admission in three Universities i.e. Punjab University, Chandigarh; Rajasthan University, Jaipur and Vikram University, Ujjain. The first call letter came from Vikram University. I had to appear for the entrance test. I appeared in the test and qualified. Destiny had paved the way for my future.

I had to go to Ujjain. At Srinagar, I found a friend, a true friend and at Ujjain I met my 'Guru' - a traditional Guru. I met Prof. Bhargava for the first time when he came to Srinagar for conducting our B.Lib. Sc. practical test At that time I had no idea that one day I will enthrone him on the seat of my heart as a traditional Guru, but these relations are predestined.

In July 1978, I reached Ujjain to join my M.Lib. Sc. class. I had to deposit my admission fees and was worried also about my hostel accomodation. I went to see Prof. Bhargava, who was the Head of the Department. As I entered his room, I found him busy with his work. That afternoon the Sun was slanting through his window. He was physically well built, stout and heavy. We all encounter our Idols at some point in our life time. I had no idea that the time would come so soon. As he looked up, I told him pointblank : "Sir, I have to deposit my admission fees, but I am short of money. I am from J&K State and I do not know any one here." He smiled and said, "You need not know anyone. I am here to look after you." He put his hand in his pocket and pulled out a hundred rupee note. "Here is a hundred rupee note, go and deposit your fees." Prof. Bhargava has a generous nature. For him it was an ordinary thing, but for me it was a turning point. As I came out of his room an inward dance of elation possessed me. My feeling towards him was peculiar and I decided to make him my 'Guru'.

My hostel accommodation was more comfortable than any other student in the University. I was provided a room with a ceiling fan. Such rooms were allotted to research scholars only, but it was done on the instructions of Prof. Bhargava, who took personal interest in my comforts.

My visits to Prof. Bhargava became more frequent. After the usual class work, I often met Prof. Bhargava. A peculiar bond had developed between us, a bond of traditional Guru and disciple. This bond has grown very strong over all these years. Gurus, in general, rank as the first and most distinguished people of society. Prof. Bhargava is a master educator, erudite scholar and a fine teacher of Library Science. I was fortunate to have heard him for hours together. He is a great talker and ever ready to discuss anything related to Library Science. His approach to teach the students was simple and lucid. The students regarded him as one of the luminaries in the Library Science profession. He used to teach us Colon Classification.

Like the great S.R. Ranganathan, Prof. Bhargava is simple in his habits. He has a belief that each library professional should not live on the profession but for the profession. Those who understand him correctly feel that he is very kind and helpful. One can see it in his black eyes, which are deeply worried about his students/ scholars and hear it in the soft, academic inflections of his voice.

When Prof. Bhargava first came to our class, the students stood in awe of him. But he made us comfortable with his smile. And he started in a simple way his subject of Colon Classification-Theory and Practice through Postulational Approach. The lecture in Prof. Bhargava's class always turned into a healthy discussion. He liked very much the idea of student's participation in the discussion. He used to create an informal atmosphere in the classroom. The practical way of teaching by citing numerous examples, rich with his vast experience, made Prof. Bhargava quite popular as a teacher among the students.

Examination was not yet over and the next few days were an orgy of farewells. On the last day of examination I made a round of duty calls, saying goodbye. The one person I wanted to meet most was Prof. Bhargava. It had been a remarkable experience to have him as my teacher in Ujjain. He had taught me more about my profession than anyone else had ever taught me. He had given me much of his time and patience.

After the examination, the students were required to write a dissertation. This was a part of the examination. I was fresh in research techniques. I had no idea of how to begin and end. Prof. Bhargava made me understand the technical things regarding my dissertation in a lucid way. I prepared the Questionnaire. Prof. Bhargava checked each column of the questionnaire and instructed me to collect data from the place of my research i.e. Jammu. I collected the research material patiently. After collection and compilation, I proceeded to Ujjain with the rough draft for final approval. Prof. Bhargava thoroughly checked and approved the draft for final typing with his blessings.

The way Prof. Bhargava taught me the trends of research methodology and techniques of teaching has a great impact on me. A true Guru, respected teacher and authority on the subject can teach in only such a way. In his praise and honour I have this to say:

I want your love in abundance;
Look how simple is my desire!
For me, it is enough that
I get a glimpse of you.

Two

Library Science Education at Crossroads in India

DR. (Mrs.) D. RAJYALAKSHMI

Introduction

As library school programmes evolved in the first half of this century, the conflict emerged even more strongly when assorted definitions associated with distinction between Library and Information Science came into conjugation. Because of these amorphous conceptualizations, the programmes of the library school of 1980's contained in many instances, an unwieldy and often unsatisfactory combination of traditional library core, appropriate library science electives, computer science, philosophy of librarianship, assorted theories of management, psychology, communications, organizational behaviour, educational development, human and machine engineering, marketing sociology and many other disciplines presumably of value to the generalist graduate of one year library school.

The idea of teaching library techniques or economics and those subjects that were perceived as particularly important in the organization of libraries, notably catalouging and classification was matched with an equal emphasis on practical or field experience.

In 1970, Reed pointed out that pioneer educators have left their impression not only upon professional library education, but also upon librarianship in general and they have tried to give the training to students to enable them eventually to put the libraries into perfect working order.

The early curriculum requirements in American library schools are familiar from well-known Williamson reports and in the landmark publication (1986) on the *Curriculum in Library Schools* by Reed. Williamson's Studies caught the attention in the Western world because they strongly documented that the quality of introduction in the library schools as well as about everything else associated with the schools was totally non professional and the differences between Professional and clerical demands had not been well defined.

The word "training" was generally assumed in the profession to hold in prospect routinized, repetitive tasks to connect the learning of methods and processes which call for little discretion and may be exercised with only remote reference to their meaning.

"Education" on the other hand, contemplates work involving problems necessitating adoptions, embracing the revision of techniques, concern and with a definite body of knowledge, possession of intellectual responsibility, judgement and initiative and appreciation of the purposes and standards of the tasks in view. In short it implies whatever is prerequisite to practising a profession.

LIS Schools in Information age

The implications of the new technologies in communication and computer science are probably not as widely appreciated, either by professionals in librarianship or by teachers of LIS Schools. Despite the emphasis in the literature on the merging of computer and communication technologies and their applications, these areas have not been paid proper attention in giving practical training for the graduates.

Most academicians are quite familiar with the difficulty of developing an interdisciplinary curricula of LIS Schools. The difficulties relate to the following area:

What is being taught in our current LIS School? What theory should be taught? How much specialization is being offered? and is required? A lot of literature on LIS education is being published internationally and nationally; but no standardization of LIS Schools, curriculum, human resources and infrastructural facilities is being followed.

Future curriculum should provide high quality education which should provide professionals with social competencies they need.

The future curriculum will resemble current programme in broad outline, but the academic unit of the MLISc degree will include other information professionals like: sociologists, psychologists, behavioural scientists, management scientists, computer professionals, statisticians, system analysts, and communication specialists who will very soon take over the professional area of the LIS Schools in India. These professionals will help and enable the LIS Schools to cope with the rapidly changing information technology world and maintain a proper database system, online retrieval system and archives.

The LIS Schools of 1990's have much in common with the schools of 1890's in spite of efforts of accrediting agencies in the Western world and the professional bodies of India and attempts to provide widely held professional parameters.

Curriculum

The curricula of library education is the existence of a core a standard essence required of each graduate of LIS School. The concept of core was reaffirmed by Conant Report of 1980. In his review of one year programmes in the Western world was included a table titled "composite course listing by categories of subjects." He also stated that library schools concentrate in the basic functions of the profession. Reference service, Bibliography, Technical background of books and libraries is a standard part of curriculum in all the schools he surveyed. Indian Schools are no exception to this.

Supporting the need to provide fundamental concepts and skills is the major need of the hour. The committees on accreditation of ALA issues guidelines for identifying the principles and procedures common to all types of libraries.

LIS curriculum always seemed to lag behind the social needs, especially in technological areas. To compensate for this lag, an interdisciplinary curriculum has to be designed as a consortial effort of major LIS Schools in India.

The curriculum should be evaluated as a whole by its major options, by each individual course. It is important to determine the evaluation of the curriculum by the practicing librarians and educators together to specify the following objectives;

- What is the overall evaluation of the graduate curricula?
- Are the perceived values by professionals in the field different from those of education?
- Is a graduate of the programmes marketable as an information specialist?
- Are LIS Schools meeting the needs of Information Age?
- Is the duration of the one year graduate programme, able to produce skilled personnel to the profession?

Professional Obsolescence

The technical competence of the professional does not embrace the future most reaches of knowledge and techniques comprising the Library and Information Science field. Library education institutions using outdated materials, and concepts in training may engender obsolescence in the graduates at the very start of their careers.

Depending upon the cognitive ability of our own training institutions, the quality of instruction and the courses offered, we all enter the workforce in the same degree of obsolescence.

Infrastructural Factors Affecting the Obsolescence

The way the organization is structured, plays a profound effect on the growth and development of its professionals. The need for a flat organizational structure with emphasis on narrow, non duplication, non overlapping definitions of duties and responsibilities, lessened emphasis on authority in the direction of a greater amount of interpersonal communication and multiple group membership.

The multiple group membership will facilitate innovation by increasing the amount and diversity of input of ideas and stimulation. Thus, exposure to new ideas will contribute to maintenance of competence in the field.

Continuing Education and Creative Research

The objectives of LIS continuing education programmes enable teachers to:

- to help broaden and deepen professional knowledge;

- to keep up-to-date in the subject field;
- to prepare themselves to meet the challenge of changing needs;
- to learn about new methods and techniques;
- to improve effectiveness of the teaching programmes;
- to assist professional growth and development; and
- to achieve job satisfaction.

The approach to continuing education programmes and motivating the faculty for creative research should be viewed as an integrated system. One of the library schools should be developed as a centre for advanced research and such a centre should be facilitated by providing facilities like human resources, financial resources; and technology by UGC.

LIS Research in India

LIS does not have a long tradition of research scholarship or organized research activity in the modern sense. This does not mean that the individual librarians have not experimented in this field.

In this country S.R. Ranganathan can rightly be called a genius and an innovate *par excellence*. He made survival contributions to almost all branches of L & IS. Some of his books have become classics in the field. During his life time Ranganathan created the entire library world for India and influenced the library field all over the world.

Some of the library schools have been actively engaged in conducting quality improvement programmes (INSDOC, DRTC) but the research work on special projects funded by national agencies, and private sector, should become a part of LIS Schools in our country.

Factors Inhibiting Rapid Research in LIS Field

- small size of LIS faculties in LIS schools and their heavy work load;
- lack of research qualifications;
- lack of financial support in the form of research fellowships, or scholarships for young people to work on full time basis;

- lack of proper library facilities;
- non availability of the essential data from libraries and parent organizations; and
- non availability of research supervisors for topics involving interdisciplinary research.

Knowledge Skills and Attitudes

Facilities of LIS schools in India are unable to cope with the needs of our society. Most of the schools are unable to provide practical skills that are required for the graduates to sustain in this multidisciplinary nature of the system. When they are going out into the market many other graduates from MCA & MBA schools are finding placements in libraries.

Right now library profession is in need of a range of intellectual equipment, professional skills and personality attitudes; when these are translated into knowledge components, library and information science will unfold itself as a largely interdisciplinary field.

The profession is in need of manifesting a true ingenuity and innovative skills to evolve a professional education programme which will incorporate the various intellectual and professional knowledge as well as inculcate the desirable personality attitudes in various categories of personnel required for Information management.

Infrastructure of LIS Schools

As an example study of LIS schools; the schools in Nagpur city offering BLISCs and MLISc Courses have been surveyed. The BLISC courses are run at three schools and MLISC is offered at Department of Library and Information Science of Nagpur university. Tables 1 and 2 give details about the various courses offered in LIS Schools and their faculty, in Nagpur.

Department of Library and Information Science, Nagpur University started with Diploma in Lib. Sc. in the year 1956 and upgraded this to BLISC in 1966 and started MLISC course in 1984. From 1956 to 1996 the department had only one fulltime Reader and three lecturers. After the retirement of the two fulltime lecturers, the Department is left with the only one full time staff of the Head of the Department and 13 contributory teachers in the current academic year. The other two schools have started their BLISC from 1993 and are run in private colleges headed by the local retired staff from the profession and with all other staff teaching as contributory staff.

TABLE 1
LIS SCHOOLS IN NAGPUR CITY

Courses	*Year of Establishment*	*Head*
BLISC; MLISC; Ph.d	1956	Dr P.S.G. Kumar
BLISC	1993	Mr S.G. Bhatt
BLISC	1993	Mr N.H. Pawar

TABLE 2
FACULTY OF THE LIS SCHOOLS IN NAGPUR

Schools	*No. of Staff Fulltime*	*Contributory Lecturers*
Dept. of Lib. Science N.U.	1	13
School of Lib. SC Dhanbad College	Honorary	All contributory
School of Lib. SC	Honorary	All contributory

With enormous growth of LIS schools all over the country along with the Open Universities offering LIS courses, a large number of graduates from the schools are evolving into the market every year. But the quality is at great stake with such huge number of schools even without proper staff.

Demands of the Next Century

Future demands will incorporate the term information science clearly created to reflect knowledge as to deal with automation; the issues with which it is concerned; attributes in a variety far deeper than simply use of computers, and it is the study of information management and the means by which organized structures, (which are called Information systems) process recorded symbols to meet their defined Infrastructural objectives. The methodology of study in large parts is a function of the choice of system being studied, but in general it will be the infrastructure to use techniques of scientific method, data acquisition with the demands through experimentation, mathematical model building and testing, to provide and analyze qualitative evaluation.

The important challenge for the information profession would be the ability not only to identify and develop relevant intellectual and professional capabilities but more crucially, the management capacity and management culture required to undertake the wide range of responsibilities.

The basic requirements for these would be:

- an insight into societal changes;
- uptodate knowledge of available and relevant technologies, and expertise;
- an innovative sense to conceptualize information configuration;
- a sense of urgency;
- a strive for excellence;
- achievement orientation;
- capacity to plan, implement information establishments; and services.

Values in Library Field Susceptible to Change

The three values that are susceptible to change are Library Values, Library Technology and Library Science.

- *Library Values*: (Attitudes, role of libraries, selection, censorship, cultural environment). These values have remained remarkably stable in librarianship. These are the products of cultural change and it is believed that social traditions will continue to influence what is regarded as suitable.
- *Library Technology*: (This implies to the technology available for use in library sciences). This is the area which will see the greatest change. Trends in our country, in this area show that additional media for bearing text, powerful technologies for handling text and much progress is anticipated in technological tools over the next century.

- *Library Science*: (This relates to how we understand our business). Our understanding of what business we are in will broaden and expand significantly. However, progress will be slow, especially as we deal with aspects of human behaviour, "If the mission of libraries is to bring information to people then the form will make very little difference".

Role of Librarians in Electronic Libraries

Electronic libraries of 21st century are built along self service lines. They are designed for use with librarians serving not as intermediaries but as consultants.

A number of present library routines like acquisition, circulation and services will undergo a considerable change in the new outfit and will be automatically generated from the databases in the electronic libraries and users will have direct access to them, without librarians intervention. If all the libraries succeed in digitizing their existing collection, and putting these databases on high speed networks for accessing by the users through library gateway or through INSDOC gateway, the electronic library movement in our country will get a major breakthrough.

[Direct Access]

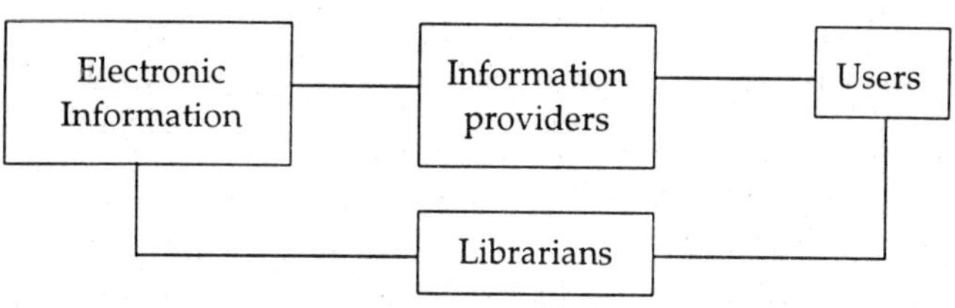

[Indirect Access]

The librarian will continue to play the role of information provider to users in the electronic library system. The role of librarian of future would be heavily involved in repackaging of information and even in a form of electronic publishing and some librarians will become hyper text engineers. The role of a reference librarian is evolving and shifting from one where online service mediation is required in the form of one-to-one tutorials, or search sessions, to that of program manager consultant and advocate.

However, the full electronic library is being setup, but without efficient staff assisting in these services, it will do a poor job and will not be able to meet the users needs in a research environment, if the library schools will not simultaneously provide the specialized skilled personnel to the profession.

It is time for the profession to meet this important challenge, institute aggressive public relations and marketing strategies for enhancement of professional image. As a prerequisite for this, the profession has to develop a sense of pride and self confidence towards their services.

Future of LIS Schools

The diversity and change should not be a weakness for any system it should become the strength because it enables us to bring wide range of approaches to a range of issues. These concern competencies of training as prescribed by practitioners, and competencies of philosophical understanding which the practitioners cannot prescribe by themselves. This LIS schools must cover a range of issues in including pre-education training, training in parallel with education, post educational training and post educational education, which will become an imperative in an environment so rapidly changing.

In order to have the library professionals to assume a central position in information age, the schools of Library and Information Science must not tie up to the past; however the schools should be based on the best ideas from the past; design and implement curricula which prepare graduates to cope up with rapid change. Without bringing the change in to our systems there is only a complacency and stagnation; with the swirl of social change there remains a little choice but to risk change so that LIS schools can successfully prepare professionals who can provide leadership for the profession.

Conclusion

According to Rothstein's analysis "Librarians are critical about library education because they tend to be highly critical people who they are, more over, in considerable doubt about themselves, their colleagues and the standing or merit of their own profession" he believes that we think of ourselves poorly but we should think of ourselves as better and much better.

Some fundamental questions should be asked for our system like:

- Is library education really bad as its critics believe?
- Does the profession want library schools to be responsible for basic education for entry-level position.
- Can the profession in India afford the luxury of returning to on the job training for every one?
- Can we learn from our past experiences and move towards the change? and
- Does library education really have a future!

The future belongs to those who prepare for it. If they don't change, in the words of Michael Buckland and Evelyne Daniel - either die a lingering death or if they don't die suffer arrested development.

In reality the programmes are not as good as most library educators want them to be, nor as bad as the critics ascertain them to be.

Library Schools do have future if we move towards the change with a lot of familiar processes but the path will be quite different.

This can only be achieved in our country if there exists an accrediting body for standardization of LIS Schools in our country to assess the total infrastructural facilities which can fulfil the demands of our present market.

REFERENCES

1. Reeds. Evolution of Pedagoguical patterns - *Library Trends*. Vol. 34, W3, pp. 451-68, 1986.
2. Grant, F.L. and Main, R.G. Meeting the needs of information age. *J. Ame. Soc. Info. Sc.* Vol. 37 N1, pp. 12-19, 1986.
3. Edward, H.G. Does library education have a future. *American Libraries*. Vol. 17, N10, pp. 702-6.
4. Rothstein, S. Why People really hate Library Schools. *Library Journals*. pp. 4-48, 1984, April 1.
5. Buckland, M. Education for Librarianship in the Next century. *Library Trends*. Vol. 34, p. 785, Spring 1986.

6. Hayes, R.M. "Accreditation." *Library Trends*. Vol. 34, pp. 5347-559, Spring 1984.
7. Ashem, L.E. Education for Librarianship: Present and Future. In Paul Koda (ed.) *Fifth Anniversary Schools of Library Science*. The book mark (Friends of the library. The University of north Carolina at chapel Hill. 51 & 52, p. 155, 1982.
8. Mohamed, O. Education for Library and Information Managers: Challenges of the Post Industrial Society. *Int. Lib. Review*. Vol. 14, pp. 185-97, 1982.
9. Dhaka, R.P.S. Electronic Library: a Myth or a Reality. *Annals of Library Science and Documentation*. Vol. 42, N4, pp. 152-59, 1995.
10. Sardana, K.L. and Kumar, K. Continuing Education for Teachers of Library and Information Science : a System Approach; In Continuing Education for Librarians. ALA All India Seminar Papers. Pragati Maidan, New Delhi, pp. 26-31, 1984.
11. Mangla P.B. Trends in Research in Library and Information Science in USA, UK and India: an Overview; In ILA Seminar Papers. New Delhi, pp. 66-79, 1984.
12. Seetarama, S. Library and Information Science Research in India: an Analytical Study based on the Input to ISORID. *Library Science With a Slant to Documentation*. Vol. 13, pp. 121-37, 1976.
13. Mangla, P.B. Library Education in India, Pakistan and Bangladesh. *Advances in Librarianship*. Vol. 10, pp. 191-240, 1980.
14. Theodore, F.N. On the Obsolescence of Scientists and Engineers. *American Scientists*. Vol. 54, N1, p. 46, 1966.
15. Shera, J.H. The Foundations of education for librarianship. Becker & Hayes, N.Y. P 202-208, 1972.
16. Rajyalakshmi, D. Challenges of Post industrial Society on Library and Information Science Education and its Future. In Hundred Years of Library Education and its future, ILA, IASLIC -GILA-IATLIC Seminar, October 10-12, 1989, Nagpur.
17. Hausrath, D. Obsolescence in Librarians: in Continuing Education for Librarians ILA 1984. New Delhi, pp. 11-21.
18. White, H. Subverted by Pragmatism. *Library Journal*, May 1. pp. 861-64, 1984.
19. Grover, R. Library & Information Professional Education for Learning Society: a model curriculum. *JELIS*. Vol. 26, N1, pp. 33-45, 1985.

Three

Teaching Methods in Library and Information Science: An Evaluation

DR SEWA SINGH

Introduction

In Library and Information Science the objectives of the courses, by and large, have been to provide a balanced training in such a way that theory and practice are well integrated covering all aspects of professional work, reflecting needs of various types of libraries, and information centres and systems.

Need of Teaching Methods

The teachers in Library and Information Science (LIS), like in other subjects, choose various teaching methods to make the communication of knowledge, ideas, and information more effective. The aim is also to develop professional knowledge, skills and capabilities so as to make the product capable enough to deal with different situations in the field.

The teaching methods have been changing from time to time across the globe as a result of the innovations and the demands of the new social systems. Some of the teaching methods, popular among the LIS teachers in India, are discussed below with an evaluative approach, offering suggestions.

Teaching Methods

Important teaching methods can be categorized as under:

Lecture Method

It is the most conventional method of teaching in LIS courses at all levels wherein teacher generally delivers lectures uninterruptedly. The teacher even dictates notes from his/her own old pages. The topic of the lecture of the day may or may not be announced in the class in advance.

Evaluation

The lecture method, in most of the cases becomes just a ritual and one-way communication, where the teacher speaks and does not teach. The teacher may not put questions to the students, or encourage students to ask questions for clarification or for discussion in the classroom. This chalk-and-talk method does not stimulate any thoughts among the students who have to become library and information professionals sometime later. There are cases where the teacher does not make use of even the chalk, the minimum tool of the teacher; and believes in talking things other than relevant to the course topics. Thus it becomes completely a teacher-oriented method of teaching, discouraging active participation of the students.

Suggestions

The lecture method can be made student-oriented by announcing the topic in advance. The teacher should provide an elaborate list of readings to the students with a view to encourage them to go to the library for literature consultation. They should be encouraged in the class to ask questions and make it a lecture-cum-discussion by active participation of the students.

Observation

It may, however, be pointed out that the quality of students joining LIS departments is declining year after year. With no good background of any subject, the students fail to evoke any interest in the new field of librarianship, and rather join it only to leave if they get a better chance elsewhere.

Seminar/Discussion Method

It is considered a prominent and forceful method of teaching followed in some LIS departments. It encourages active participation and helps to overcome the initial hesitation among the students. The discussion centres on a topic allotted generally to some students, while the rest of them come prepared for participation.

Evaluation

There are numerous advantages of this method enumerated in library literature. But unfortunately not all the teachers in a department give seminars to their students. Where it is given, it is just reduced to a ritual and not taken seriously by the students as well as the teachers. The teachers' interest gets diminished when the salubrious environment is not made available in the department.

Suggestions

The seminar followed by discussion can be made more lively by making it discussion oriented through self-thinking and cultivating the habit of extensive reading. It can help in building the students tomorrow's learned by active professionals who can face the challenge of new information environment.

Assignments Method

This method is not a complete method in itself. The teacher can supplement the lecture method with the assignments. It helps the students to familiarize themselves with the extensive literature available on the topic of assignment. All the students are given different assignments from time to time to be completed in consultation with the teacher.

Evaluation

It is observed that invariably teachers do not give assignments on the topics of their courses. Only one or two teachers in some of the university departments develop the assignment writing habit among the students. The teachers also are not encouraged much by the Heads to give assignments. On the contrary, it is observed that those teachers who regularly give assignments are rather looked at disdainfully by the fellow teachers including the Head. In some other cases, the assignments are never checked by the teachers, making the entire exercise a wasteful effort.

Suggestions

There is ample of scope of assignment writing in Library and Information Science. The students should be required to submit at least one assignment per paper. These assignments should be duly checked and improved by the teacher concerned. These should be got typed and bound together so as to make a permanent record in the Departmental Library for the successive generations of students and create literature of them.

Tutorial Method

In this method the students meet the individual teacher in small groups and discuss the individual problems in detail. This method helps in removing students' difficulties and clarifying the concepts. Sometimes one group of students is assigned to one teacher, while in some other cases tutorial groups are rested from teacher to teacher on weekly basis.

Evaluation

Tutorials should be made a part of the time-table in the Department. They should be organized regularly in the department. Unfortunately this never happens. The beginning is made with enthusiasm, but with the passage of time the initial enthusiasm among the students dies down for various reasons. The trouble starts when the teacher is not able to bind them with his skills, ability, and academic excellence; and other things start getting more weightage with them.

Suggestions

The Library and Information Science students should be made fully aware of the usefulness of the tutorials in shaping them as good professionals, by inculcating extra reading habits; infusing in them the skills and competencies they need. In tutorials students can be further exposed to the use of computer, handling of transparencies and Overhead projector, and the like. In a nutshell, this method not only helps in transferring and transfusing teacher's scholarship, but can also familiarize them with the use of computer.

Audio Visual Method

In recent times this method of teaching has also entered in Indian Library and Information Science departments. The advantage of this method is that students also take keen interest in the Audio Visual aids used in this method of teaching. The use of instructional material on tapes, slides, transparencies, video tapes, films, is made in the classroom. It makes an interesting learning experience.

Evaluation

It is believed that most of the Library and Information Science departments in the country have acquired at least one Overhead projector, and a computer. Some of these departments are making good use of equipments to infuse the needed skills and competencies for Information Technology among the future professionals. But this is not unfortunately the case in all the departments. It has been experienced that despite the availability of Overhead projector and/or computer in the department, the teachers are not permitted to use them for various reasons, thereby allowing the electronic gadgets either to gather dust, or remain packed in cupboards.

Suggestions

In view of the importance of the Audio Visual aids in communicating knowledge and having a permanent impression on the minds of the students, their use should be encouraged under the supervision of teachers. These help in demonstrating many facts, and ideas, and reduce the verbal burden.

Field Work Method

For the Library and Information Science students Field Work Method is quite significant because it helps in completing their training with practical work. Field Work provides an opportunity to work in different library and information centres, and observe their services closely.

Evaluation

Some of the Library and Information Science departments do believe in the Field Work Method and provide opportunities to their students to work in the field for some time. But in most of the cases, teachers donot give any opportunity to work in the library and information centre, even for some time. In such cases the knowledge of the students remains limited to the textbooks.

Suggestions

This method of training must be practised in Indian Library and Information Science departments in order to give students the practical training. Field work may be done as the Reference Assistant, or Circulation Assistant, or Technical Assistant in Libraries. This method would enhance their skills and capabilities and make them more competent professionals for tomorrow. However, it has to be planned properly and "a great deal of time and effort must be invested in preliminary ground work and in post visit or lecture follow up", according to Davinson.

Case Studies Method

It provides a good opportunity for innovative teaching. Case studies though prepared for learning purposes, may not reflect all the complexities of real life situations, yet they can closely reflect the problem-solving situations in each case study by the students.

Evaluation

It may be pointed out that case study as a method of teaching is not regularly followed in most of our Library and Information Science departments. The teachers do not encourage the students much to take up the case studies in different Library and Information Science courses. The students also avoid taking such case studies where they are required to go outstation for individual cases.

Suggestions

It is suggested that case study method should be regularly followed by the teachers, and students must be encouraged to take up case studies as these aim to trigger innovative capacity and develop analytical thinking so necessary for the library and information professionals of tomorrow.

Simulation Method

Through this method of teaching, the teacher brings intense motivation, personal involvement, and high quality learning into the classroom. This method is also called role-playing and is problem-oriented, wherein game is played by one of more players towards a definite objective. Students cooperate according to the model. This method encourages involvement and develops new prespectives among students.

Evaluation

Despite the fact that this method has many advantages, it is not followed in a large number of LIS departments. The reasons are not far to seek. The responsibility lies both on teachers and students; rather more on the Head of the Department, who is to provide leadership, and this unfortunately, we lack in most departments.

Suggestions

This method should be encouraged by the teachers, among the students by making provision in the time-table. The teachers may select valid models and problems, right exercises, and handle them with care. Now computer simulation is also available which is described as "a research tool for information science". It is suggested to use simulation techniques to project operational system development and make comparisons of different real life situations.

Observation Method

This method of teaching 'is a method of sensorial learning through which the individual acquires knowledge of the world around him.' The students should be trained to observe accurately and develop the ability to report what they have observed about a phenomenon or an event or a process.

Evaluation

On a critical look at the LIS department, it is observed that this method is not followed at a regular basis. It may, however, be pointed out that during the educational tour, students visit some libraries and documentation centres, and observe their working and services provided by them. But this remains only at the surface level, as the tours are arranged with an eye on recreation as well. These are so loosely planned that sometimes the very purpose of undertaking them is lost. And, not in all departments the students report back to their teachers what they had observed during the educational tour.

Suggestions

It is suggested that such an observation should be made more regular in local libraries as well as outstation libraries in the neighbourhood. Students should be given specific work assign-ments for observation in the libraries and they must report the same back to their teachers. Observation of the working and services of various libraries through guided tours, library visits on individual basis, as well as in groups, should be arranged. These may further be followed by lectures and discussion.

Project Method

In this method the students may be asked to deal with a real life problem, helpful in achieving the educational objectives. It also helps in the development of intellectual ability of the students. The role of teacher in this method is that of a guide and advisor only; and the rest of the job of collecting and analysing material is mainly done by the students.

Evaluation

Its advantages notwithstanding, the project method is not followed in all the LIS departments. Projects are not given to students even in such practice-oriented subjects as Reference Service and Sources, Documentation, Classification, Cataloguing, Computer Applications, Case Studies, etc.

Suggestions

The Project Method should be a part of the time-table and project work should be assigned on regular basis so that the students could acquire skills and competence to tackle problems in library work and services. Teachers must take full interest in assigning real life projects to the students so that they could learn their practical aspects.

Dissertation Method

For the LIS students, particularly at Master's level, dissertation method is found quite useful. In this method a topic is selected on accurate theme, according to the interest and aptitude of the students, and under the guidance and advice of teachers they prepare the dissertation. This encourages self study and aptitude for writing which prepares them for further research work in the subject.

Evaluation

This method is adopted in most LIS departments in India, but all the teachers do not do full justice to the topics as well as to the students. Some teachers after allotting the topic leave it entirely to the students to complete the dissertation on their own. This practice invariably defeats the basic purpose of dissertation for developing research acumen.

Suggestions

Teachers must pay more attention, and guide the students regularly in writing their dissertation. The chapters written by students must be carefully checked by the teachers and suggestions made for improvements supported with more and latest bibliographical references. In this way, a habit of writing on the topic of their choice can be inculcated among the students.

Brain-storming Method

This method of teaching attempts in catalysing and cultivating the creative abilities of the students. Creative sessions of spontaneous problem solving is known as Brain-storming. The brain-storm session creates conditions which activate the innovation in the mind of each participant and it is presented without any inhibition. It could be done under the leadership of teachers of the respective subjects.

Evaluation

Despite the usefulness of this method, brain-storming is not used as a regular method of teaching in LIS departments. But as the ill luck would have it, most of our departments do not practise this method as they do not encourage their students to actively participate in discussion. Mostly, the classroom teaching remains without interaction, and one way teaching only.

Suggestions

For problem-solving situation in library and information work, brain-storming sessions are found to be useful, whereby teaching itself, as a learning process, can be made more interesting. It is very useful in such areas as thesaurus construction, classification, indexing, design of an information system, formulation of a library policy, and the like. Thus, it encourages creativity among the further professionals.

Class Test Method

This is another teaching-learning process in the subject of LIS. This method could be both written as well as oral, and both are used in most of the LIS departments. Oral test is held in the class on an identified topic given in advance, leading to a lively discussion with the teacher taking the lead. Oral test is also conducted in the form of viva-voce for such papers as dissertation, classification practice, cataloguing practice, reference service and sources, database creation, and the like. In written tests, the syllabus is identified in advance and the students are asked to write, as in the final examinations. These answers written by students must be evaluated by the teachers, and discussed.

Evaluation

More class tests of short duration, should be encouraged by the teacher. However, that is unfortunately, not the case in all the LIS departments. Generally, teachers give minimum tests to their students, and the students also prefer not to be put to test.

Suggestions

This being a useful method of teaching and evaluating. More informal and formal, oral and written, tests should be given to the students. This method keeps them ready through self study as they would sift through more literature and keep uptodate.

Internship/Apprenticeship Method

It could be both pre-course and post-course internship. But it is believed that post-course internship is more useful for LIS students. Through internship in different libraries for a period of about 6-8 weeks after the examination, the students would familiarize themselves with the routing work in different sections as ordering and acquisition, classification and cataloguing, circulation, reference service, periodicals, maintenance, etc. This method makes the students fully ready to face the library environment of their own, of course, under the guidance of library staff.

Evaluation

There are hardly few LIS departments in India which follow this method, though in principle, the teachers would agree with its usefulness and necessity.

Suggestions

It is strongly suggested that post-course internship should be followed in all the LIS departments so that the students are not considered as "half-baked material". They should be attached to some recognized libraries in view of their aptitude, background, and specialization. They must maintain a daily diary of the work they perform in the library, and on completion it should be evaluated. It is further suggested that they should also be given some stipend during internship.

Continuing Education Method

This method is used to upgrade the professional knowledge, by providing information about the latest developments in the field. This helps in updating their abilities and understanding so that they would become more effective and efficient professionals in the times to come. Continuing education programmes can be planned carefully and imparted through formal and informal methods, by a recognised agency, preferably a rich university department.

Evaluation

The LIS departments organise from time to time formal continuing education (CE) programmes through Refresher courses, Summer Institutes, Winter Workshops, etc. Some such CE programmes are organised on specialised subjects such as Computer Applications, Marketing of information services, Total Quality Management, etc., which refresh and update Library and Information Science workers' knowledge and skills, and make them more efficient. However, only a few of them organise such programmes.

Suggestions

The Continuing Education method needs more careful attention from LIS departments. These programmes should be regularly arranged on topics of current developments. This is particularly essential on such topics as identified above; or at least on Computer Applications in view of their increasing use in libraries, and the large number of professionals without any hands on experience. During such programmes they should also be told about the use of overhead and slide projector, in addition to the computer.

Conclusion

It can be concluded from the above discussion that no single method of teaching is sufficient in itself. These methods have to be used in combination with each other for making LIS education and training more meaningful. The most popular and prevalent method of delivering lectures must be supplemented by other methods depending upon the availability of resources in terms of manpower and equipments.

REFERENCES

1. Agrawal, S.P. *Directory of LIS Education in India.....*, assisted by T. Mythill and Rajani Soni, New Delhi: Reliance Publishing House, 1996.
2. Chandra, A. *Curriculum Development and Evaluation in Education*, New Delhi: Sterling, 1977.

3. Davinson, Donald. Thoughts on a Nodal Syllabus for a Two Year Master's Degree Course, In Mangla, P.B. (ed.) *Library and Information Science Education in India.* New Delhi: Macmillan, pp. 102-8, 1981.
4. Dean, John. *Planning Library Education Programmes.* London: Andre Deutrch, 1972.
5. Gopinath M.A. Creative Methods and Evaluation in LIS Education. In Tejomurty, A (ed.) *Library and Information Science Education and Teaching Methods.* Jaipur: RBSA Publishers, pp. 73-81, 1991.
6. Neelameghan, A. Education for Librarians in India, In: Kent, Allen (ed.) *Encyclopedia of Library and Information Science.* New York: Marcel Dekker, Vol. 2, 1974.
7. Ranganathan, S.R. Teaching Library Science. *Library Science with a Slant to Documentation.* 3, pp. 293-388, 1966.
8. Workshop on the methods of teaching and evaluation of Library Science, Delhi, 1973. *Papers and Proceedings.* Delhi: Deptt. of Library Science, University of Delhi, 1973 (Mimeographed).

Four

Evaluation Techniques in LIS Research

DR J. YADAGIRI REDDY

Introduction

Human beings appear to stand alone among the earth's creatures in their desire to understand their existence and the world around them. This want or need can be partially satisfied by knowledge gained as a result of everyday occurrences, including trial and error, the formulation of generalizations based upon first-hand experience; and the use of logical reasoning. A more efficient and effective approach to expand knowledge, however, is the conduct of special planned, and structured investigations — a process known as research. In its largest context, research is a "systematic quest for knowledge."[1]

Studies conducted to obtain objective and systematic evidence of the success or failure of library projects and programmes are often categorised as evaluation research. When a programme is evaluated, its relative effectiveness in terms of standards, goals, and objectives is determined and described. Typically, evaluation research is an attempt to measure operations in terms of the goals of libraries or library projects or the end results sought.

According to Armstrong, the ultimate point of measurement and evaluation is its product - "Does it produce, what it is designed to produce, and does it meet the requirements of the customers?"[2] He suggests, therefore, that the ultimate product of the library is intangible.

Until recent decades, assessments of most library programmes and projects were somewhat sporadic — if indeed they were even attempted for some projects. Although earlier evaluations were based primarily upon value judgements of sponsors or project coordinators, the current trend is towards more systematic accountability of library activities; thus, the success or failure of various programs is now measured.

Essentially, the process of conducting evaluation research can be divided into six broad steps as follows:

(i) Determine what is to be evaluated and the reasons for the evaluation.

(ii) Establish the desired level of performance of the object of the evaluation with particular reference to existing standards, goals, and objectives.

(iii) Select appropriate investigative techniques, and if necessary, prepare a suitable scale or instrument to measure levels of performance.

(iv) Measure or test subjects (objects) to determine actual level(s) of performance.

(v) Compare the programme's goals with its objectives (i.e. determine the extent to which goals were achieved).

(vi) Evaluate the project on the basis of analysed data.

LIS Research

LIS research is a natural outcome of LIS education. Research is an important human activity. It is essential for the progress of any discipline. Research creates new knowledge and finds solutions to problems. LIS Research however, had a late start in India. S.R. Ranganathan started the Ph.D. Programme in LIS, for the first time, in 1948 at the University of Delhi. The first candidate who completed his research was Dr R.B. Krishna Rao in 1957. Most of the other Universities have taken up research activities during the 1970s. Research in LIS has numerous uses. Research activity in LIS has been quite inadequate. The provision of funds are meagre. Until 1986 there were only 58 Ph.Ds in LIS.[3] Now the number is growing faster.

Most of the LIS teachers and Librarians have done their Ph.D. not only to fit into the UGC qualification stipulations but also to explore the subject field for effective organization of libraries and their services as also for LIS education.

Need for Evaluation

Evaluation is an integral part of the planning process. No library can afford to ignore it if it has to serve the readers satisfactorily. Evaluation enables us to:

(a) know how best we are fulfilling/realising the objectives/goals set for the library;
(b) check whether the library is moving in the right direction or not; and
(c) take necessary corrective measures.

In India, we do not have a rich tradition of evaluation in LIS. Not many significant studies have been done in this area.

Evaluation Techniques

Performance Assessment

The heart of the management approach is of course to define objectives, develop methods of meeting those objectives and to assess how effective this whole process is. Schauer (1986), perhaps some what unrealistically, argues that goals of libraries must be expressed in such specific terms that changes are both observable and measurable. Monitoring performance is an integral part of good management and is really undertaken for two reasons:

(a) to convince the funders and the clients that the service is delivering the benefits that were expected when the investment was made;
(b) as an internal control mechanism to ensure that the resources are used efficiently and effectively.[4]

Cost Benefit Analysis

Wolfe et al., (1974) emphasises that "while profit maximising, public decisions must include in the decision calculus the external or spillover benefits and costs that accrue to other parties".[5] However, most LI Services including those in the private sector operate in a non-market environment as a free-service. Schauer (1986) identified a number of approaches to cost benefit analysis:

(a) maximum benefit for a fixed cost;

(b) minimise costs for a given level of benefits;
(c) maximise the ratio of benefits over cost;
(d) maximise the net benefits (present value of benefits minus present value of cost); and
(e) maximise the internal rate of return.[6]

Unobtrusive Testing

Unobtrusive testing or obtrusive measurement, is a 'qualitative' based method of performance evaluation which has attracted a great many conflicting opinions regarding its validity and reliability. The origins of the technique dates back to Webb's (1966) review of the theory and utility of obtrusive measures for social research. Since then it has been used extensively by LIS researchers to determine the quality of library reference services. It invariably involves the use of trained enquiries or proxies to ask questions (for which answers have been predetermined) of library staff members who are unaware that the service is being evaluated. During the past two decades, there have been a considerable number of studies employing unobtrusive tests designed to assess the ability of reference services to provide accurate answers to short factual and bibliographical questions.[7]

Attitudes of Users and Non-users

Attitudes will influence user assessments of services, but measuring attitudes is a complex business. The problem with attitude studies is that, users rarely have strong views about libraries and, therefore, one needs a sensitive measuring instrument to identify these differences.

Outcomes

Performance assessment should be based on what users actually do rather than what they say they do. This was one approach that Blagden (1980) took in the context of assessing the performance of two special libraries. It was also the approach adopted by Stone (1983) who interestingly also recorded prior expectations of utility of documents requested through inter library loans and then compared these with ratings of the documents usefulness after they had been received.[8]

Inter Library Comparison

One way of answering the question as to whether a library is good or bad is to try and conduct controlled comparisons between similar types of libraries. The application of this technique to libraries in the UK however, has been primarily due to the work of the centre for inter-firm comparison, whose first report for the British Library for public libraries appeared in 1981.[9]

Case Histories or the Expanded Anecdotes

Blagden (1980) summarized a number of spectacular technological disasters which could perhaps have been avoided if the technologists had access to information that had already been published prior to the disaster. Of course, this assumes that libraries would have been able to retrieve the information at the time it was wanted and that the overall costs of library investment did not outweigh these potential savings.[10] Clearly all LI services can benefit from the recording of one of the success stories as Wilde and Cooper report (1988), where access to information significantly increased the profits or significantly reduced the costs of the organization that the service is supporting. These case histories do not answer the question referred to earlier as to whether, in general terms, the benefits from the library service, outweigh the costs unless the library can demonstrate large off cost reductions or profit improvements.[11]

Document Delivery and Availability

An area which has developed a sound methodology which will give generalised representative results, is the area of document delivery and availability. High methodological standards were set by Richard Orr and others way back in 1968[12] when they developed a methodology for assessing a library's ability to deliver known documents. This technique has been extensively used and reviews of its strengths and weaknesses have been presented by Lancaster (1977).[13] It should be emphasised that this technique is only assessing document supply success rates and speed of delivery.[14] Revill (1987) reviews availability rates, i.e. on the shelf when sought, and quotes availability rates from other studies. He admits that given the development of on-line public access catalogue these studies may be less useful in the future.[15]

Conclusion

A wide variety of evaluation techniques are available to measure the performance of LI Services. The choice of appropriate technique depends on the various factors such as type of library (public/academic/special, etc.,) level of modernisation, maintenance of relevant statistical data, availability of sufficient staff in LIS and nature of library operations and services, etc. It is true that the benefits and social impact of LI Services are difficult to measure. The results are considered to be intangible. But, by selecting appropriate evaluation techniques, which are reasonably valid, objective and reliable, we can have a fair gross estimate of the performance of a library.

REFERENCES

1. Busha, Charles H. *Research Methods in Librarianship: Techniques and Interpretations*. London: Academic Press, 1980.
2. Armstrong, Charles M. Measurement and Evaluation of the Public Library. Chap. 2 In Herbert Goldher, (ed.) *Research Methods in Librarianship: Measurement and Evaluation*. Illinois, University of Illinois, 1968.
3. Pathak, Vijay and Ramaih, L.S. *Bibliography of Research in LIS in India*. Gurgaon : Indian Documentation Service, 1986.
4. Schauer, Bruce P. *The Economics of Managing Library Service*. Chicago, American Library Association, 1986.
5. Wolf, James N. et al. *The Economics of Technical Information Systems*, New York: Praeger, 1974.
6. *Op. cit.*, (4), pp. 14-30.
7. Webb, Eugene, J. et al. *Unobtrusive Measures: Non-reactive Research in the Social Sciences*. Rand McNally, 1966.
8. Stone, S. Inter.Library Loans; a study of Antecedents and Outcomes of Inter-library Loan Requests. CRUS occasional paper No. 7. Centre for Research on User Studies, 1983.
9. Blagden, John. *How good is your library*? a Review of Approaches to the Evaluation of Library and Information Services, London: Aslib, 1990.
10. Blagden, John. *Do We Really Need Libraries*? London: Clive Bingley, 1980.
11. Wilde, D.V. and Cooper, N.R. Justifying your information Centre's Budget. Proceedings of the 9th National Outline Meetings, 1988, pp. 421-27.

12. Orr, Richard H. et al., Development of Methodologic tools for planning and managing library services. In measuring a library's Capability for Providing Documents. *Bulletin of Medical Library Association*. Vol. 56(3), pp. 241-67, 1968.
13. Lancaster, F.W. The Measurement and Evaluation of Library Services. Washington D.C. Information Resources Press. 1977.
14. Lancaster, F.W. *If You Want to Evaluate Your Library*, London: Library Association, 1988.
15. Revill, D.H. Availability as a Performance Measure for Academic Libraries. *Journal of Librarianship*, Vol. 19(M), pp. 14-30, 1987.

Five

Book Selection

DR SONAL SINGH *and* DR SURENDRA SINGH

Introduction

Any written or printed composition of some length is called a book. The word "book" has a very wide connotation. "It covers all kinds of reading materials in any form which serves the purpose of the readers whether for general or recreational reading, or for study and research, or for mere consultation as source of information."[1] The books contain the wisdom of the philosophers and sages of many centuries.

Library is a dynamic instrument of education. Its basic function is to satisfy the intellectual needs of the readers. Unless a library possesses adequate recent documents supplemented with latest reference and bibliographical tools, it can not serve its clientele. Among the three important functions of the library, namely collection, storage and dissemination of reading and kindered material, the collection occupies the most vital position. The library implies the close collaboration of the trio i.e. the books, the readers and the staff. Infact, the books are basic material with which the readers are to be fed. The books have a pivotal position in the library world. Without books there will be no library worth the name. No service to the readers can flow without books. So, the fundamental function of a library is to build up a collection which is dynamic and capable of meeting the changing needs and demands of present as well as future users. It is the document collection that gives a library a character more so, than either staff or building. A well-equipped and well managed library is the foundation of modern educational set up, which makes it possible to share the experience of many other persons by reading about their thoughts and achievements. Library is a place where the experiences of the past can meet the needs of the present.

Library is the heart of an institution. A quality education is impossible without a quality library. A library with a rich and varied collection is the foundation of modern educational setup. Hence, the collection should be balanced, upto date and in accordance with the needs of readers.

Any kind of library service that is desigried to provide books and to being together readers and books, must be based on intelligent book selection. The selection of reading material is an objective task. It should be done carefully keeping in view the principle of appropriateness. It requires acquaintance with literature, accurate knowledge of reader's need, the existing book stock and available books in print. Library, in order to be a creative, useful and affective instrument of education, should contain the right type of books. Today, collection development is the most important, most interesting and most difficult of the professional librarian's responsibility. Modern library collection calls for a librarian who not only loves books and keeps them in order on shelves but he must possesses the initiative to be able to adjust to the changing conditions of the readers, of work and of the society at large. He must be willing to learn and adopt new techniques and be dedicated to service and no service to the readers can flow without collection development. The collection development will come out only when its librarian and the library staff are in the know of new trends, new publications, newer editions and understand the various dimensions of subjects in the growing universe of knowledge.

Principles of Book Selection

Today, we are living in the world of "Knowledge Explosion". Financially libraries are not in a position to purchase all books needed. The books themselves are of various kinds and suit various tastes and age groups. Similarly, libraries are of different kinds catering to different needs of their special kinds of readers. It has been, therefore, very essential for the libraries to select the most useful and suitable books. While selecting books for a particular library, we should keep alive in our minds the purpose of the particular library and the means through which this purpose can be fulfilled properly.

"Book Selection is one of the most important techniques with which librarianship is connected for it is the book stock which gives a library its character more so, than either staff or building".[2] To select the best out of the vast and for the mass is the process of book selection. No book should be purchased without a selection decision.

Successful librarians on the basis of their rich and long experience have formulated some principles of book selection. They have provided some valuable suggestions and have decided some standards. The oldest principle has been formulated by Melvil Dewey.

Principle of Melvil Dewey

"Best books, for the largest number, at the least cost". This principle was formulated by Dewey keeping in mind the principle of economy and the condition of libraries at that time.

The condition of libraries was very poor at that time. American Public Libraries were lacking financially. They did not have funds either for collection development or for library staff. Donations, gifts and endowments were the main sources of library. University libraries were also facing financial problem. Hence, Melvil Dewey formulated the principle that best books should be purchased, for the largest number, at the least cost. While formulating this principle. Dewey has also kept in mind, the "Principle of Economy", which is most widely accepted principle. An intelligent person always trys to purchase best useful things at the least cost.

According to this principle, there are three aspects on which book selection depends:

1. Best books.
2. Largest number.
3. Least cost.

Best Books

The present trends in the development of knowledge create certain problems in book selection. When specialisation was the trend in the development of different disciplines of knowledge, the book selection work was not a problem. The book selector could easily decide the purpose and usefulness of a particular book. But today there is interaction of subjects. The result is that, many new subjects are coming into existence. The knowledge is growing infinitely and multidimensionally. With the growth of knowledge, published literature is also growing continuously. It is growing today in various forms and various languages. It is very difficult for a book selector to decide the best book out of the published literature. Book selection is done according to the types of libraries. A book may be very useful for a special library so it will be a best book. But the same book is useless for a college library. Different types of libraries are having different type of readers. It means that needs of readers differ from library to library. So book selection work should be in accordance with the need of the reader. The book mostly demanded should be treated as best book. By selecting best books, demands of the readers will be fulfilled and library will gain popularity.

Largest Number

Best books should be selected for the largest number. Maximum number of readers should get the advantage of best books. So while selecting best books, the book selector should keep in mind that the subject content of the book is according to the need and level of the readers. Different aspects of a subject are clearly defined in that book. Its language is easy, sentences formation is correct. There should be continuity of the though content. Then only it will be used by largest number of readers. To select best books for the largest number it is necessary to know the demands and reading interest of the readers. Keys, guide books, guess paper, book series, etc., must not be purchased, no matter how much it is demanded by largest number of readers.

Least Cost

Best books should be purchased, for the largest number, at the least cost. We have to satisfy maximum readers. But due to financial limitations, book selection work is not an easy job. We can not purchase all the books. So only those books should be selected which are demanded by the majority of the readers. In a country like India, the libraries are always lacking financially. Library cooperation is the only way to select best books at least cost. This system may be applied on local level, district level, state level, national level or even international level. Book selection work should be done in a cooperative way. It will avoid duplication of reading material also.

Principle of Dr Ranganathan

According to Dr Ranganathan, book selection work should be done in such a way that the five laws of library science are satisfied. These five laws are as follows:

1. Books are for use.
2. Every reader his/her book.
3. Every book its reader.
4. Save the time of the reader.
5. Library is a growing organism.

The first three laws are concerned with the reader book relation, fourth law with time and fifth law with development of the library. While selecting books for a library, if these laws are kept in mind, the aims of the library will be fulfilled.

Books are for Use

First law accepts careful book-selection for its satisfaction. Readers should actively use the books. For this we should consider some qualities of a book.

(i) Format: The physical makeup of the book should be very attractive. The shape, size and weight of the book should be normal so that it is easy to handle. Its cover page should be very attractive. It should be durable. The paper should be of best quality and binding should be strong. Printing should be clear and easily readable. A popular size, good shape, good type of printing and binding will attract the readers to use the books which is the most common theory of demand of book selection.

(ii) Internal qualities of a book: Its language should be easy, sentence formation should be correct. Books with short sentences should be preferred. Paragraphs should be short and there should be unity of thoughts. If the book is illustrated, it will be more attractive. In addition to text a book must have a table of contents, preface, appendices, index, references, bibliography, etc. The book should be a standard book. The book selection work should be according to the interest and level of the readers. Book collection in all the subject fields should be made strong. It means all the subjects should be treated equally. If any subject has weaker book collection, then the books of that particular subject should be selected first.

Every Reader His/Her Book

According to this law, books should be selected in accordance with the needs of the readers. Books or their lists should be displayed before the readers for their valuable suggestions about the book selection. List of newly published books should also be shown to the readers to choose the latest books of their own choice. Readers should be asked to provide a list of books which they require and such lists should be taken into consideration before deciding the final list. Reference librarians should maintain the list of books which are not in library, but are demanded by the readers. Readers interest can be determined by going through the issue registers. The books which are continuously in circulation are supposed to be the useful books. More copies of such books should be purchased. So as to satisfy the second law. For proper book selection work, libraries should maintain a statistical record of issued books so that there will be an authentic and ever ready record of useful books, their subject, standard and language. Reference books should also be selected keeping in view the readers needs. Books on local needs, local industries, local personalities should also be selected. All possible demands of the future should also be considered.

Every Books its Reader

According to this law, no book in the library should be kept unused. So only those books should be purchased which are useful for the readers. Books should be selected only in that language which our readers can understand. Book selection varies according to the type of library. The type of library is important because that determines the type of clientele. There are mainly three types of libraries: (1) Academic Libraries (2) Public Libraries and (3) Special Libraries. Academic libraries are intended to serve the students, research scholars and staff members. Public libraries serve the cross-section of the community. Special libraries are mainly meant for those who are specializing in special fields. Each library has two objectives : (I) General education and (II) Special Objectives with respect to its parent body's function. So functions and objectives of a library are to be borne in mind while doing book selection. Then only we can satisfy the third law.

Save the Time of the Reader

According to this law, books should be selected on such lines that it may save the time of the reader and staff. Different types of bibliographies and bibliographical periodicals and serials should be selected. Reference books related to different subject fields should also be selected. Duplicate copies of books on frequent demand should be selected. Indexing and abstracting periodicals should also be selected. Thus, if books will be selected according to needs of the readers, then readers will get the books of their own choice, at once. Thus, satisfying the fourth law.

Library is a Growing Organism

Library is a trio of books, readers and staff. With the growth in the number of readers, number of books also increased. Proportionally number of staff is also increased to provide proper service. Thus, library is a growing organism. Utility of library depends upon the quality of reading material. So latest reading material should be purchased. Keeping in view the fifth law, only useful books should be purchased. Book selection should be based on the percentage of staff, space and equipment. Microfilms and other microforms are less spacious and are proved to be more helpful in providing the adequate information. The usefulness of a library is determined by the variety and quality of materials it has on its shelves. As the education is becoming increasingly library-centered, the need for good books in the library cannot be over emphasized. Every year thousands and thousands of books are published all over the world. In fact, there has been an increase of 250 per cent in the number of books published each year over the last 25 years. From the vast mass, every library has to select suitable books and related material for the community it serves, keeping of course, its financial limitations in view. To satisfy the fifth law, duplication of books should be avoided unless it is absolutely necessary. All libraries have to face the problem of weeding out books. Unless books are weeded out, the expansion of the stack room will have to be a continuous process. Old editions can be removed from the library and must be either stored or destroyed. Thus, keeping in view the demands of the readers and our financial limitations, we can try to make a balance and adequate collection.

Thus, book selection is the primary function in any library. All other activities radiate from selected books. Therefore, book selection work should be done very carefully. The sole purpose of book selection is to meet the demands of the readers. In short, we can say that we should try to select the best for the masses out of the vast.

Sources of Book Selection

Today we are living in the world of "Literature-Explosion". The literature is growing continuously. It is growing in various forms and various languages. From this overwhelming mass of new books and periodicals, every library has to select reading material for its community of readers, keeping in view its financial limitations. Book selection is a very responsible job. Librarians should know reader's needs, financial limitations and the literature published. To make book selection effective, the librarian must know the policies of libraries, the characteristics of readers and the resources including source materials and staff. Book selection procedure varies from library to library, due to peculiar circumstances of each library.

For book selection, one must know the relevant sources from which books can be selected. There are mainly three sources of book selection:

1. Reader's suggestions
2. Book reviews
3. Bibliographies

Reader's Suggestions

Reader's suggestions are an important and direct source for book selection. Readers should be encouraged to make their wants known. Sometimes readers suggestions prove to be very valuable in filling a gap in collection. So readers should be encouraged to suggest good books which are not available in the library. A definite system should be followed for getting the suggestions from the readers. Some libraries maintain a suggestion register. Some libraries use separate suggestion cards for their purpose. Library should keep a suggestion box preferably near the entrance of the library. Suggestions may also be oral. Library should give priority to the reader's suggestion and to order the book as early as possible after the approval. If some how, the suggested books are not approved for purchase, then concerned readers should be informed, if possible verbally, of the reasons for its rejection. Otherwise readers will feel that libraries do not take their suggestions seriously.

Book Reviews

"Book Reviews" means reviews or criticisms found in periodicals usually on new books. It is an important source of book selection. Almost in every important periodical and newspaper, there is a separate section on book review. Value of book review depends upon the standard with which they are written. Broadly reviews may be of two types: (1) critical and (2) journalistic. Critical reviews are based on subjective approach while journalistic reviews are objective. Journalistic reviews summarize the contents of the books, noting the style and the treatment. It may even point out the physical qualities of the book such as the paper binding, printing, illustrations, standard of exposition, index and other bibliographical details. Critical reviews differ from person to person. Critical reviews may be either judicial, moral or impressionistic. The judicial type compares a book with other titles which have been accepted as good. The moral weighs the book according to ethical standards. The impressionistic type, the most common, judges a book by the critics personal reaction to it rather than by objective standards. Some reviews are descriptive in nature. They describe briefly the contents of the book. Some are analytical reviews. They are usually short providing concise and critical information. A review may be in a narrative form. It provides general information about the book. A review may be abstracting review. These are not critical in nature. Abstracts are given which can be long or short.

Book reviews are published with several names: Book Reviews, New Thought, New Publications, See Your Books, Current Books, Your Books of the Week, etc.

Mostly, the reviews published are not of a high standard. Many times magazines are of poor standards because they do not have their organizational set up to appoint persons for reviewing of books. Book review is an important media to publicize, for that reason authors and publishers wish to have a favourable review for their books. Sometimes, they influence the reviewers for their purpose. Book reviews are an important source of book selection. Reviews must keep up certain standards, then only they can be relied upon for book selection. The main purpose of a review is to inform the reader regarding the contents of book including the physical qualities. The information given should be specific, brief and complete. The main purpose of the book should also be made clear so it must be done by authoritative persons in the field. They must be scholars in the subject.

Bibliographies

Bibliography means list of books including periodicals. It is an important source for book selection. Its utility and importance in book selection will be clear by studying the types of bibliographies.

Subject Bibliographies: Subject bibliography is usually a list of books, articles and other materials on a given subject. It helps in selecting the books of a particular subject.

Selective Bibliographies: It is a list of best books on a subject or a group of subjects. It helps in selecting books for an average library.

Author Bibliographies: An author bibliography is the list of writings by an author together with the works on him by others. It helps in selecting books by a particular author.

Reading Lists: It is a list of readable books on a particular subject. Such lists are published by the library associations also.

Prospectus: Universities and other examination centres published the prospectus. It provides a list of books for every examination and for every subject. It is useful in book selection.

Year Books: Some publishers publish year books which provides a list of books published in a particular year. They provide subject wise arrangements of the books published in a particular language.

Library Catalogues: Bigger libraries publish their catalogue. It also helps in book selection.

National Bibliographies: It is the record of books published in the language of one country or of books produced in the country, whatever their languages. It is almost a complete record of printed output in a given country, accepting no limitations in the subject fields, nor in the form of literature.

Book Seller's Catalogues: Book sellers publish catalogue of available books and send them to the libraries. It provides information about the books available in the ready stock of a particular book seller.

Publisher's Catalogues: Publishers also send the list of books published by them. It provides informations about newly published books.

Catalogues of Copyright Books: State Government receives books under the copyright act. List of these books is also published at regular intervals. It also provides information about newly published books.

Bibliography of Bibliographies: It is a list of bibliographies. It helps in selecting bibliographies for a library, which is an important tool of book selection.

Thus, bibliography helps in selecting best books in a easy way. It is time saving and helps in providing right book to the right reader at the right time.

Book Selection Tools

The library is a temple of learning, the doors of which are open to all without the distinction of caste, creed, sex or religion. It means we have to satisfy each and every reader coming to the library. A library cannot fulfil its aims and objectives unless it is supplied with the latest reading material. It means the librarian must know the latest reading material published in various branches of knowledge. But today, it is the world of "knowledge explosion". Every minute two thousand documents are published. Librarians are well acquainted with the book selection procedure but are not the master of all subject fields. It is impossible for a librarian to make a satisfactory selection in every branch of knowledge without guide books. "An acquisition section incharge without latest bibliographical tools at his desk is just like a soldier in the battle field without his gun."[3] It means that all possible book selection tools on every branch of knowledge must be acquired in the library regularly. Every subject field now possess bibliographical aids which may be general, special and trade bibliography. Reviewing periodicals and other cumulative book indexes should also be acquired. It is better if a standing order is placed for the acquisition of all important and latest bibliographical tools.

Important Bibliographical Tools

Some important bibliographical tools which are useful in book selection are as follows:

Books Published in Great Britain

British Books in Print

London, J. Whitaker & Sons, 1965 - Annual

This publication is a continuation of Reference Catalogue of Current Literature which started publication in 1874. Previously it was known as *Reference Catalogue of Current Literature*. Since 1965, it is being published under the present title. It provides information about 4,00,000 of those British books which are in print and are available from about 10,000 British book sellers at a particular time. Since 1976, author, title and subject entries are arranged in a single alphabetical order. Each entry provides full bibliographical details, with International Standard Book Number. In the preliminary pages, it contains table of book sizes, lists of abbreviations of publisher's name, list of publishers, identifiers in numerical order, i.e. International Standard Book Numbers and the names of publishers. How to obtain British books i.e. British Publisher's Overseas agents and representatives, series publications and their publishers. Since 1971, it is computer based. The entries are taken from the weekly publications *Book Seller*, which is also J. Whitaker' weekly publication of British books as they are published.

Whitaker's Cumulative Book List

London, J. Whitaker & Sons, 1924- Quarterly and Annual.

It covers all British Books published during the quarter. The arrangement is classified under various subject headings, with an alphabetical index of authors, titles and subjects. Each entry provides the name of the author, title imprint, collation, price and the class number by Dewey Decimal Classification. It is issued quarterly and cumulated annually. Larger cumulations (four yearly and five yearly) are also available. It is prepared on the basis of the weekly publications *Book Seller* which is also J. Whitaker's weekly publication of British books as they are published.

Book-Sellers, the organ of the book trade

1858-1908, Monthly; 1909- Weekly.

It contains each week the full list of British books as they are published, in an alphabetical arrangement, with full bibliographical details. It is issued weekly and cumulated monthly, quarterly and annually.

Paperbacks in Print

London, J. Whitaker & Sons, 1961 - Semi annual.

It is a reference catalogue of over 70,000 paperbacks in print and on sale in Great Britain. The entries are arranged under various main headings. It also provides author and title index.

Whitaker' Books of Month and Books to Come

London, J. Whitaker & Sons, 1970 - Monthly.

It is a monthly list of books published in UK and the books which are in publication. It provides full bibliographical details. The arrangement is alphabetical. It is issued monthly and cumulated annually.

British Book News

London, British Council, 1940 - Monthly.

It is selective in nature. It reviews 250 best books only which are published in UK and the Commonwealth each month. The entries are arranged in a classified order. Each entry provides the name of the author, titles, series, imprint, collation and price. A succinct review is also appended. Index is cumulated. It is an important book selection tool.

Times Literary Supplement

London, *The Times* (daily newspaper)., 1902 - Weekly.

It mainly covers the British books in humanities and social sciences. It is a reviewing periodical. The reviews are given by subject specialists and signed.

International Bibliography of Social Sciences

London, Tavistock Publications, 1968.

It provides a list of British books in Economics, Anthropology, Sociology and Political Science.

ASLIB Book List

London, ASLIB, 1935 - Monthly.

It provides a monthly list of about 100 recommended books on technical and scientific subjects. Entries are arranged in a classified order by UDC in four parts : Elementary, Intermediate, Advanced and Reference books. Each entry provides the name of the author, title, imprint and collation. A short annotation is also given.

British National Bibliography

London, Council of British National Bibliography, 1950 - Weekly.

It provides a subject list of new books published in Great Britain based upon the books deposited at the copyright office of the British Museum. The entries are arranged in a classified order by Dewey Decimal classification with modifications. In addition, a full author, title and subject index are also provided. Each entry provides DC class number, name of author, title of the book, imprint, collation and series. Reference to previous edition is also made, wherever applicable. AACR 1967 is followed for cataloguing. It is published weekly. It has monthly, quarterly, year and quinquennial cumulations. The cumulation of author index is published every month. It is printed through computer - controller photo type system.

Books Published In the United States of America

Books In Print

New York, R.R. Bowker, 1948 - Annual.

It is an annual trade bibliography listing all in print and forthcoming books of America. It covers more than 6 lakh titles from about 13,500 publishers. Certain classes of publications, for example, Government publications and some paper bound books (which are covered in paper bound books in print) are excluded. It provides author and title approaches. Full bibliographical details are provided in author and title index. It provides name of author, title, price, edition, binding, publisher, year of publication, illustrations and series, if any and the International Standard Book Number.

It annually invites, all the publishers to submit their listings for inclusions. Then the information is rearranged in different sequences. It is produced from the Bibliographic Information Publication System (BIPS), data base of R.R. Bowker. It is produced from records stored on magnetic tapes, edited by computer - controlled photo composition.

Subject Guide to Books in Print

It covers American books in print. It is a subject guide to the books which are listed in books in print. It does not include some publications like Government publications, most professional law books, subscription reference sets, some paperback books and the books priced less than 25 cents.

The arrangements of entries is alphabetical, by subjects following the Library of Congress Subject Headings list. In many cases there are more than one subject heading assigned to the same title, with a number of cross references. Under each subject heading the entry is arranged alphabetically by author. Each entry provides author name, title, imprint, series, price, number of volumes, edition, illustration, type of binding (if other than cloth binding), International Standard Book Number.

It is produced from Bibliographic Information Publication System (BIPS) data base of R.R. Bowker. It is produced from records stored on magnetic tapes, edited by computer programmes and set in type by computer - controlled photo - commission.

American Book Publishing Record

New York, R.R. Bowker, 1960

It is a list of current American Books. It is published monthly and cumulated annually. Larger cumulation are also available. It does not include following publications : Federal and other Government publications, Subscription books, Dissertations, Periodicals, Pamphlets under 49 pages, Publication of Transitory nature or intended as advertisements.

The entries in classified are arranged according to Dewey Decimal Classification. Author and title index is also provided. The classified part is followed by many other sections like Juvenile fiction, Adult fiction, Paperback books, etc., arranged separately in each issue.

It is extremely useful for the libraries, for the selection of books, for verifying bibliographical details and technical processing.

There are a number of other publications brought out by R.R. Bowker & Co., New York:

1. *Publishers Weekly*, 1872 - Weekly.
2. *Weekly Record*, 1974 - Weekly.
3. *Books in Print Supplement*, 1973 - Annual.
4. *Text-Books in Print*.
5. *Paper Bound Books In print*.
6. *Forthcoming books*.

Book Review Digest

New York, H.W. Wilson, 1905 - Monthly.

It is published monthly except in February and July. It has half-yearly, yearly and quinquennial cumulations.

It gives the digest and index of about 5000 book reviews published in about 85 English and American periodicals. The entries are arranged alphabetically by the name of the author. In addition, a separate title and subject index is also provided. The bibliographical details in each entries include author name, title, imprint, collation, price, description, annotation and quotation taken from one of the reviews. Indication of favourable and unfavourable review is given.

Cumulative Book Index

A world list of books in English language

New York, H.W. Wilson & Co., 1898 -

It is issued monthly except August. It is cumulated quarterly, annually, half-yearly and two yearly volumes.

Initially CBI was used to record only American publications. Since 1928, it covers publications of the entire world published in English language. It excludes reading materials like Government publications, pamphlets, music, miniature editions and emphemera.

The arrangement of entries is alphabatical, by author, title and subject in one sequence. Each book is listed under as many subject headings as its contents require. Subject headings have been derived from Library of Congress Subject Headings List. Author entries give full information i.e. author's name, full title, imprint, edition, series, if any, illustration, binding if other than cloth binding, price, Library of Congress Card Number, and International Standard Book Number (if available).

This tool is extremely useful for selecting books published in English in the whole world. It also provides a selective list of world publishers at the end.

The National Union Catalogue

Washington, Library of Congress, 1948 - Monthly.

It is published monthly and cumulated quarterly and annually. It covers new printed books received in the Library of Congress and the titles reported by other American libraries. However, the books covered by the National Library of Medicine Catalogue and the Bibliography of Agriculture are excluded. The arrangements of entries is alphabatical by author. Each entry provides the author' name, title, imprint, collation, prices, etc.

The Library of Congress Catalogue, Books: Subject

Washington, Library of Congress, 1950 - Quarterly.

It is published quarterly, cumulated annually, superseded by quinquinnial cumulations.

It covers recently published books. The entries are arranged alphabatically by subject. The bibliographical details in each entry includes author, title, imprint, series, price, number of volumes, edition, illustrations, type of binding (if other than cloth binding). However, it does not provide notes and tracings which are found in the LC Author Catalogue.

Scientific, Medical and Technical Books

ed. by R.K. Hawkings, 2nd ed. Washington, National Academy of Sciences, National Research Council, 1958.

It provides list of books published in the United States of America. It covers selected books on Scientific, Medical and Technical subjects. Each entry provides complete bibliographical information.

Books Published in India

Indian National Bibliography

Calcutta, Central Reference Library, National library, 1957-Quarterly, 1964 - Monthly.

It is an authoritative source for Indian books. The material included in it are the ones received in the National Library, Calcutta according to the delivery of Books and Newspapers Act of 1954 and the amendment of 1956. It is a consolidated list of all subject books received with the periodicity of the publication. It covers all books published in India in English and other languages recognized by the Constitution of India.

It is divided into three sections. The first section is the classified section. The entries of books included in the bibliography are arranged in a minutely classified order. The classified section gives information about general books as well as government and quasi-government publications, in a single sequence. The second and the third sections consist of the indexes. The system of classification used for main part is the Dewey Decimal Classification with verbal expansion. Entries in classified part are constructed according to A.L.A. cataloguing rules with modifications wherever necessary. Arrangement followed in general, is helpful for book selection purposes.

It excludes materials like musical scores, keys and guides to text books, ephemeral materials such as trade catalogues, reports and financial statements of statutory companies, cheap novel and periodicals and newspapers, except the first issue of a new periodical and the first issue of the changed title of a periodical.

Each entry provides full bibliographical details like title, sub- title, imprint, collation, series, reference to previous editions, if any, the language of the book and the title in the original language. All entries are given in Roman Script.

It is issued monthly and cumulated annually. Besides, separate language annuals in respective script are issued through the State Governments.

Indian Books in Print

Compiled by Sher Singh and S.N.Sadu, 3 Vol. Delhi, Indian Bureau of Bibliographies, 1986.

It is a selective bibliography of English language books published in India.

Its first edition containing information about books published between 1955 and 1967. It includes more than 40,000 books and pamphlets by about 1500 publishers. It also includes a large number of publications brought out by various societies and institutions, and government publications. The bibliography consists of five parts:

(i) Classified Part
(ii) Author index
(iii) Title index
(iv) Subject Index and
(v) List of Indian publishers.

In classified part the entries have been arranged according to Dewey Decimal Classification (16th edition) with suitable feature headings. The author and title index parts also give complete bibliographical detail. The subject index provides subject approach. The entries in general have been prepared according to the rules given in the classified catalogue code (1964) by S.R. Ranganathan. The book is a major contribution to bibliographic organization of Indian materials and is very useful for librarians, books sellers and publishers.

Its second edition was published in 1972 covering English language books for the period upto December, 1971. It is published in three volumes - Vol. 1: Author index; Vol.2: Title index; and Vol. 3: Subject guide. It contains complete bibliographical details of about 70,000 Indian books in English language in print.

Its third edition was published in 1973, covering the period upto 1972. Its fourth edition was published in 1979 covering the period upto 1977.

Its present set is in three Volumes. Vol. 1: Author Index, Vol.2: Title index and Vol. 3: Subject index. Author and Title indexes have been arranged in alphabetical order. Subject index is in classified order giving DDC number with feature headings. It is edited by Sher Singh. It covers the books published upto December, 1985. About 85,000 titles are included in it. At the end of third Volume, a directory of Indian Publishers is also given.

National Bibliography of Indian Literature 1910-1953

New Delhi, Sahitya Akademi, 1962.

In enlists all Indian publications of literary merit and abiding value. It is published in four separate volumes.

Vol. I — Assamese, Bengali, English and Gujarati.
Vol. II — Hindi, Kannada, Kashmiri and Malayalam.
Vol. III — Marathi, Oriya, Punjabi and Sanskrit.
Vol. IV — Sindhi, Tamil, Telugu and Urdu.

The entries are in Roman Script. The entries are first grouped under language and then arranged alphabetically by author under sub divisions such as general works, philosophy and religion, social sciences, linguistics, arts, literature, history, biography and travel and miscellaneous items. Literature is further divided into poetry, drama, fiction, essays, letters, humour and satire and miscellaneous items. At the end of each Volume an alphabetical index is provided. Annotations are given in English.

Index

Reference Catalogue of Indian Books.

New Delhi, Indian Book Exports & Imports Co.

1690 - Supplement 1960-62.

It gives a list of important books published and in print in India. It is divided in two sections. In the first section alpha - betico - classed arrangement in broad alphabetical subject groupings. In the second section the entries are arranged under author, title, catchword title and series. The bibliographical details are given in both the sections, Government publications are dealt with separately.

Indian Scientific and Technical Publications

Exhibition: 1960

New Delhi, Council of Scientific and Industrial Research, 1960.

It is a selective list of scientific and technical publications of India. It is published in English as well as in other Indian Languages. The entries are arranged in classified order. It has two parts. Part I contains published work in Indian Languages and Part II contains English Books. One consolidated subject index is provided. Alphabetical indexes are also provided.

Documentation on Asia

Ed. by Girija Kumar and V. Machwe.

New Delhi, Allied Publishers, 1960 - Annual.

It contains a selection on India. It is a comprehensive bibliography of current literature on Asia. The entries are arranged in order of geographical areas and sub-arranged according to subject.

Asian Social Sciences Bibliography

Ed. by N.K.Goil, Delhi, Vikas Publications, 1970.

It is an annotated and selective bibliography. It contains six branches: Social Science, Socio-data Education and Communication, Political Science, Economics, Sociology, Social Anthropology and Social Psychology and Demography.

Central and State Government' List of Publications

The Central and State Government publish periodically various lists of books published by them respectively.

(i) Catalogue of Government of India: Civil Publications. Delhi, Government of India Press, 1966, p. 761.

Government Publications of India

A survey of their nature, bibliographical Control and distribution systems.

By Mohinder Singh, assisted by J.F. Pandya, Delhi, Metropolitan Book Co., 1967.

It includes over 1500 titles published by 250 Government of India Officers, Ministers and Departments including the Planning Commission, the Election Commission and the Union Service Commission.

Publisher' Catalogues

(i) *Publisher' monthly*: Delhi S. Chand & Co.,
It enlists books published by M/s S.Chand & Co., Delhi.

(ii) *Asia Bulletin*: Bombay, Asia Publishing House.
It is a monthly Bulletin. It enlists the publications of M/s Asia Publishing House, Bombay.

(iii) *Indian Publisher's and Bookseller's monthly*: Bombay, Popular Book Depot.
It consists of important books published during the month by the publishers.

(iv) *Oxford University Press Catalogue*: New Delhi, Oxford University Press.
It is a consolidated list of publications issued by M/s Oxford University Press.

(v) *Book Talk*: Ed. by B. Bhattacharya. New Delhi, Wile Eastern Ltd.
It publishes list of books on Science and Technology every month. The books are listed under various subjects and each entry provides a detailed annotation.

Bookseller's Catalogue

Many big and small booksellers issue lists of books stocked by them.

(i) *UBS's Catalogue*: Delhi UBS Publishers.
It Publishes a consolidated list of books published by about 110 foreign and 150 Indian Publishers represented by the firm. It is a classified list by subject headings.

(ii) *Indian Book House's Catalogue*: Bombay, India Book House.
It publishes a catalogue of books of about 20 publishers represented by it.

(iii) *Rupa & Co.'s Catalogue*: Calcutta, Rupa & Co.
The catalogue enlists books published by many publishers represented by the firm.

Other Publications

(i) *Indian Book Chronicle*: Ed. by Amrik Singh. Vivek Trust, New Delhi.
It reviews book published in India and books about India published anywhere in the world.

(ii) *Indian Book Industry*: Editor-in-chief : O.P.Ghai. New Delhi, Sterling Publishers Pvt. Ltd.
It is a monthly journal linking the activities of Publishers, Book Sellers, Librarians, Scholars, Research Bodies, Universities and other trades and industries connected with the production and distribution of books i.e. paper, printing machinery, etc.
It provides information about the English books published every month in India. It also provides articles on important topics. It also includes book reviews of selected books.

List of Periodicals

Today we are living in the world of "Knowledge-explosion". Knowledge is growing very rapidly due to rapid research. Nascent thoughts are arising continuously. Increasing population pressure and social pressure are accelerating the rate of research. Periodicals publish at a regular intervals and inform us about the results and progress of different researches. In this way, periodicals inform researchers about the latest researches and also helps in avoiding duplication of work and wastage of time, money and labour. A number of periodicals are publishing in India and around in various subject fields. Ultimately there is a need of an authentic source which can inform a reader about the periodicals of his interest. Some important sources are:

Ulrich's International Periodicals Directory

New York RR Bowker & Co., 1932.

It is a comprehensive list of periodicals, worldwide in scope. It is a classified guide to current periodicals, foreign and domestic. This publication was started in 1932 with a list of about 6000 periodicals. Its 22nd edition was published in 1983. It is in two volumes and lists about 64,000 periodicals of all kinds from all over the world in 556 subject areas. There are 1,16,000 entries from 63000 publishers from 180 countries. It includes periodicals which are currently in print, issued more frequently than once a year and usually published at regular intervals. Annual and irregular serials are covered through a companion volume, entitled "Irregular serials and annuals : An international directory".

In first ten editions, it followed an alphabetical arrangement under subject headings. Eleventh and twelfth editions were divided into two parts viz. Vol. I - Scientific and technical periodicals : Vol. II ; Arts, Humanities, Social Sciences, etc. From the thirteenth edition it again followed classified arrangement under main subject headings and subheadings are arranged alphabetically. For periodicals dealing with more than one subject, cross references have been used to direct the readers to the subject under which the complete entry will be found. Each entry provides full bibliographical details like DDC number and International Standard Serial Number, Name of title, translated title, language of text, year first published, frequency, annual subscription, editor's name, sponsoring body/publisher's name and address, whether indexed/abstracted, whether bibliography, book reviews, advertising included, circulation figures, former title if changed, etc. In the beginning, it provides user's guide, abbreviations used, key to subject in English, French, German and Spanish. At the end, additional information such as lists of periodicals which ceased publication, index to publications of international organizations, title index has been provided. This bibliography is in a continuous contact with various publishers to get the necessary information through a complex computerized mailing system. Its new edition and supplements are published in alternating years to keep the directory uptodate, an another publication "Ulrich's Quarterly" has been started from 1977.

Indian periodicals - an annotated guide

Complied by N.N. Gidwani & K. Navlani. Jaipur, 1979

It is the first guide to Indian periodicals which is annotated. It is very useful for academic and research librarians. It is also useful for specialists, booksellers and publishers.

It is a classified guide to Indian periodicals in English listing more than 5000 entries. It provides very useful information with a special mention of newsletters, house organs, embassy publications etc. It excludes ephemeral publications and the publications meant for children.

It is in two sections first section provides a list of periodicals annotated and arranged by subjects in alphabetical sequence. Under the subject, each entry provides full information about title, subtitle if any, year of origin, periodicity, subscription, name of editor, publisher and other necessary information. The second section provides the alphabetical list of titles.

In addition to these, other important sources providing information about publication of periodicals are :

(i) Regional Union Catalogue of Scientific Serials. Bangalore, 1967.

(ii) Regional Union Catalogue of Scientific Serials. Delhi, Medical Libraries, 1967.

(iii) Regional Union Catalogue of Scientific Serials. Dehradun - Roorkee, 1971.

(iv) Catalogue of Serials in the National Institute of Sciences of India, Delhi, 1968.

(v) World list of Scientific periodicals published during the period 1900-1950. Ed. by W.A. Smith and others. London, Butterworth, 1952.

(vi) Readers Guide to Periodical Literature. New York, Wilson, 1900.

(vii) Union List of Serials in Libraries of United States and Canada. Ed. by Winifred Gregory. New York, Wilson, 1962.

(viii) Union Catalogue of Learned American Serials in Indian Libraries. Delhi, Indian Council for Library Development, 1966.

Conclusion

Thus book selection is the primary and the most important function of a library. It is a very responsible job. The success or failure of a library's programme depends upon it. Through the selection of good books, library gains popularity. Book selection work must be done in accordance with the type of the library and its users. The librarian's ethics for book selection requires to meet the demand of users to a maximum extent with greater economy and efficiency. Well planned and properly thought out selection of documents helps in strengthening the library's resources for education, information, recreation, knowledge and research. The basic aim of a library should be to build up a collection which is dynamic and capable of meeting the changing needs and demands of present as well as future users. The collection development will come out only when its librarian and library staff are in the know of new trends, new periodicals and newer editions. Thus, all possible source materials such as books, trade lists, reviewing periodicals and other cumulative book indexes and lists should be acquired regularly.

REFERENCES

1. Mukherjee, A.K. *Reference Work and its Tools.* 3rd Ed. Calcutta: World Press, p. 40, 1975.
2. *Encyclopaedia of Librarianship.* 1st ed. p. 46.
3. Mittal, R.L. *Library Administration: Theory and Practice.* 5th Ed. New Delhi: Metropolitan, p. 197, 1984.

Six

Library Authority and Library Committee

DR H.R. CHOPRA

Library Authority

Government, Management Committee, Board of Trustees, Senate, Syndicate, Executive Council or similar other bodies authorised to do certain job or control the working of certain organization is called "Authority". The agency authorised to control the working of a Library is called "Library Authority". Such a body generally supervises the working of the library, its librarian and the related activities. The main function of the Library Authority is to levy duty, sanction funds, appoint library staff, sanction posts and have control over the functioning of the library within the framework of its Constitution. The Library Authority can authorise some of its agencies, sub-committees or persons to perform its duties. In other words, it can delegate its authority to some smaller or subordinate agency or committee to perform its function. Library Authority is the highest governing body of the library, empowered by law, to sanction funds or posts, reward or punish library staff, make rules & regulations and authorise subordinate agencies or persons to perform its duties and day to day activities.

Library Committee

A committee comprises of a group of persons authorised to perform certain duties or undertake certain responsibilities, as authorised by the higher authorities. A committee constituted with the purpose of providing collective advice on all matters of the library concerning its activities and services is called "Library Committee" or "Library Advisory Committee". It is appointed by the Library Authority for a fixed period and under certain defined conditions . Library Committee comprises of certain library professionals, experts from different fields, representatives of the Library Authority, representatives of the library users and representatives of the locality concerned. The number of Library Committee varies from five to fifteen, depending upon the type and size of the library concerned. The head of the institution or his representative/nominee (e.g. Vice-Chancellor, Dean, Principal, Director, Municipal Commissioner, M.P., Managing Director, Headmaster, etc.) is the chairperson of the Library Committee, while the librarian of the library concerned is its Secretary, Convenor or Secretary-General.

Need and Purpose of Library Committee

In order to run the library through a democratic process, to check the undue authority of the librarian, and to avoid his monopoly, involvement of the Library Committee is very essential. Since it has certain experts in different fields as its members, experts opinion is made available regularly and freely. Collective advice and guidance is made available to the librarian for better and efficient library management. He can get help in policy making and implementing plans with confidence. He gets delegation of powers for prompt action and implementation of policies made by the Library Authority and Library Committee. Librarian gets directions for future development of the library. It is a good method to decentralise responsibilities of the librarian. Thus, the librarian can play a positive role objectively to manage the day to day functioning of the library with confidence. Moreover, he has a spokesman in the Library Authority to support and argue his suggestions, policies and recommendations for betterment of the library services, sanction of more funds, additional posts and better facilities. Thus, it is evident that Library Advisory Committee plays a very important role to help the librarian and for betterment of the library. Library Committee is needed for every type of library.

Types of Library Committees

There are different types of Library Committees depending upon the size, scale of activities, operations and types of libraries. Some of the important types of Library Committees are as under:

Statutory Committee

It is constituted according to the legal requirements of Library Act. For example, Library Advisory Committee for State Public Libraries.

Standing Committee

It is constituted by Executive orders of the Library Authorities. For example, Grievance Committee or Book Selection Committee.

Ad-hoc Committee

It is constituted by the Executive orders of the authorities for certain specific purposes, such as Promotion, Assessment, Review or Selection Committee.

Reporting Committee

Such a committee has sufficient powers to take decisions and need no approval of the higher authorities. Rather, these only report to the higher authorities the decision taken by it, for example, Leave Sanction Committee.

Working Committee

It is also called Task Forces. It is appointed by the head of the library to assist him in technical or administrative matters, for example, Classification Committee, Reprographic Services Committees, etc.

Recommending Committee

Such a committee does not have a real power. It only makes recommendations and the higher authorities may or may not accept its recommendations, for example, Selection Committee, Enquiry Committee, etc.

Sub-Committee

It is a subordinate committee to assist the higher committee in certain specific matters. It can be constituted by the Statutory Committees.

Executive Committee

This committee is the most powerful because it has full powers for certain matters which are delegated to it by the competent library authority. It is a kind of Self-Perpetuating Committee, having the sole authority in the control and management of the library under it.

Committees in Different Types of Libraries

Public Libraries

Only ten States in India have enacted Library Act (by the end of 1994). The Constitution of Library Committees in these States (Madras, Karnataka, Andhra Pradesh, Maharashtra, West Bengal, Manipur, Haryana, Kerala, Goa and Mizoram) has been defined in the Library Act concerned.

University Libraries

As provided in the statutory document, the constitution of the Library Committee is defined. The members include Dean, Principals, Professors, Syndics and the Librarian as its Secretary.

College Libraries

Generally the principal, members of the management committee of the college, senior faculty members and the Librarian are members of the College Library Advisory Committee.

School Libraries

Library Committees of schools comprise of headmaster, members of the management committee, nominees of the State Government, principals of the neighbouring institutions and the librarian of the school library concerned. This constitution varies slightly in case of government schools, government aided schools, missionary schools, private schools and minority group schools.

Special Libraries

Libraries attached to the industries, research institutions, commercial organizations, societies, associations and similar other agencies have different constitution of their Library Committees, which comprise of nominees of the parent body, researchers, scientists, outside experts and the librarian concerned.

Functions of the Library Committee

The primary functions of a Library Committee are to give advice and guidance to the librarian in the policy matters. It approves budget estimates, plans, policies, Annual Reports, Statements of expenditure, Library Rules and similar other matters concerning the library and its staff. It also approves staff recruitment, evaluates programmes, allocates funds, constitutes selection committees for recruitment, scrutinises major purchases and appoints sub-committees for various specific purposes. Library Committee also makes library policies for library cooperation, standard library services and library audit and accounts. It renders advice to the librarian in all important matters concerning library management and policies.

Librarian and Library Committee

The librarian is generally the Secretary (or Secretary General or Convenor) of the Library Committee of his library. Very often he recommends the names of the members of the Library Committee because he knows who can help or guide him in certain matters. The Library Authorities generally approve his recommendations. It is the librarian who prepares the agenda for the meeting of the Library Committee; gives explanatory notes, records the proceedings of the meeting and implements the policies and decisions approved by the Library Committee. The follow-up work within the time limit is also the responsibility of the librarian. He has skill of communication, recording and implementing. He keeps the chairman of the Library Committee informed of the developments in the library from time to time, maintains cordial relations with him and possesses coherent views. Thus, it is evident that the librarian has very close and significant relations with the Library Committee.

Meeting of the Library Committee

A Library Committee is generally constituted for a period of two or three years. The meetings of the Library Committee are conducted quarterly or four monthly. In certain cases, these meetings are held even twice or only once in a year, depending upon the agenda or urgency of the matters before it. The agenda is scrutinised by the chairman of the Library Committee well in advance, before sending it to the members of the committee, time and venue of the meeting is also fixed with prior approval of the chairman of the Library Committee. Due notice is given to the members of the Library Committee and agenda is sent well in time in order to enable them to study it carefully and make it convenient to attend the meeting. Conditions for payment of travelling allowance, dearness allowance, arrangement for stay and other details are also communicated to all the members along with notice for the meeting and the agenda. Proceedings are recorded by the convenor and confirmed by the chairman of the Library Committee. Recorded proceedings are circulated among all the members regularly, which are confirmed by the Library Committee in its next meeting. In case of an urgent matter, meeting of the Library Committee can be convened with short notice also. The librarian keeps a record of all the previous proceedings of the meetings and implementation of its decisions as well as follow-up action.

Some Apprehensions

Despite the usefulness of the Library Committee, a few negative aspects are often discussed in the library community. These apprehensions are worth consideration. First of all, it is considered that meeting of the Library Committee is merely a formality and no real contribution has been seen or found in such committee meetings. Secondly, the cost of these meetings is very high when we calculate the cost on stationery, postage, ministerial assistance, travelling & dearness allowance for the members, hospitality, and other miscellaneous expenses. Thirdly, unnecessary delay in taking decisions by the Library Committee is another negative point. Fourthly, the members of the Library Committee tend to dominate the proceedings and may have conflict with the librarian, which is not a healthy practice. Finally, it is thought that all the members of the Library Committee do not possess expert knowledge to render genuine advice to the librarian for better management of the library concerned.

But, despite these apprehensions, the necessity of the Library Committee prevails. The librarian remains cautious, alert and answerable to the Library Committee. In difficult cases or circumstances, he gets help, advice and guidance from the Library Committee. Monopoly of the librarian, if any, can be eliminated and responsibility can be shared in case of expensive purchases, controversial policy decisions, difficult library rules, and development plans of the library. The Library Committee does play a vital and significant role in the betterment of library management, check on the role of and assistance in the functioning of the librarian. Above all, the Library Committee acts as a shield for the librarian in case of controvercial decisions, and supports the librarian in case of plans for expansion, development and better library services. The role of the Library Committee cannot be underestimated despite certain apprehensions.

All the apprehensions mentioned in para 91 above need thorough discussion, viable suggestions and appropriate recommendations, in spite of the fact that role of Library Authority and Library Advisory Committee is very important.

Seven

Personal Effectiveness And Job Involvement of Library Professionals

[With Reference to Social Science Libraries in Delhi)

DR J.N. GAUTAM *and* DR MAHAVEER SINGH

Introduction

Personal effectiveness refers to integrated qualities of a person. It is personal effectiveness on which the success of a job depends. According to Sutton and Ford, 1982, personal effectiveness can be defined as an ability to solve four system problems. These problems are adaptation, goal attainment, integration, and latency. It also refers to an ability to perform the job effectively.[1]

An individual in an organization is said to be high performer if he or she accomplishes his or her job successfully, that is assigned to him. It is difficult to measure the performance of an individual in an objective and quantifiable manner. There may be other indicators or job performance such as profit of a unit, company, products, etc. But they are not accurate indicators, because some unaccounted factors also might affect these criteria.

Dimensions of structure such as specialization, formalization, and centralization are related with job performance. Specialization or the divisions of work have a very important role in the efforts to achieve high performance. Dalton, Todor, and Spendolini (1980) concluded that lack of hard performance criteria, one cannot establish clear relationship between specialization and performance.[2] Child (1975) found that poor performance is related with less staff specialization, formalization, and less developed systems of procedures.[3] Routamaa (1981) in his study showed that positive relationship exists between specialization and performance.[4]

Researches have shown that climate has significant influence on performance (Kaczka & Kirk, 1968).[5] Fredrickson (1966) reported that innovative climate would yield greater productivity.[6]

Litwin and Stringer (1968)[7] found that achievement oriented climate was most productive whereas democratic and friendly climate produced higher work satisfaction. Pritchard and Karasick 1973[8] related several organizational climate dimensions with individual job performance. Only two aspects of climate, namely, level of rewards and achievement were positively related with performance.

The present study is focused on looking into the impact of individual performance on the job involvement of the library professionals who are serving in the social science libraries in Delhi.

Job Involvement

Job involvement is the internationalisation of values about the goodness of work in the worth of the person. According to Lodahl and Kejner, 1965; "Job involvement is the degree to which a person is identified psychologically with his work or the importance of work in his total self image."[9] Thus job involvement measures the ease with which the person can be further socialized by an organization.

Although there may be many such factors which influence the job involvement of the members of the organization but in the present study only personal effectiveness factor has been taken in account.

Personal Effectiveness and Job Involvement

Sample

The present study was undertaken on 261 library professionals in 61 social science libraries in Delhi. Out of 261 library professionals, 141 were male and 120 were female library professionals. The sample was selected on the basis of non-probability "Accidental sample" technique.

Measures

The scale used for measuring personal effectiveness in the job was developed by Sutton and Ford (1982). There are 4 items followed by a five point scale ranging from 1 (True to almost no extent) to 5 (true to a very good extent). Higher scores are indicative of greater personal effectiveness. Coefficient of this scale was found to be 0.68. Item total correlation was found to be at a moderate level.

"Measuring job involvement in India" a scale developed by U.N. Agarwal, (1978)[10] is used in this study to determine the Job Involvement of the professionals. The Scale consists of 32 items relating to different factors like job-longing, work underload, emotional involvement, persistence, energy expenditure and planfulness, etc. Each item is to be answered with the help of a 5 point scale, ranging from strongly agree to strongly disagree.

The reported split-half reliability coefficients ranged from 0.85 to 0.87 and convergent validity is 0.33. This scale is found to correlate highly (4 =0.85) with the Lodahl and Kejner's (1965) abbreviated Job Involvement scale.

Data Collection/Analysis

The "measures" were administered individually to each respondent who was assured that information provided by him will be used only for research purpose. The scores on each statement with five-point rating scale were measured. The data were analyzed for personal effectiveness in terms of level with job involvement. The statistical analysis of data is reported as shown in Table 1.

Results and Discussion

Table 1 indicates that there are only three persons who find their job to be highly personally effective and they are also high on the job involvement which means that it is not necessary that those who find their job personally effective are more involved in their job. Again the table refers that the individuals, who solve the problems by involving themselves personally, that is, the individuals who are effective, do not directly stand in ratio with job involvement. Both the facts are poorly proportionate to one another. A large number of respondents stand in the line of involvement in job in degrees of agreeable magnitude. Strong job involvement has to be traced somewhere else.

Table - 1
Cross Tabulation between Personal Effectiveness and Job Involvement

Level	*Strongly Agree*	*Agree*	*Neither Agree Nor Disagree*	*Total*
1.00-1.99	0	2 (100)	0	2 (.8)
2.00-2.99	0	17 (89.5)	2 (10.7)	19 (7.3)
3.00-3.99	1 (.8)	93 (77.5)	26 (21.7)	120 (46)
4.00-4.99	3 (2.5)	95 (79.1)	22 (18.3)	120 (46)
	4 (1.5)	207 (79.3)	50 (19.5)	261 (100)

Conclusion

The successful accomplishment of one's job assigned to him is certainly because of one's personal effectiveness which may be an attribute of his integrated qualities like specialization, formalization and centralization or division of work. But, this success is achieved only when one puts in effectiveness. It is the need of the hour to the factor which makes one put in one's effectiveness. Though demographic and organizational are some of the factors which motivate a person to put in one's effectiveness, but these are found to be lean and weak motivators. In our opinion one's heritage of good breeding, disciplined and planned education and bringing up of the person, urge him to put in his effectiveness in his job.

REFERENCES

1. Sutton, R.L. and Ford, R.H. Problem Solving adequacy in hospital Sub units. *Human Relations* 35, pp. 6754-701, 1982.
2. Dalton, D.R., Tadar, W.D. and Spendolini, M.J. Organizational Structure and performance: A critical review. *Academy of Management Review* 5. pp. 49-64, 1980.
3. Child, J. Managerial and Organizational factors Associated with Company Performance Part II. *Journal of Management Studies*. 12, pp. 12-27, 1975.
4. Routamaa, V, Organizational Structure and Performance. Proceedings of the University of Vassa. Discussion paper No.32. p 1-15, 1981.
5. Kaczka, E. and Kirk, R. Managerial Climate, Work groups and Organizational Performance. *Administrative Science Quarterly* 12, pp. 253-72, 1968.
6. Fredrickson, N. Some effects of organizational climate on administrative performance Educational testing service. Research Memorandum RM - 66-21, 1966.
7. Litwin, G.H. and Stringer, R.A. *Motivation and Organisational Climate.* Boston: Harvard University Press, 1968.
8. Pritchard, R.D. and Karasick, B.W. The effects of organisational climate on managerial job performance and job satisfaction. *Organizational Behaviour and Human Performance* 9. pp. 126-46, 1973.
9. Lodahl, T.M. and Kejner, M. The definition and Management of Job Involvement, *Journal of Applied Psychology* 49, 1965.
10. Agrawal, U.N. Step to developing job involvement (JI) Scale. *Indian Journal of Psychology* 55 (1-2) pp. 35-42, 1980.

Eight

Qualitative Librarianship through Kaizen Approach

A.R. SETHI

Kaizen Philosophy

Each society has a unique cultural configuration or gestalt, consisting of traditions, values, axioms and norms that regulate the life of its members. For instance, the basic tenets guiding the Hindu life are four *purusharthas* (aims of human life), namely *dharma* (duty), *artha* (power), *kama* (pleasure), and *moksha* (renunciation). The philosophy guiding the Japanese life is known by the term Kaizen.

Kaizen, or the philosophy of continuous improvement, is based on a simple but fundamental belief that life deserves to be continuously improved. "Let us make things better" is the constant refrain of this approach. The approach lays emphasis on process rather than on product. A correct action is bound to lead to correct result, is the promise of this philosophy (a, *la karma* philosophy enunciated in the *Gita*). Kaizen philosophy makes its adherents quality conscious, not quantity-minded.

5-Ss Keys

Also, Kaizen is a philosophy of total life, it does not believe in addressing select problems in a select way. It has messages, though, couched differently for different purposes. For instance, to deal with formal organizations, Kaizen advocates a *5-Ss* strategy consisting of:

Seiri = organization, that is, proper arrangement of work place, equipment, and work activities.
Seiton = orderliness of work place, inventory and work activities.
Seiso = cleanliness, or individual responsibility.
Seiketsu = standardisation.
Shitsuke = discipline, to follow rules and make waste removal a habit.

(*OSADA*, 1995. pp. 604-5).

It is this economic aspect of *kaizen* approach which enabled a politically defeated, economically ruined, socially disoriented Japan of late 1940s to emerge, phoenix like, from its ashes by 1970s, and pose an economic challenge to the whole world. The threatened West, intent on finding out the secret of Japanese success, came out with the revelation that it was their own evolved concept of Total Quality Management (TQM) introduced by Deming to the Japanese industry in early 1950s, which was at the root of this economic miracle in that country. It was difficult for America to digest that TQM itself was the American version of *kaizen*, though in the process of adaptation, they transformed the great Japanese idea the same way as they did the Indian practice of Yoga, by reducing this godly and spiritual exercise to mundane physical exercises for trimming their bulging waistlines.

Total Quality Management (TQM)

It must be said to the credit of Total Quality Management (TQM) that a renewed interest in quality has emerged in societies that by force of habit had always sworn by it but had, of late, jettisoned it in favour of 'mass culture', driven by the urge to compete with, or march with the societies that lived in and thrived on 'quantity'.

Theoretically speaking, TQM consists of :

one objective: continuous improvement;
three principles: customer focus, process improvement, and total involvement;
six supporting elements: leadership, education and training, supportive structure, communications, reward and recognition, and measurement. (Brophy & Coulling, 1996. p. 69).

The claim of the votaries of TQM approach is that it admits no national origin, nor exclusive use by any one. It works successfully in any organization, whatever its size, whatever its nationality, whatever the product or the service, whatever the industry.

On the practical level, however, the literature being doled out by the Western media makes TQM appear like a passing phase, a fad, a fashion of the elite countries. The approach of these countries to TQM suffers from its slant towards industrial organization, and not necessarily the service institutions; it emphasizes product rather than the process; it is practised with an eye on maximisation of profit rather than user's satisfaction; it is moving towards confirmance to standards, rather than confirmance to individual requirements; it is relying more and more on measurement and statistical techniques.

Qualitative (Kaizen) Librarianship

A modern library is a complex organization like any other formal organization with the important difference that it is a non-profit, service organization. The TQM approach, with its slant towards industrial organization, emphasises on result, and an eye on profit, is not exactly the philosophy to guide the management of libraries. A more subtle and substantive approach, like the *Kaizen*, is the need of the hour.

The Kaizen approach, with its emphasis on constant and continuous improvement, quality, rather than quantity, process rather than product, synthesis (totality) rather than analysis, lends itself beautifully to transform the practice of running libraries into *Kaizen* librarianship.

The tenets of *Kaizen* librarianship may be stated as:

1. Library user defines 'quality'
2. Aim 'better', not 'bigger'
3. Quality approach leads to quality product
4. Empower/improve library staff
5. Quality is culture bound

Messages of Kaizen Librarianship

The above tenets have the following messages for practical librarianship:

For Qualitative Approach

(i) Quality management is prevention, not detection.

(ii) The user has a right to zero-defect product/process/service. Quality is not something negotiable, adjustable, or correctable. It is doing things right, the first time, everytime, all the time.

(iii) Quality is not measured by confirmation to specifications, but by meeting user's expectations.

(iv) Quality, management is a journey, not a destination.

For Qualitative Service

(i) every library has its readers. The library that thrives and prospers and feels good about what it does, is one that consistently satisfies its users;

(ii) from the point of view of users, only excuse for your being in the library is to satisfy them;

(iii) user's define value in their two terms;

(iv) dissatisfied/demanding/picky users are not problems, they are golden opportunities. Keep satisfying them, and they will keep coming back and telling others for life;

(v) always treat a user as if he will remain a user. Never treat him as if this is the last time you will see of him;

(vi) when a user provides honest comments, he is doing you a favour - and that is how he looks at it. Give him a reason to do you the favour.

(vii) the user uses five dimensions for judging services, viz. tangibles (e.g. shelving of books, dress-habits of staff, positioning of staff); reliability of information; responsiveness; competence, and empathy of library staff.

For Qualitative Staff

(i) Involve everyone on staff in the new vision of organization;

(ii) Communicate openly, eliminate all barriers;

(iii) Recognise efficiency, reward distinguished service;

(iv) Devolution of responsibility has no meaning without devolution of commensurate power;

(v) Provide opportunities for staff training, education and development;

(vi) Expect mistakes, teething troubles, staff resistance in the initial stages, to envisaged programmes.

(These messages are largely based on Clay Carr's, *Keys to Quality Improvement*.)

Concluding Remarks

Japan is a living and thriving example of success of *kaizen* approach. A country, once having the dubious reputation of poor-value products: toys which came off quickly; cars which broke down and rusted; electronic goods that failed the moment the all too short warranty period was over; transformed itself, within a short span of 50 years, into a country that produces more than 10 per cent of world's economic value, makes more than 50 per cent of world's ships, 25 per cent of its cars, and almost 90 per cent of its videos, with the help of *kaizen* approach to life.

A noteworthy feature of the kaizen approach is that it is culture/environment/soil bound. It derives its philosophy, principles, and practices from the environment in which it is practised. Thus, though it is 'universal' in its sway in the sense that it can be applied by any organization anywhere in the world, it is 'localised' in the sense that it is rooted in the culture of the practising institution.

It is time India too, before taking a firm stride into the future, makes a dive into the deep ocean of its culture and comes out with a *kaizen* like mantra to guide its march towards constant and continuous improvement. If India improves, can its libraries lag behind?

REFERENCES

1. Brophy, Peter and Coulling, Kate. *Quality Management for Information and Library Managers*. Hamtshampire: ASLIB and Gower, 1966.
2. Carr, Clay. *Frontline. Customer Service*. New York: John Willey, 1990.
3. Osad, T. The 5-Ss: Five Keys to a total Quality Environment. In Manji, Gopal K, Ed. *Total Quality Management*. London: Champan & Hall, 1995.

Nine

A TQM Approach For Sustainable Library Development

ROSHAN RAINA

The Need

In todays competitive environment, information is valued as a critical resource for development. Organizations made greater use of information as an economic resource, to introduce innovation and to increase their effectiveness and competitive position. People, in order to ensure better standards of living, use information more intensively in their day to day activities so as to firm-up their choices between alternative products and services.

In this scenario, availability of right information for the right user at the right time and at right cost becomes all the more vital. The scenario has, posed major challenges to the information sector, whose prime function is to satisfy the complex and increasing demands for information products and services. The times, when the Librarians and Information Managers (LIMs) used to remain busy (and satisfied) with functions aimed at acquiring, organizing and providing reading materials, only when there was a request for the same, are over. The profession today is being geared to aim at something beyond that. Something beyond, in the context of Library and Information Centres (LICs) means that the LIMs will have to chip in and accept the challenges by playing a more pro-active role.

Mere possession of information will serve no purpose unless

it is put to effective use by those who need it. LIMs will have to bring the user and information together. However, increasing technological advancements are putting increasing pressures on LIMs. First, the technology of information work is vastly extending the scope of their work. It is now possible to gain access to and process much greater quantities of information than was possible only five years ago. Computers and CD-ROMs have found increasing acceptance in LICs; Multimedia has shown much potential for LICs; and information networks have broken down time and space barriers. Second, user expectations are rising constantly, creating a demand for ever more sophisticated, high-quality in information products and services.[1]

In the same breath, it is also appreciable that information is becoming increasingly expensive and so is its packaging and repackaging. Value addition of the information, makes it even more expensive. There is a further rise in the cost of information when IT (acquisition and upgradation) is to play its role in designing and delivering information services and products. Further, the age-old concept of certain social services like health, education, justice, etc., being made available, free of cost, is becoming irrelevant as the time goes by. This is true with library and information services (LIS). The institutions engaged in all such services are being asked to become self- sufficient, if they are to survive in cost conscious and competition oriented social and environmental set-ups. Public funding for such purposes is being questioned.

The Challenge

It is true that by using a variety of IT tools and techniques, LICs are now able to generate and develop various kinds of information products, resources and services in addition to performing the routine tasks. But, it is a little unfortunate that these remain largely underutilized, or even, in cases, wholly unutilized.

The reasons cited are several and include the following:

- efforts in building learning resource materials of LICs lack involvement of those for whom they are built;
- level of information awareness or consciousness among the users needs to be raised a lot further; and

- information products and services are "generator" driven rather than "user" driven and in that there remains a "linkage gap" between the generators and users of such products and services.

LICs have, over the years, spent enormous amounts of money, expertise and other valuable resources to come up to a stage where they are at present in terms of service delivery. They continue to do so, even as of now. Mobilizing resources, particularly the finances, may not be that easy an affair now as it has been in the past. But, in the demands and expectations from their users, there won't be any looking back. In such a situation, not only will mere survival of the systems to the expectations of their users be a major challenge for the LIMs but their sustained development will be a big question. The only way out seems to be that the development of LICs will have to be only in accordance with more exact and specific needs of their users. Towards this end and keeping the concept of a resource constrained regime in mind, the services offered will have to be internally efficient and extremely effective. It is in this context that the concept of 'Total Quality (TQ)' becomes relevant for the sustainable 'Management (M)' of LICs.

TQM Philosophy

Total Quality Management (TQM) is an approach aimed at satisfying the customer requirements on a continual basis (Quality - first time, every time, all the time) by involving everyone (Total) in the system, and at a lower cost (Management). The philosophy of TQM is based on three basic premises, these are: (i) to become more customer driven rather than be more self focused; (ii) to concentrate on process rather than be preoccupied with results; and (iii) use the workers' heads in addition to their hands.[2] In today's fast changing competitive environment, there is no doubt that it is the customer who is responsible for the survival or otherwise of the business itself. However, if customer focus alone is emphasized, TQM will be reduced to mere lip service since the other pivotals have been left uncared for. In this approach, emphasis is on prevention of errors rather than on their mere detection. It believes in doing things differently and not in doing different things. In line with this approach, 'Quality', has been very aptly explained as: (i) a strategy to survive in a competitive era, (ii) a key to globalization, (iii) a path to excellence, and (iv) an eternal philosophy of continuous learning.[3]

Application of TQM

Dr S.R. Ranganathan's Fourth Law: *Save The Time of the Reader* has similar implications as are advocated in the TQM process.[4] The focus, even in 1931 was on the customer, symbolized by 'user satisfaction'.

LICs, over the times, have operated in relative isolation, as mere storehouses of knowledge. They were managed by the so called caretakers, obsessed with internal processes and controls than user needs and satisfaction.[5] Competition and users turning to other sources for their information needs were unthinkable. To cope up with the increasing demands from the customers, as well as the pressures from the environment, a need was felt that the LICs should reorient themselves keeping the customer in the focus. TQM, incidentally, is a philosophically strong approach adopted by organizations (including LICs) to operationalise the customer centeredness.

TQM and Sustainable Development

In the context of LICs, adoption of TQM approach will help them not only in their effective growth but they will also be able to sustain their development if LIMs develop strategies and mobilize their resources in such a manner that they are able to:

- gauge the requirements of their users more accurately and precisely;
- cater to the exact needs of such users; and
- remain cost effective in every area of operation by doing things right the first time, everytime, all the time.

The above is possible if LIMs become responsive to the following agenda:

- Understand the TQM process.
- Develop TQM as a strategic focus to effect continuous improvement in various activities and services of a modern LIC, encompassing acquisition, organization and dissemination of information.

- Appreciate and overcome barriers in continuous improvement in the context of LICs.
- Make continuous improvement a way of life for everyone involved in LIC in any organization.

While the LIMs are deluged with advice as to how to satisfy the complex and ever increasing information needs of their users, the LICs are looked upon as out-reaching as well as revenue generating centres. Needless to point out that the LICs were, one time, very well accepted as cost centres to cater to the information needs of their respective (mostly internal) clientele. This situation gets further compounded when the question of a resource constrained regime comes into the picture. LIMs have, in all earnestness, started taking active interest not only in building a strong image for their LICs but also in developing their resources, facilities and services, exactly in accordance with the needs of their users. This approach is finding increasing acceptance among the library authorities as well as library users who are constantly subjected to several pressures, including the ones posed by resource constraints.

Other Approaches

LICs have, over a period of time, built rich learning resource materials. These remain largely underutilized as their use is generally limited to the clientele of the organization of which the LIC is a part. In such a scenario, while on the one hand there is an increasing demand for availability of right information, on the other, it is not possible for everyone to go in for huge investments in terms of developing appropriate information infrastructure. Hence out-reaching is the solution to bridge this gap.

LIMs will have to take up the challenge of looking out for ways and means to increase their client base in the external sectors and open up their resources, facilities and services to meet the information needs of the clientele in those sectors, of course, without, in any way, jeopardizing the interests of the internal clientele. For this out-reaching measure to be a success, LIMs will have to fine-tune their resource development and utilization policies to meet this challenge.

Some Hindrances

Misunderstanding

LIMs feel that adoption of approaches, like TQM may result in commercialisation of their services or mere publicity or public relations.

Passive Role

LIMs will have to change their role from a passive provider of information to a more proactive one.

Internal Marketing of the Concept

Since LICs generally exist in relation to their parent bodies, they are viewed as a sub-system of the main system. Hence TQM will find its way in the sub-system only when there is such an orientation in the main system itself. Within the sub-system itself the approach has to be accepted by all involved, rather than leaving it to be the domain of only public relations staff like circulation and reference. It will yield more encouraging results if everyone involved in the sub-system is groomed to appreciate the client orientation.

Obsession with Systems & Procedures

LIMs, because of various well-known compulsions like physical verification, audit, etc., have been more concerned with storage and security aspects of the information rather than its use. The methods, systems and procedures followed in the LICs are therefore, more biased towards this aspect rather than the use or user aspect. This also has to change. Systems and procedures should lay more emphasis on the use and the user of information rather than on other aspects.

Information is (not) Free

The concept that information should be made available free has to go, as it costs quite a bit to acquire, organise and retrieve it. The way we don't mind paying for our other essential needs like food, clothing, shelter, health, etc, we should be prepared to pay for the information, we need.

Conclusion

It is not that all TQM initiatives are success stories. Such cases are not to turn back on the concept and discard it. Instead they provide enormous learning opportunities. As a noted management consultant has put it 'if TQM fails, it is because of the errors in its implementation; the approach itself is not flawed. Implementing TQM as a program will doom an organization to eventual failure. A programme has a beginning and an end; it does not change the basic approach of a company in running its business. If TQM must succeed, an organization should integrate its philosophies and practices into the day to day running of its business.[7] And definitely, TQM is a human relation oriented philosophy, which requires fundamental changes in people management, treating them as an ever appreciating asset.

To sum up, a change-over, as advocated above, in the LIC context, would call for: (i) sensitizing top management to TQM approaches; (ii) constant interaction between the user, producer and provider of information; and (iii) training and retraining of LIMs in newer ways of identifying and understanding the user and his/her requirements.

REFERENCES

1. Moore, Nick. The Information Society. In *World Information Report: 1997-98*. Paris: UNESCO. pp. 271-84, 1997.
2. Chakraborty, Subrata, What on Earth is TQM all About? *Images*. Lucknow, IIM Lucknow, 1995.
3. Schonberger, Richard J. Total Quality Management Cuts a Broad Swath Through Manufacturing and Beyond. *Organizational Dynamics*, (Spring) pp. 16-28, 1992.
4. Raina, Roshan. Total Quality Management in Library and Information Services. *University News* 33 (24), pp. 4-6, 11, 1995.
5. Stuart,Crit and Drake, Miriam A. TQM in Research Libraries. *Special Libraries*, (Summer), 1993.
6. Mackey, Terry and Mackey, Kitty. Think Quality: The Deming Approach Does Work in Libraries. *Library Journal*. pp. 57-61, May, 1992.
7. Lulla, Suresh. It's a frame-up. *Economic Times* (Corporate Dossier), 22-28 Nov., 1996: 3.

Ten

TQM and Reengineering for Library Services

(With Special Reference to M.D. University Library, Rohtak, Haryana)

K.C. DABAS

Introduction

In the era of globalisation, privatisation and liberalisation the buzz word "quality " has led to a total rethinking on management philosophy. The school of thought developed in Japan during the problem solving era of 1945 was 'Kaizen' i.e. continuous improvement. Kaizen was based purely on Japanese culture and philosophy of life. The TQM is the American version of 'Kaizen' and was developed by an American Dr William Edward Deming, the god father of quality movement from a narrow technical concern to a broad, holistic, strategic and customer oriented management framework. Dr Deming applied TQM to the war shattered and economically ruined Japanese industry in 1950. TQM provides customer feedback which helps in understanding level of quality of effectiveness of an organization. Quality level has a direct relationship with quality management level.[1] Organizations that emphasise the parallel development of new products to suit the changing needs and tastes will alone survive the competition.

Reengineering or innovation can not occur without systematic abandonment of obsolete practices and products. Quality improvement programme tend to enhance the existing processes rather than break through changes. The core values of TQM and Reengineering are similar to those of higher educational institutions i.e. customer (internal & external), knowledge and continuous improvement. Recognising that information is the key resource for socio-economic, scientific and technological progress of mankind and information technology organizations are in the business of providing information services and universal access to multiple information resources in all possible formats from a single work station; we in academic libraries are pre-occupied with the future and our ability to maintain our market share and to prosper; for this TQM & Reengineering library services is the answer.[2]

This study attempts to describe how MD University Library is implementing TQM & Reengineering to meet out the challenges posed by information revolution and other information providers on the basis of literature survey, observations and experiences of the authors. Interview and interactions methods were applied to make it more objective.

Total Quality Management would be incomplete without mentioning the names of Dr W.E.Deming, Dr Joseph Juran, Philip Crosby, Kaoro Ishikawa, G. Taguhi, & A. Feigenbaum. Peter Drucker credits Dr Deming for supplying scientific methodology for analysing the process. Deming believes in a democratic and humanistic partnership. He is known as the father of modern quality movement.[3] Dr Juran initiated the important transition from analysing the technology to critically examining the commitment from the top management and also initiated a shift from inspection of the product to examining the overall process. Philip Crosby is known for promoting zero defects approach (1960) and for his best selling book *Quality is Free* (1979). Ishikawa believes that TQM is a thought revolution and it is easier to implement it in a culture dominated by one race and language. There are differences among quality gurus but each share the concept of continuous improvement. TQM is a basic business strategy that provides goods and services that completely satisfy both internal and external customers by meeting, their explicit and implicit expectations. The strategy utilizes the talents of all the employees, to the benefit of the organization, in particular and society in general, and provides a positive financial return to stakeholders.[4] It is a way of managing to improve the effectiveness, efficiency, flexibility and competitiveness of a business as a whole, and it involves the whole organization getting organized and commitment to quality in each department, each activity and each person at each level.[5]

Reengineering

All profit and non-profit organizations look towards customers concerned with competition and preoccupied with an environment that has and will continue to experience transformational change. Service oriented organizations know that just to survive and then to grow, they have to do more in the form of new and improved processes, new features, new products and services to distinguish themselves. Service with distinction is the competitive edge. Reengineering or reinventing are becoming common for profit and non-profit organizations to flourish.[6]

Elements of Reengineering for Libraries

While reengineering libraries, the main focus should be on certain key issues which are important to get optimum benefits. These are as follows:

The libraries should be users centred focus, State of the art Information Technology, focus on processes, breakthrough not small changes, and break with old traditions and rules. Philip Tompkins argues forcefully that team based working groups for specific projects and problems and collaboration with faculty and computer professionals is essential for reengineering. Peter Drucker states that successful innovation cannot occur without systematic abandonment of obsolete practices and products.[7]

Reengineering and Total Quality Management

Though reengineering is not implementing total quality management even then it shares many common elements with quality management

1. Customer (internal and external) focus.
2. Process improvement and breakthrough.
3. Continuous improvement.

Reengineering is not merely an automatic existing process

though automation may assist in redesigning processes. This is not reorganization, delayering or flattering of organizational structures, though this too may occur as a biproduct of reengineering. It emphasizes the parallel development of new products and services to suit the changing tastes of the customers and for survival of the organizations.

Need of TQM and Reengineering for Academic Libraries

The corporate literature on TQM and reengineering has much to offer academic libraries in a time when budgets are decreasing and customer expectations are increasing, Daniel Seymour in his book on *Q: Causing Quality in Higher Education*, discusses his belief that significant change does not occur in organizations unless pressure from outside the organization, prompts it to do so. He cites four forces for change:

1. Survival in an increasingly, competitive environment.
2. The escalation of costs of doing business.
3. A trend to make organization more accountable for their actions and outcomes.
4. Blurring of the distinction between products and services.[8]

In addition to the above, the information super highway and digital technology has tremendously affected all aspects of print culture, which is directly related to libraries and information centres. Management skills and the state of the art technology of the libraries must match these internal and external changes in the environment. The exploitation of quality management and reengineering is timely.[9]

Philip Tompkins argues forcefully that library quality will be increasingly dependent on merging the print culture with the electronic culture.[10] Quality is the ultimate state of being and quality control is the process of getting there. Output, performance, and effectiveness are equal to quality.[11]

Quality can be Defined as Such

1. Quality is conformance to specifications. This can be applied for various electrical, electronic, mechanical and other stationary items needed in the library and not for library services.

2. Judgement of the Customer : Academic libraries exist for the academic community. Users of library services are the external customers and library staff is the internal customer of small activities i.e. parts of library processes. If both the customers are satisfied and happy then the quality is maintained.
3. Conformance to standards : Standards may be regional, national and international. Though standard criteria is more reflective than the specification, but they also fit for engineering goods.
4. Inputs to an organization: The greater the inputs, the greater the quality output. Collection was considered to be a sole criteria for quality library services but now access is more important than collection. Law of diminishing marginal utility will neutralize the additional satisfaction of every additional unit of inputs.[12]

Implementation of Quality Management and Reengineering in MD University Library

The historical and cultural roots of MD University Library go back to Punjab University, Chandigarh. It was established as a library of Punjab University Regional Centre Library, Rohtak, in 1967-68. It was renamed as Kurukshetra University Regional Centre Library, Rohtak. The same library was renamed as MD University Library Rohtak in May 1976 after the Haryana Vidhan Sabha had passed an Act no. 25. "M.D.U. Act 1975". Since then the University is growing, at a very slow pace. As soon as the great military strategist, educationist, visionary and mission oriented Lt. Gen. O.P. Kaushik (retd.) joined as Vice-Chancellor of this University, situations started changing dramatically. Like, Carl, M. White Report 1965, V.C did not consider the University Library as an inherited and conventional accessory[13] but fully endorsed the impressive terms used for University libraries by various Educational Commissions and Committees and visited the heart of the university immediately after joining as V.C. alongwith P.V.C, Registrar and four deans. From the very first day this team of seven people meets regularly at 9 a.m. and are known as 'saptrishi'.

The V.C. had a long discussion with the librarian, staff members, students and teachers about the library and himself observed the functioning of the library from very close corners and told the librarian that we stand nowhere. We can't withdraw back from the changes and challenges before us or to count the days until retirement. He realigned the philosophy, attitude, and behaviour of employees and stressed the need to learn from others who have better processes, techniques and practices. Suggestions were invited from all the stakeholders and a cash award of two thousand was given for the best suggestion. The vision, mission, goal and objective statements were prepared. He addressed all the employees that the head of this family marks attendance at sharp 9 a.m. and spare only 30 minutes for lunch.

This much commitment and involvement of the top for quality service was a clear message to the lowest level of employee and helped in setting a quality mindset and commitment. The Employees were first enabled then empowered and provided Identity card along with chain. This helped them to be more accountable, responsible, friendly, responsive, cooperative, credible, apathetic and trustworthy. Instead of this is not my job, I can't do this, an I can do work culture was adopted.[14] Technical services were put under line of command whereas the front line staff was empowered to serve the external customer. As the TQM and the reengineering is applicable in a democratic and humanistic atmosphere and also supposed to stand the organizational chart at their head. The organizational hierarchy in the M.D.U. Library is suitable for TQM and reengineering i.e. Chief Librarian, Assistant Librarians, Restorer and attendants, cleaners, and other para professional staff.

Education and Training

Professional staff was facilitated to attend refresher courses, seminars, conferences and correspondence courses. For in- house computer course and computerisation of the library, a library professional with advanced computer training was appointed as assistant librarian. A fully air-conditioned and well furnished computer laboratory having two Pentiums, one PC/AT-486 and one PC/AT-286 along with CDS/ISIS 3.07 version, SCO UNIX and WS4, Dbase was set up with the close cooperation of the Engineering cell, Administrative wing, Computer Science Department and Computer Centre.

E-mail service, Video library service, Newspaper clipping service and Book shop service has already been started in a proactive and benchmarking method. Now MD University Library has a benchmark regarding the above services over the other libraries of the region.

The faculty members and research scholars are ready to pay for some services. The V.C. reduced Xeroxing charges to a minimum of 30 paisa and provided an additional plain paper copier from Bee Electronics, Japan. Cheap photocopying service minimised the mutilation and theft of books. Microfilm reader was also provided in the library to facilitate the researchers.

Inhouse database for periodicals (current & back Vols.), thesis and dissertations has already been completed. Database for current and most used books is in progress with CDS/ISIS packages and UNIX OS. Library inhouse computer training was provided to all the professional staff to enable them to reengineer and reinvent the library services in a proactive rather reactive way in the face of the new information providers, for example, publishing houses, broadcasting and cable channels, Internet and other information super highway agencies. A high power generator was installed near the library to maintain a regular supply of power for all the three reading halls and periodical halls and a UPS of 3 KVA capacity with maintenance free batteries for two hours backup was installed in the computer section.

A meeting of the head computer science, director computer centre and Xen engineering cell and Chief Librarian was called for greater cooperation and collaboration with regard to connectivity, installation, maintenance, networking and training for library automation and reengineering.

Staff members of low esteem and calibre were given the sensitive touches. This changed the attitude and behaviour of staff members. Resistance to change was pacified and professional staff made committed to accept the challenges of the environment. The V.C. articulated his vision, ability in ways that motivate followers to commit themselves to the hardwork of realising that vision. He weaved relationships and created structures among employees to enhance the worksmanship of each individual and produced an organizational fabric capable of supporting excellent service. Open decision making through brainstorming and brainwriting methods of different teams helped the staff to come out of the shell and quite ordinary people began to move mountains. An atmosphere of trust and goodwill promoted two way communication. Intercom telephone connection was right step for greater cooperation and collaboration among internal and external customers. Knowledgeable staff members with sober and sophisticated manners and temperament were posted as section incharges and front line staff. Greater emphasis was laid on asking the questions from users instead of answering. The overall objective of TQM and reengineering is to make the system effective. Effectiveness leads to customer satisfaction, and satisfied and happy customers are a proof of service quality. Service quality cannot be maintained without qualitative management and reinventing library service.[15]

IFLA standards and guidelines 1986 states that—quality in university libraries can be attained by defining the purpose, system and status of the library. Services, collection development, conservation, facilities, budget, technology and staff must relate to the purpose of the library.[16] Table 1 gives some measures of quality in libraries with their respective particulars.

TABLE - 1
QUALITATIVE INDICATORS

S.No.	*Qualitative Indicator*	*Description/Details*
1.	Number of clients	4667
2.	Proportion of stock size added annually	4%
3.	Funds	1996-97 50 lacs; 1997-98 64 lacs
4.	Staff numbers	17 professionals and 23 others
5.	Seating capacity	650
6.	Items issued and supplied	350 average
7.	Opening hours	9 am to 8 pm working days 9 am to 12 pm (3 months) 9 am to 5 pm Sundays and holidays
8.	Enquiries handled	35 average
9.	Number of visits	390 average
10.	Study hours provided	360 days

A perusal of the recently published literature of library and information science indicates a renewed interest in measuring the satisfaction of library users with library services. Satisfaction and service quality are subjective concepts. Service quality is antecedent of customer satisfaction. Satisfaction can be measured by interacting with employees of the library, the services used and organization as a system. Evaluators view satisfaction by asking general questions, measuring attributes such as knowledgeability, self-confidence, helpfulness, friendliness, patience, interest and enthusiasm of the staff and the relevance, amount, exhaustiveness and helpfulness of the product of information provided. Specific measurement applies general and attribute measurements to use of a specific service. How well a service is provided is not enough. Service quality or satisfaction view organization and services from customer perspective and head to outcome measures. Service quality approach helps in developing research strategies and outcome measures are beneficial to library planning and management.[17]

Continuous improvement means continuous change. For this continuous change there must be some common purpose that binds people together as a cohesive unit. Learning, research and teaching are a continuous process in the university and they must be matched by continuous improvement in system and processes of the library.

Library Effectiveness

Professional literature shows a thread relating library quality with library effectiveness. It is concerned with the effect the organization has on its environment.

Measurement of Library Effectiveness

1. Effectiveness by prescription of inputs
2. Internal processes
3. Contract fulfilment
4. Professional standards
5. Tradition
6. System approach
7. Organic approach
8. Coalition approach.[18]

Conclusion

Absence of direct competitor to University library does not mean that customer will develop loyalty.[19] To meet out the challenges of internal and external competitors, exploitation of quality management and reengineering skills is timely. Reinventing the library in the context of what customers think is important for qualitative library services and for survival and growth. Quality is an antecedent to customer satisfaction, reducing the gap between expectations and service provided and by working in a proactive way like the MD University Library style leads to qualitative service.[20]

Application of digital culture with print culture will definitely improve effectiveness (goodness and value) and quality of service.[21] Quality has been and will continue to be an issue of strategic importance upon which depend survival and growth of academic libraries, the sure way to ensure quality service.[22]

REFERENCES

1. Johansen, Carl Gustav. Quality management and innovation: findings of a Nordic Quality Management Survey. *Libri*. 45 (3/4), pp. 131-44, 1995.
2. Shapiro, Bath J. & Long, Kevin Brook. Just say yes: reengineering library user services for the 21st century. *Journal of Academic Librarianship*. 20 (5/6), pp. 18-30, 1994.
3. Aguayo, Rafael. *Dr. Deming: The Man who Taught the Japanese about Quality*. New Delhi, Viva books Pvt., 1990.
4. Bropy, Peter and Couling, Kate. *Quality Management for Information and Library Managers*. Mumbai: Jaico Publishing House, 1995.
5. Sherikar, Amruth and Sangam, S.L. Study for implementing total quality management in information technology products in 20th IASLIC Conference papers: Information technology products of 1990s and library & information centres 1995. IASLIC. Calcutta, pp. 57-60, 1995.
6. Catt, Martha E. The Olympic training field for planning quality library services. *Library Trends*. 43(3), pp. 18-30, (Winter) 1995.
7. Shapiro, Bath J. *op. cit.*, p. 287.
8. Mullen, Janet A. Total Quality Management: a Mind set and Method to stimulate change. *Journal of Library Administration*. 18 (3/4), pp. 91-108, 1993.

9. *Ibid.*, p. 93.
10. Tompkins, Philip. Quality in Community College Libraries. *Library Trends*. 44(3), pp. 506-25, (Winter), 1996.
11. Prichavd, Sarah M. Determining Quality in Academic Libraries. *Library Trends*. 44(3), pp. 572-94, (Winter) 1996.
12. Shaughnessy, Thomas W. Assessing library effectiveness. *Journal of Library Administration*. 12(1), pp. 1-7, 1990.
13. Shrivastava, Anand P. A University and its Library: Academic Culture and Ethos. *Uni News*. 30(35), pp. 63-67, 1992.
14. Rout, R.K. Managerial Revolution and the University Libraries. *Uni News*. 30(35), pp. 139-44, 1992.
15. Hernon, Peter and Schwartz, Canady. Measuring Customers Satisfaction. *Library and Information Science Research*. 18(4), pp. 295-96, 1996.
16. Boekhorst, Peter Te. Measuring quality: the IFLA guidelines for performance measurement in academic libraries. *IFLA Journal*. 21(4), pp. 278-81, 1995.
17. Shaughnessy, Thomas W. Information. *Library Trends*. 44(3), pp. 459-63, Winter.
18. Brophy, Peter. *op. cit.*, (4).
19. Dabas, K.C. and Dabas, Sheela. Impact of automation on library management techniques in human relations in librarianship : Seminar papers 41st all India conference Vijayawada. Jan. 7-10. ILA, pp. 313-23, 1996.
20. Sethi, A.R. Towards qualitative librarianship. *Uni News*. 33(12), pp. 5-10, 1995.
21. Raina, Roshan. Total Quality Management in Library Information Services. *Uni News* 33(24), pp. 4-6, 11, 1995.
22. Cullen, Rowena J. and Calvert, Philip J. Stake holder perception of University library effectiveness. *Journal of Academic Librarianship*. 21(6), pp. 438-48, Nov. 1995.

Eleven

Services of Special Libraries

(With Special Reference to Madhya Pradesh Institute of Social Science Research Library, Ujjain

DR SONAL SINGH

Introduction

In the modern world of Information explosion, communication of information has become increasingly important. The phenomenal growth of periodical literature and various types of special material has complicated the process of retrieval of information. The concept of modern librarianship has entirely been changed. Today, it is the foremost duty of the librarian to serve his reader pin-pointedly, exhaustively and expeditiously in the procurement of documents and the local information. The increasing complexity of present day culture with the spread of literacy increased the dependence upon graphic records which further intensifies the role of library with respect to information. The role of library, as a centre of information sources is more important today than it has been ever before. Today, library is considered as the most indispensable part of every academic institution, government department, research institution, business or industrial organization. The trend for developing these libraries, documentation centres; or any other kind of information centres has been on the rise as information resources in any country are now recognised to be as important as any other resources such as energy and minerals. The acquisition, organization and dissemination of these information resources provide an essential basis for the socio-economic development of a nation as a whole, which is the aim of any nation. Thus, special libraries play a significant role in providing qualitative information needed for the nation's progress.

Special Libraries

Special libraries are the product of the twentieth century. They have come into existence to promote research and development activities and for fulfilling certain social needs. The term special library denotes specialist libraries that means the libraries which specialize on a particular subject or group of subjects. Special libraries are generally set up by the Government, learned and professional societies, business and industrial organizations and they exist as units of their parent organizations. The special libraries are established particularly for the research and development wings of various industrial organizations. Their main aim is to provide right information to the right user at the right time and in the form most useful to him. Here, the librarian serves as a collaborator of researchers who finds and files information and disseminates it as quickly as possible. Research is an intellectual act and is essential for the sake of good life. Research is indispensable to satisfy the growing demands of the society and to maintain the standard of living. Due to population pressure, a number of social problems are arising continuously. In addition to it, man is trying to make his life more smooth and comfortable. He is always engaged in solving the complex problems of society. Problems are ever growing so research is a continuous process. Today, a number of research institutes both in the field of Science and Social Science are engaged in research work in India. Development in the field of Social Sciences in India is very little as compared to Natural and physical Science. Social research is a complex procedure which requires complete planning and management of work procedure on scientific grounds. Social research is limited not only upto data collection but it aims to draw scientific conclusions, from reliable and authentic data. In social research, documentary sources i.e. published documents, reports, statistics, letters, diaries, etc., are very important. Thus, a library is an indispensable part of social science research institute.

Historical Background of Ujjain City

Ujjain is a historical city and the cultural capital of India. In the olden days, it was known as: Vishala, Kanak Shriringa, Amravati, Pratikalpa, etc. Ujjain which had always been known for its sanctity, is situated on the fertile land of Malwa, on the right bank of river 'Kashipra'. It is one of the seven sacred cities of the Hindus.

Ujjain was the capital of the famous King Vikramaditya who was also famous for his judgement and navaratna of scholars. In addition to historical, cultural and religious importance, Ujjain has long been a seat of scholars. From here, the rays of knowledge had flooded the entire country in the ancient period. Before Nalanda, Kashi Universities, Ujjain was the 'Gurukul of Sandipani' which can still be seen. It was so famous at that time that Lord Krishna, his elder brother Balram and their well-known friend Sudama came here for higher studies. Mahakavi Kalidas. the Shakespeare of India, has given a vivid description of Ujjain in his famous work *Meghdoot*. He had also added glory to Ujjain.

Ujjain is still a centre of learning, being the seat of Vikram University. The Vikram University was established in Ujjain after the name of the great, just and brave ruler Vikramaditya. The foundation stone of Vikram University was laid by the then Home Minister of India, Shri Govind Vallabh Pant on Tuesday, Kartika Krishnapaksha Chaturthi, Vikrambada 2013 i.e. on the 23rd October, 1956 The function was presided over by the Rajpramukh of the Madhya Bharat State, Late Jiwajirao Scindia.

Vikram University conducts seventeen study centres. Fifty three Colleges are affiliated in its jurisdiction. Scindia Oriental Research Institute, Maharaja Jiwajirao Pustakalaya, Vikram Kirti Mandir, Museum and the University Information and Employment Bureau, etc., are also among the University run institutions.

Besides, there is also a social science research institute.

Madhya Pradesh Institute of Social Science Research, Ujjain

Madhya Pradesh Institute of Social Science Research (MPISSR), Ujjain, MP was founded in 1983 as an autonomous non-political, non profit making research institute registered under Madhya Pradesh Societies Registration Act, 1973, Vide No. 11830 dated January 13, 1983 by Dr R.S. Gautam. The primary objective behind the establishment of the Institute is to promote research in social science, the focus of such research being the State of Madhya Pradesh. Keeping in view this central objective the MPISSR has engaged itself in research activities pertaining to the social, political, economic, cultural, administrative, agricultural, industrial and civic aspects of the State of Madhya Pradesh.

After its establishment, MPISSR carried its research activities with its own financial and human resources for nearly a decade. However in 1993-94 the Institute was included in the grants-in-aid scheme of the Indian Council of Social Science Research, Ministry of Human Resource Development, Government of India, New Delhi. There after Ministry of Higher education, Government of Madhya Pradesh, Bhopal also started providing a matching grant. Thus, the Institute is presently being supported by two governmental agencies, the ICSSR and the Ministry of Higher Education, Madhya Pradesh.

The MPISSR is also registered under section 6(1) of the Foreign Contribution Regùlation Act, 1976 by the Ministry of Home Affairs, Government of India New Delhi.

Objectives of the MPISSR, Ujjain

The objectives of MPISSR are as follows:

(1) To undertake and promote research in those areas which are identified as thrust areas due to their socio-economic significance current relevance and policy implications with particular reference to the developmental problems of Madhya Pradesh.

(2) To develop specialization in research on Tribal Development, Panchayat Raj, Rural Development, Environmental Issues and to conduct evaluation studies on developmental programmes and schemes.

(3) To provide facilities for research, training and extension work related to the development of Scheduled Castes, women, minorities and other weaker sections of the society.

(4) To extend training facilities for Panchayat representatives and functionaries and to contribute to promote anticipatory development in rural areas through action research and better involvement of NGOs.

(5) To undertake studies on problems of industrial development in Madhya Pradesh with special references to regional disparities and labour issues.

(6) To create institutional infrastructure for empirical research, survey work and data analysis.

(7) To offer consultancy services to the State and Central government and to carry out development studies and research projects sponsored by governmental and non governmental organizations, international agencies and foundations.

(8) To invite social scientists and researchers to the Institute to pursue their own advanced research and/or to contribute to research and other activities at the Institute.

(9) To organize seminars, symposia, workshops and special lectures on developmental problems and burning national and State level issues.

(10) To publish research works of high standard in the form of books, monographs and occasional papers.

(11) To bring out *Madhya Pradesh Journal of Social Science* for the advancement of knowledge in social sciences and to encourage dialogue on developmental problems.

(12) To start doctoral and post-doctoral research at the Institute and to institute fellowships and awards in honour of distinguished social scientists.

(13) To develop a professionally managed well equipped social science library and documentation centre with database to fulfil a long-standing demand for establishment of a social science resources centre in Madhya Pradesh.

(14) To forge close functional relationship with sister institutions, centres of higher learning and research foundations in India and abroad.

(15) To achieve the status of deemed university in due course to reach the peak of excellence in advanced research and higher education.

MPISSR Library

The library of MPISSR is situated on the ground floor of the Institute in a hall where in 30-35 students can be accommodated at a time. Reference books, text books, and other reading material is arranged in glass door almirahs. The furniture is comfortable.

The Director, himself, is the chairman of the library committee and the librarian acts as a convenor. Librarian possesses academic qualifications and is professionally trained. He is M.Sc. M.Lib Sc.

Finance

Finance is the motive power for providing proper and efficient services. Infact, it is the backbone of any library. As library is a growing institution, a perennial source of supply of adequate finance must be tapped because financial demands of libraries are recurring in nature.

MPISSR, Ujjain is presently being supported by two Governmental agencies, the ICSSR, Ministry of Human Resource Development, Government of India, New Delhi and the Ministry of Higher Education, Madhya Pradesh, Bhopal.

Library Collection

Library collection is an important constituent of the library, which should be rich quantitatively as well as qualitatively. The quality of services provided and the satisfaction of user depend largely upon the kind of collection. The collection should be able to meet the changing needs and demands of present as well as future. The collection should be alive, balanced and uptodate one with regard to subject content and the kinds of materials and the areas of specialization and special interest should be covered in depth.

In MPISSR, Ujjain the library collection is growing steadily both in forms of published and unpublished materials. The library presently possesses more than two thousand reference books and thirty periodicals. Publications are being received regularly. The library has two hundred back volumes, twenty maps and charts, twenty reports, five encyclopaedias and eight dictionaries.

The library also maintains an extensive collection and documentation of newspaper clippings from, five dailies, out of which three are in hindi and two in english on over thirty subject headings.

MPISSR, in accordance with its policy, has started publishing a journal of its own, under the title *Madhya Pradesh Journal of Social Science*. Three volumes have been published so far.

Library Services

Library service is a social service which aims at self development and improvement of skill and efficiency of the people in all walks of life. It is a vital input for research and national development. Library service is not simply supplying of a few documents demanded by the users. It is more comprehensive in nature, providing complete informational and intellectual aid to every user in an informal academic environment.

The library of MPISSR, Ujjain remains open for seven hours, that is, from 10.30 am to 5.30 pm. It also provides services on Sunday and other holidays in special circumstances.

For classification, Dewey Decimal Classification, 18th edition is used and for cataloguing, card form of catalogue is used.

The library is having a closed access system. The reading material is to be used in the library premises only and is not meant for home issue.

Reference service is provided by the librarian to users of this library. Ready reference tools are provided for short range queries, and for long range queries. A prolonged and intensified search is made through other social science libraries of the country.

It is very necessary to keep the researchers posted with the latest information on the topic of their interest appearing in periodical article and variant forms of literature so as to match their needs. Thus, current awareness service is also provided by MPISSR library. In addition to it, SDI Service is also provided, which is the most effective way of promoting library use. The selective dissemination of information is an advanced kind of service directed towards individuals so as to cater to individual requirements. The basic concept of SDI consists in matching of the information with the interests of the clientele. It also enables the librarian to obtain feedback on the value of the service.

Indexing services are also provided which make a link between the specific subject or topic and the identified document. Abstracting services are also provided where summary or abridgement of the thought context of the publication or article is made. An index produces a clue to the location of the information and the abstract helps the reader to decide whether he needs to refer to original document or not.

Literature is being published in various languages. The language barrier can be overcome by translation services, by translating the required article from its original language to other desired language. At present MPISSR Library is not providing translation services.

Conclusion

A special library is an integral part of its parent body. It is expected to procure, process, store, retrieve and disseminate information, documents, and data. MPISSR, library is successfully running on progressive lines, but due to limited funds, limited staff and limited space, it still needs improvement. Problems of the libraries cannot be solved until the problems of our society are solved. Separate library building, sufficient staff and computerization of library are some of the suggestions for providing quality library services by the MPISSR library.

Twelve

Concept of Resource sharing in University Libraries at Regional Level

DR (Mrs) NEERA SAHNI

Introduction

Resource sharing is a kind of cooperation among various libraries of a region by which they share their resources for the benefit of users whose numbers have grown fast and whose interests have become diversified. It is an arrangement by which resources of all the participating libraries are coordinated and are made available to the users at each of the participating libraries. In the contemporary world, the resource sharing among libraries of a region has become essential. This system avoids duplication of materials, saves funds for collections and provides better services to the clients. In this age, no library can grow in isolation. It must become a part of the system to achieve more efficiency in service. No library, however privileged, can hope to achieve self sufficiency in the materials required by its users. This is especially true of today when a vast amount of literature is being produced and demanded by the users. In order to cope with the needs, a library requires huge funds which may not be available. As a result, the cooperation among libraries has gained further significance. The same is being advocated strongly by the professionals. A limited success has been achieved in this regard. However, a lot needs to be done. The success in this field has been especially slow in the developing countries. In third world countries, a little has been achieved in sharing the uses of information or textual resources, facilities of qualified staff and also of technical units and equipments.

Types of Resource Sharing

The cooperation and resource sharing among the libraries of a region are of various kinds. In this regard the following five types need mention:

1. Inter-Library Use.
2. Joint acquisition programme.
3. Cooperation in technical bibliographical work and scientific information service.
4. Joint storage for less used library materials.
5. Studies of mutual problems.

Inter-Library Use

Inter-Library use or Inter-Library loan refers to the sharing of materials among participating libraries on loan basis. It is practised among the University and academic libraries on a very restricted and limited way and there is no uniformity in the practice. Some of us put very rigid conditions, some do not lend rare books, dissertations and backfiles of periodicals while others do not care to reply to inter loan requests from other universities. The present condition is not at all satisfactory and rules framed by UGC seminar on work flow on libraries and Dr Ranganathan's book are not comprehensive. For streamlining the present non-uniform practises we badly require a code for inter library loan uniformally applicable to all the academic libraries of India. The code makers shall carefully consider the following points:

1. Problem of cost.
2. Frequency of requests.
3. Limitations of loan issues.
4. Inequalities between libraries
5. Character of loan items.
6. Security against loan issues, and
7. Period of loan.

Another new problem is how to make inter-library loan effective with foreign universities.

Further, in order to make inter loan easy or less costly the postal department should be approached for introducing a special concessional rate. This is an important issue and it requires fresh attention.

Joint Acquisition Programme

Joint acquisition means the purchase of library materials on cooperative basis. It may also include the exchange of library materials among participating libraries of a region. However, a little has been done in this field. This is especially true of India. In this country academic libraries suffer from lack of balance of total book collection. That is why research scholars and fellows working on specialized subjects face so many difficulties in our academic libraries. The only way to eradicate this major drawback is to allocate special fields to the different universities and academic libraries. This can easily be done on zonal basis and this will greatly minimize unnecessary duplication of costly backfiles of learned journals, reference and research publications. At the same time this policy, if pursued, will provide a zone with copies of all printed materials published in a particular subject. Research scholars should be attached to the universities where the library is well stocked with the publications with which the scholar is directly concerned. This type of specialized zonal cooperative acquisition policy can really enrich our academic libraries and help higher learning and research in the truest sense of the term.

Besides purchase, exchange is another important source of acquisition. Universities and other academic institutions publish their research works, pamphlets and serials, journals and dissertations. At present exchange is practised in a limited way after due consideration of the volume and value of publications, their frequency, etc. It is entirely based on profit and loss basis. Further, like Germany and other advanced countries we, do not exchange dissertations. Not to speak of exchange, sometimes it is difficult to get them on loan. As dissertations obtain latest trends of thought, new interpretations and recent lights on new aspects of knowledge, it is necessary to make some suitable arrangement for exchange of these publications. Each thesis or dissertation should be cyclostyled and should be distributed to all the academic libraries of allied interests on an exchange basis.

Further it is advisable that the UGC appoints a committee for considering the varied aspects of exchange system as well for streamlining the exchange policy.

On joint acquisition, another point may be stressed i.e. the introduction of cooperative purchase of library materials by a zonal central body as a whole with the cost divided among the co-operating libraries proportionately by an agreed formula. For instance in West Bengal, the librarians authorize one central body to make all the purchases (except text books) and store them in a central place for distribution. This will help in avoiding unnecessary correspondence, cost, labour and it will also minimize the harassing audit queries on purchase. This process may be taken up in the near future with the cost proportionately divided to some agreed formula. UGC Library committee take note of this point, discuss and work out, details.

Cooperation in Technical Bibliographical Work and Scientific Information Service

Cooperation in bibliographical work and scientific information service is another significant aspect of resource sharing. It facilitates the inter-library loan on exchange. Participating libraries can pinpoint loan-materials and exchange them only if a common catalogue is available or such an information about each library is pooled and made available to each participating library.

Some of the academic libraries publish and exchange cyclostyled lists of library bulletins, catalogues of current periodicals, etc., and thus maintain happy relations in the field of co-operation. Others should come forward and join in this programme and make the purpose more effective. This is the only satisfactory way to make the information available in some way to librarians and scholars such as the location of volumes which someone would like to use. This is a useful method used to obtain bibliographical control.

Photo-Duplication Service and Document Reprography

No Indian academic library has a full fledged photo-duplication laboratory which is essential to gear up service. Procurement of equipments, their installation and selection of technical personnel are costly affairs and difficult issues. INSDOC may help us with necessary advice and UGC can provide us with funds. Considering the present financial position of UGC as well as difficulty in procuring foreign goods I suggest that such costly technical units may be started on zonal basis and the libraries of the respective zones will contribute to a common pool and share dividends. Sporadic developments will not solve our problem.

Documentation and Translation Services

Like bibliographical and document reprography services—documentation and translation services have become a necessity to feed the academic needs. A centralized indexing service of scientific literature has been started from 1954 from Indian National Scientific Documentation Centre [INSDOC]. INSDOC has developed the following services — Documentation, Translation, Bibliographical and Document reprography services. But INSDOC is mainly concerned with Scientific literature. Recently All India Special Libraries Association has also developed reprography and translation services which have proved useful. Research workers and advanced students of Science are utilizing services of these agencies. But there is no such agency for documentation of subjects which comes within the region of Humanities. At present some of the universities have started documentation of works in the Arts subjects by having a full time documentalist on their staff. As a result there is the risk of unnecessary duplication of indexing and abstracting the same document. For subjects under Humanities, I suggest that the Advanced Centres of Studies attached to the Universities may be authorised to cover their respective special fields for documentation and the UGC should provide them with a full time documentalist. The documentation lists should be circulated and sister universities or academic bodies may exploit that to the fullest.

Joint Storage For Less Used Books

University and research libraries tend to grow more rapidly than the libraries of other educational institutions because they add new titles to their collections and rarely discard them. Growing university libraries face the problem of shortage of shelving or stack space and they gradually encroach on the functional space. As a result the total library system gets disturbed and fails to function smoothly. This problem can be solved if we believe in joint storage of less used textual materials, public documents, periodicals sets, Newspapers, etc. They cover a substantial part of the stack space. We can, by mutual agreement, transfer these collections to a Central Common Storage at a reasonable rent. This method can solve our evergrowing problem for space and give us considerable relief.

Studies of Mutual Problems

At present there are numerous problems in the organizational sector, Technical services, bibliography and documentation services, cooperation and specialization issues and also in planning and utilization of space and equipments. In future also other problems will crop up. Individual attempts to solve these problems will not be satisfactory and they are bound to be influenced by local conditions but they are amenable to cooperative study and solution. A sample of such problems is stated below:

Organization Section

(i) Purposes and services of departmental libraries and their relationship with the Central Library.
(ii) Whether service can be provided to non-university readers?
(iii) Whether professional library staff will enjoy the privileges of the faculty?

Technical Services

(i) To compile an Index of Indian names (author).
(ii) How to improve the financial sides of the University Libraries?
(iii) How can publicity methods be improved ?
(iv) To enlarge Asian Sections of Dewey's schedules.

Bibliography and Documentation

(i) How bibliographical control, translation services and photo-duplication services can be improved?

Co-operation and Specialization

(i) Problems already stated.

Planning and Utilization of Space and Equipments

(a) To compare the current products of library equipments and furniture and assess how close they are the ideal requirements?

(b) What improvements can be made on noise and dust controls of university library buildings?

To solve problems of such nature there should be scope for team work and cooperative study. Either the University Grants Commission should provide with a common platform or there should be a living association of Academic libraries.

Conclusion

Academic libraries face the problems of financial implications of ordering, purchasing, processing and storing of continually increasing masses of acquisitions and they are ever eager to find out ways and means of preventing unbalanced budgets. It is their responsibility because the teachers and staff as well as the students and scholars fail to understand the real problem.

The libraries have glimpses of the real position. The choice before us is to have enough courage and initiative to put such a programme into effect and achieve what other advanced countries have already done. In the words of Mr Metcalf - "Whether it is considered grasping at a straw to keep afloat or a logical solution of the problem, inter library co-operation is one of the possibilities that ought to be examined. It would be misleading if I said that I thought these difficulties could be completely overcome, for they are bound to recur, and a co-operative enterprise must continue to deal with them as long as it lasts." We all agree with Mr. Metcalf and appreciate the ideas and that is why we previously made several attempts from different levels at different times to discuss the question with the hope of developing a firm basis for library cooperation. But a little has been achieved. Why?

Firstly, the teachers of the University who are guides of library committees and Academic Council and who have an insatiable appetite for textual material, ready at hand, do not try to understand the financial implications of purchasing, processing and storing of materials and have little sympathy for library cooperation.

Secondly, some of the libraries are still very conservative and consider other sister institutions as rivals. They think that by introduction of cooperation, they will loose freedom of action and they like to see their libraries supreme both from the point of view of qualitative and quantitative aspects.

Thirdly, there is no institution or society which can coordinate our efforts, take the responsibility of running the machinery of cooperative projects and to remove inter-institutional jealousy. "It must be remembered that a cooperative project is like a machine. No matter how well it is designed, it will not work or run without a vigilant operator. Neglect may lead to a costly breakdown. Any successful inter-library cooperation must have an able supervisor, alert to the symptoms of trouble and an equally alert board of directors representing the cooperative institutions". Library co-operation is highly desirable today and the proposals, if you approve, deserve serious consideration in order to make university and other academic libraries potent instruments for the improvement of the academic standard of our mother country. And it would perhaps not be too optimistic to predict that a history illuminated by this new rounded outlook is in the offing.

Thirteen

Prospect of Automation in Cotton College Library

ZABEEN AHMED

Background

Cotton College - Down Memory Lane

Even today in the last decade of the 20th century, the newspaper contains frequent references to postal delays in Assam. One can well imagine the condition of things in the beginning of this century. Only a privileged few who were either rich or fortunate enough to receive merit scholarships offered by the government, could proceed to Bengal for obtaining college education. This state of affairs quite naturally agitated the public in general and enlightened personalities in particular, who made strong appeal to the authorities for providing college education in Assam. But the proposal took shape under the strong leadership of Late Manik Ch. Baruah, a highly erudite and outstanding personality of Assam. Ultimately the proposal was accepted for the establishment of a government college at Guwahati for which sanction from the secretary of state for India was received in June, 1899. The then Chief Commissioner of Assam, Sir Henry John Steadman Cotton took immediate steps to lay the foundation of the college which has been gratefully named after him destined to be the alma mater, being a common forum of the people of hills and plains of Assam. The college was formally opened by Sir Henry Cotton himself on 27th May, 1901 as a second grade college and it was upgraded to a first grade in 1912 with the Calcutta University grantings honours affiliation to its many subjects and a post-graduate affiliation in 1914. To ensure success, the college was endowed with a liberal system of scholarship, excellent faculty, hostels, library and facilities of extra curricular activities.

The history of Cotton College is inseperably associated with the development of higher education in Assam, specially in the Brahmaputra Valley. Nevertheless, it will not be wrong to say that modern Assam is by and large the product of Cotton College. The alumni from this premier college have made their mark in every field of national activity in arts, literature, science, education, administration, industry and politics helping thereby to shape the destiny of Assam. The college which has grown up with the passage of time has been upgraded to a Centre of Excellence on October 17, 1992 to enable it to play increasing role in the field of higher education and research.

History of the Library

In 1901, the library was located in a large hall. By the end of the first quinquennium, it contained about 2000 books nearly all well chosen and useful. No deposit was required a fact which conduces to the free use of the books. The quinquennial review 1907-12 states that considerable attention has been paid to the improvement of the college library. During the same period, a librarian had been appointed and this increased the facility for day study. In 1913, the management of the library was vested in a committee selected from among the academic staff of the college. This resulted in several reforms, closer contacts, wide expenditure and proper utilization of the library by faculty members and students.

In 1924, an attempt was made to introduce open-shelf system with the thought that anything is better than the cabining of books against use. But it had to be closed in the second year for frequent theft of books.

By 1915, the number of collection crossed 5000 and in 1920 it swelled upto 8000. In 1939, it touched the figure of 16,891 and at present the number of library collection available in the library has crossed one lakh.

Of these about 3000-10,000 books can be treated as rare and old books helping to shape the destiny of Assam.

Present Position of the Library

Cotton College, one of the oldest institutions of its kind in the country has now grown into a postgraduate college offering integrated courses from the higher secondary to the postgraduate level in 21 subjects in the humanities, social science and pure science faculties.

Today, Cotton college has 5000 students on its rolls. The number of teaching staff has gone up to 250 and a number of non-teaching is about 260. Most of the faculty members are in the pursuit of advanced studies and research in the respective subjects and area of specialization.

Therefore, the library is very well used by the student community and faculty members. The average visitor of the library constitutes of:

Students	:	500
Teachers	:	20
Others	:	10

A look at the library staff structure given below, brings to the light that the structure is inadequate for such a library:

The qualifications of the staff are as follows:

Librarian	:	Dean of the College.
Deputy Librarian	:	M.A., B.Lib. Sc.
Library Asstt.	:	B.A.
Issue Clerk	:	Under Graduate
Book men	:	Matriculate
Bearer	:	Under Matric.

It is clear from the above that there is no uniformity what so ever. But systematic pattern of staffing is very helpful in proper organization of the functions of the library.

Organizational Structure of Cotton College Library

An organization has to be structured in order to achieve its goals and objectives. Libraries are generally organized on the basis of their functions viz. collection, development, technical processing, user's services.

The functions of Cotton College library is divided into several sections to render efficient, effective and profitable services to the users. They are: Acquisition section, Cataloguing section,

Classification section, Reference Section, Periodical Section, News-paper Section, Academic information Section, Circulation Section and Repographic Section.

Organizational chart for Cotton College library is shown in Figure 1. An organizational chart highlights the inter-connections, inter relations, and inter dependence between all the units of the library.

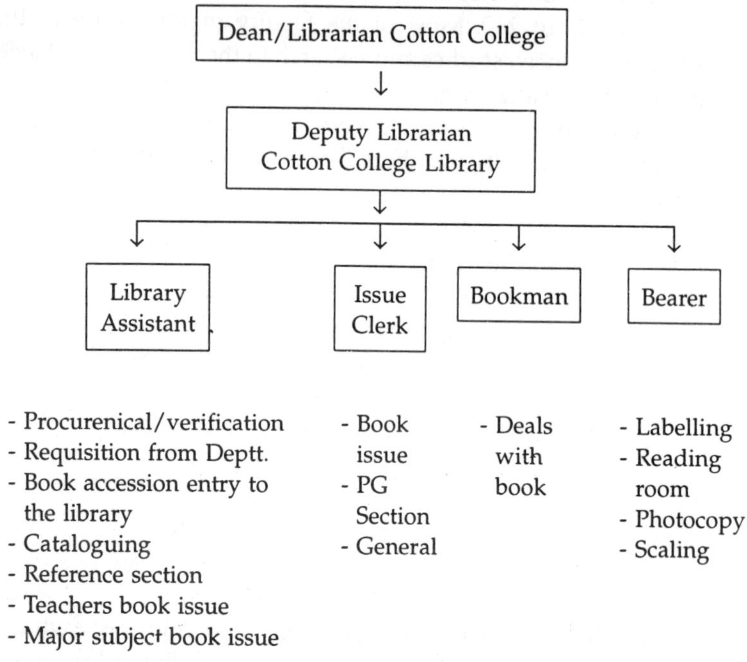

Fig. 1 — Organizational Chart of Cotton College Library

Factors Affecting Smooth Functioning of the Library

There are certain factors for which smooth functioning of the library has become difficult.

Budget

Due to financial crisis in the State there is irregularity of funds for which expenditure could not be incurred fully on the annual availed hence earmarked balance remained to be carried over for the next financial year. Due to rise in prices, the books added every year to the library collection depends on the grants received.

Physical Facilities

Physical facilities are not adequate in comparison to the number of its members, as the addition of volumes continued every year the library has become terribly congested. The foundation stone for a new library building has already been laid down. Once it has been completed, it will be able to provide the facilities to its readers.

The Library Staff

The library staff is inadequate in number and that too they are under qualified. Except the deputy librarian, no one has got professional qualifications.

Library Computerization: Present Scenario

Library is a growing organism. The truth of this law is realized with all its modern forms of automated services. The law urges the librarians that in order to act as agent to social change, they must keep themselves alert to the changing needs of the modern societies. To meet the demand of this law in the present context, there is need to be farsighted in the planning of the library buildings and library services. These have to be geared towards the use of computers in the library.

Benefits of Automation

Automation in libraries refers to the processing of the routine library functions. It enables managing of the ever increasing volumes of information. Several factors have led to the application of computers to some of the library operations and services.

A machine readable record prepared at the time of acquisition can be used repetitively for several purposes and significant savings in terms of effort, time, resources can be attained.

Other benefits of automation in comparison to manual processing include the following:

(i) Creation of a machine readable database of bibliographic information relevant to the product profile of the organization.

(ii) Improved control over library collection and library operations.

(iii) Improvement in the existing library services as well as introduction of new services.

(iv) Speed, efficiency, consistency, reliability are the key factors of information retrieval which is only possible through computerization.

(v) Various library functions done more efficiently through computerization are: acquisition, processing, serial control, circulation and generation of accession list.

(vi) Avoiding duplication of work.

(vii) Enabling scholars, researchers, teachers and students to have access to information and documents available in libraries.

(viii) Computer networks using computer and communication facilities for effective sharing of resources among the libraries, for example, INDONET, NICNET, INFLIBNET, DELNET, etc.

(ix) The purpose of computers came into force, where the literature search in science and technology was becoming unmanageable in libraries.

In light of the above it is obvious that Cotton College library, an important source of National Information Resources, was lagging behind libraries of peer institutions in others parts of the country, in utilisation of available information retrieval technology.

With a library collection of more than one lakh volumes, a student community of five thousand and the college's active curriculum and research programme, the decision for an automated library system needs to be implemented urgently.

Factors to be kept in Mind while Deciding on Automation

The following factors should be taken into consideration for automation requirement, hardware and software selection and its performances.

Collection or Size of the Library and its Planning

Planning is one of the most important skills in solving library problems. Library planning generally consists of two broad categories namely: Short range and Broad range. It involves: (i) Survey, (ii) Feasibility study and iii) Time factors in planning.

Time plan means: (i) Record entry time, (ii) Record searching time.

Manpower Strength for Library Services

There are some institutions in India having computer infrastructure such as INSDOC, DESIDOC, DRTC, NISSAT, etc., and are providing training in computer applications to library and information workers.

Any academic library on its way towards installing some computer system can very well depute a couple of its professionals with such an orientation to obtain hands on experience.

Users Education Programme

This will have to be designed to provide more information about the computerised databases, on-line searches, user- friendly system, etc.

More effective and well brought out current awareness services need to be provided to the academicians.

Library catalogues need to be made more effective and responsive.

Tools Required for Library Automation

The tools required for computerisation can be outlined in terms of Hardware (H/W) and Software (S/W) requirement of the system. Hardware is the term given to all physical devices (largely electronic) from which the computer is made up and software is the expression used to describe all programmes which are used in a particular computer installation.

CDS/ISIS software package is rapidly becoming useful for library and information centres. The package can perform a variety of functions related to information storage and retrieval. Its main three functional components are file maintenance, retrieval, sorting and printing.

This package will enhance skills help in gathering experience and because of its sophistication, retrieval of data will be fast, accurate and pin-pointed. It is developed by UNESCO and mainly designed for handling non-numerical information. To promote computerization in India, this software was distributed free of cost by NISSAT. But now it charges a nominal cost of Rs 1500 for its 3.07 versions.

Library Fund

Finally the fund at the disposal of the college authority will be a determining factor in the choice of the automation equipment.

Computerization in Cotton College Library

Expert Committee

The first and foremost step of computerization in Cotton College library is the formulation of an expert committee, comprising of Dean of the college as chairperson, librarian as convenor, a few teachers representatives, two computer scientists and two library and information science experts as its members.

The committee will be entrusted with the responsibility of:

(a) feasibility study which generally covers the location of the centre, benefits of automation to its readers and so on;
(b) management of the library which is an important function of the library.

A library can be well managed at a cheaper cost and within its financial capacity with the help of computer. Figure 2 shows a flow chart to show the Cotton College library information system and interface of the system with external entities. This chart reflect the distribution of work, authority and responsibility, nature of duties, input of job, outflow of work, discipline mechanism and so on.

Sanctioning of Fund

Cotton College is a government institution. It receives funds mostly from State Govt. and University Grant Commission. A proposal for computerization of Cotton College library has been prepared with the help of National Information Centre (NIC), Assam State Unit and it has been sent to State Govt. University

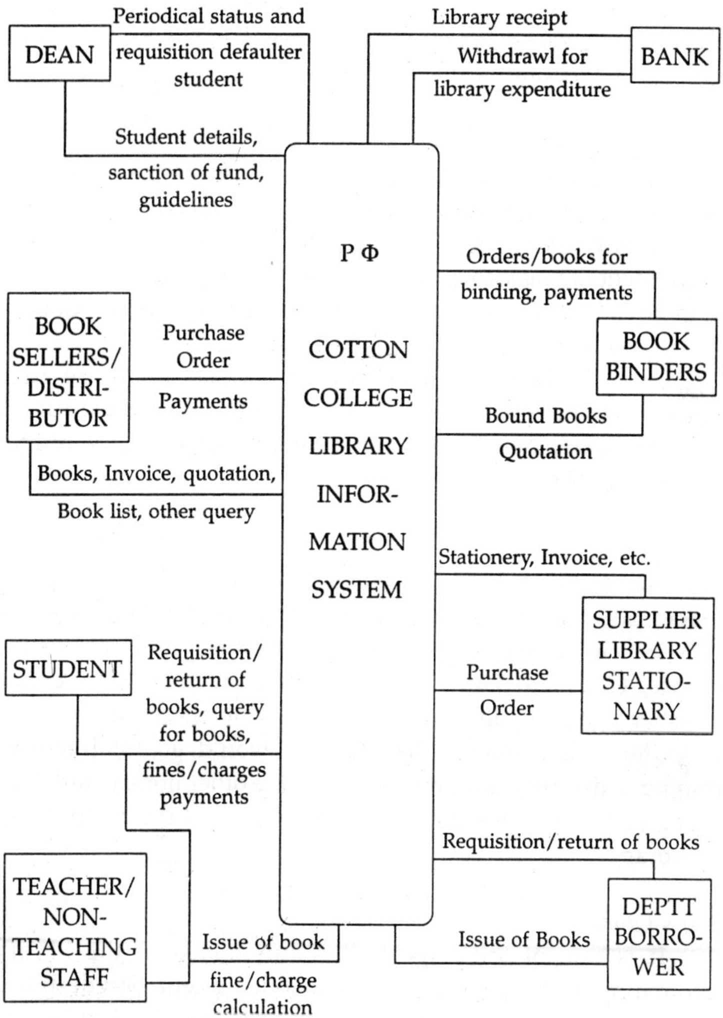

Level Φ DFD (Data Flow Diagram)

FIG. 2: INTERFACE OF THE COTTON COLLEGE LIBRARY INFORMATION SYSTEM WITH EXTERNAL ENTITIES

Grant Commission and INFLIBNET for financial consideration for the installation of the computer. We are very much optimistic in this regard. We are hopeful that funds will not be a contraint for automation of Cotton College Library.

Selection of Hardware and Software

Beginning can be made with PC/AT - 386 hardware and the use of MS-DOS platform based CDS/ISIS software available at a nominal cost from NISSAT. The details of hardware and software requirements alongwith the cost for Cotton College library is shown in Table 1. The layout of computer system in Cotton College library is shown in Figure 3.

From Table 1 it can be calculated that total one time expenditure amounts to Rs. 6,20,000 and recurring expenditure of Rs. 94,500 annually will be required for installation of a computer system at Cotton College library.

Staff Training

The librarian of the college is familiar with the computer system She has already undertaken one short term course on CDS/ISIS organised by the department of Library and Information Science, Guwahati University sponsored by NISSAT and one refresher course from Aligarh Muslim University. Moreover if computer is introduced, the librarian would go for intensive training in due time. For the training of the other library staff, NIC has agreed to train them after the installation of the computer in the library.

User's Education

It is one of the important requirements of the library automation. User education is an expanded orientation designed for self help by the user and the use of all media is necessary. Using the library effectively is the route to intellectual treasure.

The user of Cotton College library comprises of teachers, students, and others. They need to be oriented if computerization takes place. A plan has already been designed to train them. Moreover we are hopeful that once the staff of the library is trained, it will not be difficult to train the user.

TABLE - 1
BUDGET OF HARDWARE AND SOFTWARE REQUIREMENTS OF COTTON COLLEGE LIBRARY

Sl.	*Item*	*Qty*	*Price (Rs.)*
Hardware Requirement			
1.	Intel 80486-DX2 based IBM compatible computer system with processor upgrade technology of the following configuration: — 66 MHZ Clock speed — 32 MB RAM — 256 KB on-board Cache — AT Compatible keyboard (101 keys) — 1*1 - 2 MB FDD (5½" floppy) — 1*1 - 44 MB FDD (3½" floppy) — 1*540 MB HDD with 32 bit SCSI controller — 1*150 MB SCSI CTD with 16 bit SCSI controller — 14" VGA monitor (colour) — 2 nos of multiport communication card/ device in support upto 16 terminal parts — MS - Mouse — Multilingual terminals		
2.	24 pin, 500 cps, 132 column Dot Matrix Printer capable of generating letter quality output		
3.	Uninterrupted Power Supply (UPS) at 3 KVA rating with one hour battery backup of SNF batteries		
4.	Modem (Hayes compatible) (1200/2400/4800/9600/14400) BPS		
5.	Dual speed external SCSI CD ROM Drive of 600 MB capacity		
	Total :		
Software Requirement			
1.	MS-DOS ver 6.2		
2.	SCO UNIX		
3.	Foxpro for Unix		
4.	Lotus for Unix		
5.	Word perfect for Unix		
	Total		
Recurring Expenditure			
1.	Stationery		
2.	Printer Ribbon		
3.	Floppies/Tapes		
4.	Annual Maintenance Contract (AMC @ 10% of H/W Cost)		
	Total		

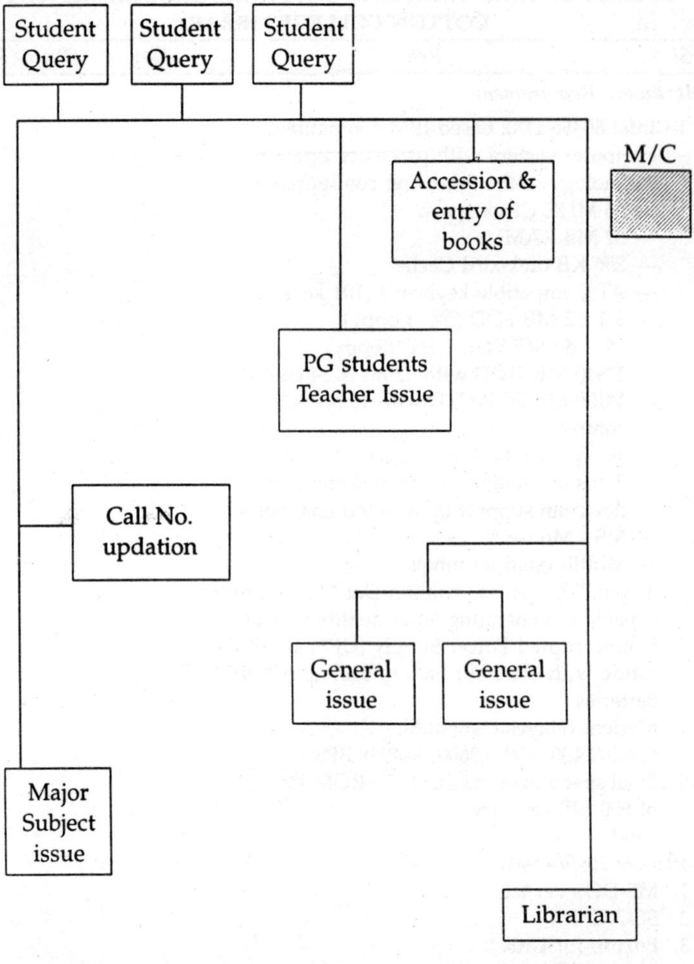

— the shaded box indicates the position of the machine

— the un-shaded box indicates the location of the multi-lingual terminals along with the activity.

FIG. 3: LAYOUT FOR COMPUTER SYSTEM COTTON COLLEGE LIBRARY

Conclusion

If education has to be of national responsibility, a proper academic environment must be created through a richer and better library system. Library being a dynamic organization should adopt to the changes and to remain effective in satisfying the changing information needs of their users. This change is also necessary due to the growing importance of information in all sectors of modern society. The development of increasingly sophisticated technology in itself constitute the importance of information. The changing technology in itself constitute a driving force for change in libraries.

Thus, for anyone who knows about the functions of modern libraries and about what computers can do; the reason why a medium sized library like Cotton College Library of about one lakh documents and an average of 500-1000 transactions per day needs to be computerised, should be obvious.

The father of library science of India, Sri S.R. Ranganathan said that computer is one of the versatile forms through which electronics can help mankind. We must accept the computer. We must derive all benefits it is capable of giving us.

In this spirit Cotton College library should adopt the increasingly sophisticated information technology to re-evaluate and adjust to the way in which they generate, collect, organize and disseminate information. The library should adopt this technology to implement information management in support of education, teaching and research.

REFERENCES

1. Desidoc Bulletin of Information Technology: Special issue on Library Automation: *Software*. Vol. 15, No. 3, pp. 30-32, May, 1995.
2. Lahkar, Narendra: Library Network with special reference to N.E. Region in Buragohain, A. and Baisaya, K (eds). *Librarianship and Information Technology*, p. 177, Guwahati: Omson, 1994.
3. M. Esperanza, A.C. *Library and Information Science*, 1995.
4. National Information Centre Assam State Unit: A proposal for computerization of Cotton College Library.
5. Satyanarayan, N.R. and Satyanarayan, R. *Problems of Information Science*, 1996.

Fourteen

Library Resource Sharing Network: Modern Trends

BHASKAR MUKHERJEE

Introduction

In the modern world of information explosion, resource sharing has become a prime necessity. Resource sharing is a way of library cooperation. Cooperation means, working together with same effort to achieve the objectives i.e. common work for a common goal. The various facets of cooperation are:

(i) Grouping of individuals having a common interest.
(ii) Action by a group, for pursuing certain aims and target.
(iii) Setting up of a permanent organization as an operational unit.[1]

Resource sharing is a need based concept on the principle of give and take policy for mutual benefit. According to Allen Kent "Resource Sharing is a mode of operations whereby functions are shared in common by a number of libraries." With the explosion of multidimensional and multidirectional information and its high costs, the librarian faces a tedious problem to acquire relevant documents for the readers. These conditions have led to the creation of various databases on various subjects for pin pointed, exhaustive and expeditious information to its clientele. Today, library services are getting computerised, to provide right information, to right user, at right time. Most of the countries are now planning to launch these modern technologies for optimum utilisation of resources and for providing better services to users.

Network technology has already come into being in libraries for resource sharing. A network is a form of arrangement for an administrative structure that links a group of individuals or organizations who have agreed to work together and/or share resources. A group of specific subject libraries come forward and pool their resources through network which is technically called library resource sharing network. UNISIST working documents defines Library Resource Sharing Network (LRSN) as - "A set of interrelated systems associated with communication facilities, which are cooperating together more or less formal agreements and instructional agreements in order to jointly implement information handling operation, with a view to pooling their resources and to offer better services to the users. They generally follow identical and competable rules and procedures."[2]

Need of Resource Sharing

Due to limited fund and limited staff, it is impossible for any library to acquire this unlimited and endless knowledge. The only alternative is Resource Sharing. The need of resource sharing can be further explained through following points:

1. Proliferation of literature in each and every field of knowledge.
2. Multiplicity of documents in different subjects, languages and formats.
3. Development of new subjects and subject specialization.
4. Increase in reading community and information seeker.
5. Diversity of user group and their information needs.
6. Demand of pinpointed, exhaustive and expeditious information services.
7. The increased access to information and services at existing cost; and
8. Access to existing information and services at less cost.

Areas of Resource Sharing

In recent past the sharing was being done in various areas. They are generally:

(i) Inter Library Loan;
(ii) Co-operative procurement;

(iii) Co- operative technical operation;
(iv) Preparation of Union Catalogue;
(v) Co-operative Storage;
(vi) Browsing privilege of co-operative member;
(vii) Co-operation in documentation;
(viii) Exchange of publication;
(ix) Exchange of experts.

In modern times the libraries do all these above works, but some modifications have been adopted for better services. They are the networking facilities for quick and better use of latest information.

Characteristics of Library Resource Sharing Network

The Library Resource Sharing Network is having the following characteristics:

(i) Two or more libraries with common goals.
(ii) Two way communication system for free flow of information from one source to another.
(iii) Distribution of information in many forms; such as catalogue card, print out etc.[3]

On the basis of the above characteristics, we can conclude the Library Resource Sharing Network in brief as any independent organization for satisfying the common desires of a group of member libraries with a two way communication facility for distributing the information through computer.

Objectives of Library Resource Sharing Network

The main objectives of library resource sharing network are to:

(i) improve the sharing of resources among the member libraries;
(ii) centralize the information processing system; and
(iii) reduce the communication gap among the libraries.[4]

Thus, Library Resource Sharing Network is very important for Bibliographic controlling of the explosion of literature and knowledge. It also avoids duplication in purchase of costly documents. It facilitates the adoption of new areas in every field of knowledge and improves the mobility of data. Library resource sharing network is a helpful way to develop the flow of information among the special information centres/libraries and other types of libraries.

Ways of Operating Library Resource Sharing Network

Previously the resource sharing was done through inter-library-loan with the help of union catalogues and union directory of periodicals. Nowadays generally the Library Resource Sharing Network is operated in two ways.

(i) By telecommunication network.

(ii) By database in optical media.

The telecommunication facility originated in 1844 with its 40 km range. In the early part of twentieth century the tele-communication networking facilities were adopted in the library for dissemination of information through satellites.[5]

Due to high cost of telecommunication network, the database on optical media was introduced in library activity. The huge information is stored in optical disks for easy transferring from one place to another. Optical media can be divided into two main classes (i) Digital and (ii) Analogue. Further these are subdivided into Read only, Write only and Erasable. CD ROM is a typical example of digital, read only memory device which is widely used in library and information field. It can carry 550 Megabytes of digital data.

There is another technology which is widely used in resource sharing work that is online network. In this process the information is simultaneously stored and retrieved through computer terminal which is connected via a modem (modulator and demodulater) to telephone. The query entered through the terminal gets converted to the analogue mode and travels through the telecommunication lines and reaches the computer systems in which the data is loaded. There would be another modem at the other end of computer system to convert the analogue signals of the query into digital signals which the computer understands. The records of the data base are searched and the search result is converted from the digital mode, back to the analogue mode by the modem at the computer system, travels back in analog mode, reaches the modem at the terminal and gets converted into digital mode and search result appears on the display unit at the terminal. All this happens in a few seconds the user feels that all this is happening instantaneously.[6]

Some Basic Differences of CD ROM and Online

(1) In CD ROM the searcher gets quick results than online. Because in online command is required to search the information.

(2) CD ROM has graphic facilities. It is able to provide graph, diagrams, maps, illustrations, etc. But in online (except the availability of TCP/IP account) only textual information can be retrieved but the biggest disadvantages with CD ROM is frequency of updating. Humanities index is updated twice per week for online but quarterly on CD ROM. This is because of production of master discs, their replication and mailing to subscribers is an expensive and time consuming process.

(3) For retrospective research-document sharing, online is the only alternative because major database are available from 1966 onwards; whereas CD ROM database are available from 1980.

(4) All CD database do not use the same search software; at least two different kinds of software are currently in use. As a result, it is difficult for the user to refer to different manuals for different databases whereas online vendors adopt common command language (CCL) for searching all databases.[7]

Networking and its Development in India

There are mainly two types of network found on the basis of area coverage (a) Local Area Network (LAN) and; (B) Wide Area Network (WAN).

Wide area network is designed to serve an area of hundreds to thousands of miles. There is a network spanning a sizeable geographical area with communication based on telephone or microwave transmission. Application of WAN in Resource Sharing is in the following three areas viz. Inter library Loan, Interlinking CD ROM database and providing access to bibliographical information.[8] Some of the examples of such networking are INDONET (INET), National Information Centre Network (NICNET) and Information and Library Network (INFLIBNET).

INET was established by the department of telecommunication in 1992. It is a nation wide Packet-Switched-Public Data Network (PSPDN) having nodes in eight cities viz; Delhi, Mumbai, Bangalore, Pune, Ahmedabad, Calcutta and Hyderabad, connected through high speed (ranging from 9600-64000 bps) link. It provides fast, reliable, flexible and effective service to the Government and Private organizations. It can access the International data network through Gateway Packet Switched Service (GPSS) of Videsh Sanchar Nigam Limited (VSNL), Mumbai. The data search on Internet can also be possible through this network by providing the account number and password given by the corresponding DoT office and enter specific number of VSNL for various metropolitans. (for Delhi it is 404311017777; for Mumbai it is 404322017777 and for Calcutta it is 404333017777). Any businessman can easily get the required information from this network by making a single dialup. They also get connected to subscriber of Remote Area Business Message Network (RABMN) of the DoT. The cost of communication are lowest, volume dependent (i.e. amount of data) and are independent of distance. It supports CCITT Standards interface/ protocols x.3, x.28, x.29, x.25 and x.27.[9] The facility which is provided by Inet.

* Reverse Changing
* Close User Group (CUG) and
* Permanent Virtual Circuit (PVC)

This is a revolutionary breakthrough for the business community as well as Government organization. An organization with a simple PC, modem and telephone can search and retrieve their relevant information through this network facility.

NICNET

A unique infrastructural network established in 1977 is National Information Centre Network (NICNET). The total network is designed in three phases. The first phase of NIC came into limelight during IX Asian games. This computer network with its 34 terminals spanning the 17 States started functioning in Delhi. NIC has reached the second phase of extending NICNET service to State government thereby improving the information exchange between the Centre and State. In the third phase NIC has connected with INSAT-ID and helped to bring all the districts of India within the limit of NICNET. It is unique in the sense that it uses almost exclusively satellite based communication, using low cost of roof top micro earth station to connect 450 district headquarters and 32 State and Union Territory Capitals with the Central point at Delhi. Another distinct feature of NICNET is that it uses 500 very small aperture terminals (VSAT's) each of which is connected with a specific outbound and inbound channel on the satellite's transformer. NICNET is designed primarily to be a government information network. Its objectives are to promote the collection, storage, analysis, transmission and exchange of data at districts, State headquarters, central ministries and various departments at New Delhi, for using in planning, management and monitoring of projects and government sponsored programmes. This is extensively used during emergencies caused by natural calamities.

INFLIBNET

During the seventh Five year plan (1985-90) the Report of the Steering Group on Science Technology and Environment and the Report of the Planning Commission Working Group on Modernisation of Library Services and Informatic, emphasise the need for Computerisation of Libraries and Library Network interlinking all special libraries in India by 2000 AD. The INFLIBNET Proposal has emerged as a logical consequence of the New National Policy on Education (1986) and the National Policy on Library and Information System (1986). These proposals were activated during the VII Five year plan (1990-95) and establish a network namely as INFLIBNET which is now an independent organization.

It is envisaged as a computer communication network of libraries and information centre using satellite cum terrestrial networking.

The overall structure of INFLIBNET is as follows:

(a) A national centre to coordinate, oversee and manage the policy making affair of network (Located at Ahmedabad).

(b) Four regional national centre (N, E, W, S) will maintain Regional Union Catalogue and database of projects, institution and specialist.

(c) Many sectoral information centres in each discipline, 4 UGC information centres of Arts, Science, Engineering and Humanities and seven NISSAT and other national level agencies like DESIDOC, INARI, INSDOC, etc.

(d) 184 Universities, 23 Deemed Universities, 6100 colleges and over 200 libraries affiliated to the organization.

(e) 400 ground terminals situated at 150 University libraries, 50 postgraduate colleges and 200 R & D institution.

INFLIBNET is being planned as a multi service network and will provide.

(a) Catalogued based service including shared catalogue, Union Catalogue, Online Catalogue access, Cataloguing production on Books, thesis and serials.

(b) Database service including bibliographic database service for retrospective search, SDI, CAS and non bibliographic database service.

(c) Document supply service, including document delivery through FAX, and non FAX.

(d) Communication based service, including E-mail for transfer and receipt of message, Bulletin board service for viewing and updating.

Local Area Network (LAN) is a communication system that is used to link the terminals, computers, word processing stations and other data processing resources, in order to be shared, within the inter connection of processors located within the same building or in general, within one kilometre of one another.

The few major characteristics of LAN are:

(1) The connection between the work station are usually at a distance of few hundred feet upto several thousand feet within the specific range.

(2) It transmits data between user station and computers.

(3) The LAN transmission capacity is usually greater than that of a wide area network; typical bit rate range from 1 Mbit/s to 20 Mbit/s.

DELNET, CALIBNET and MALIBNET

DELNET, CALIBNET and MALIBNET are the typical examples of these networking systems which is now ongoing in libraries of metropolitan cities like Delhi, Calcutta and Madras.

DELNET, the Delhi Library Network, a public switch network is supposed to connect 35 libraries of Delhi. The participating libraries have already started to enter their serial and monograph collection on a specific format using CDS/ISIS. Records are in conformity with the Common Communication Format (CCF). The participating libraries of DELNET have already prepared the Serial database which is available at one of the libraries in the network. In addition the monograph database is also searchable through the dialup access and participating libraries can also use and update data according to their need. It is proposed that their network will have E-mail, File transfer and bulletin board facilities.

CALIBNET, the Calcutta Library Network will network 38 Science technology libraries in the Calcutta metropolitan area. The plan is for introduction of automated system, in the participating libraries before networking. Each library is expected to automate their book acquisition cataloguing, serial control, finance accounting and circulation control. The network centre will provide on-line accesses to the networks, union catalogues and current awareness services including SDI. As with DELNET each cluster of libraries will be serviced by packet switching exchange.

Libraries participating in CALIBNET will use AACR II for bibliographic description. The software, MAITRAYEE supports MARC records and will also enable records to be imported/ exported via the CCF format. CALIBNET will be linked to DELNET via dialup access and to external networks via the GPSS (Gateway Packet Switched Services).[10]

In February 1993, MALIBNET (Madras Library Network) was registered as society in Madras with the support received from various institutions in Madras. A main computer system has been acquired, installed and made operational with no direct funding from Government. MALIBNET was inaugurated in June 1993 to link with five institutions viz. Anna University, IIT Madras, CLRI, Madras University and Mat Science.

MALIBNET will offer the following information service initially:

(i) Currently acquired serials holding in about 50 libraries.
(ii) Contents information of about 400 important journals.
(iii) Specialized database giving abstracts of articles.
(iv) Door delivery system for document photocopies.

There are also some organizations which set up networking for the dissemination of information of their subject field. They are

(i) SIRNET— Scientific and Industrial Network, CSIR Network, Government of India, New Delhi.
(ii) ERNET— Education and Research Network, Deptt. of Electronics, Govt. of India, New Delhi.
(iii) OILNET— Oil and Natural Gas Commission (ONGC) Network, Govt. of India, New Delhi.
(iv) PUNET— Pune Network, Pune

Conclusion

Ranganathan's First Law says "Books are for use." In modern time we are not only dealing with books but also non-book materials such as microfilm, microfische, audio-visual material, etc. Now it is better to say "Documents are for use", and the documents, containing information are an important national resource for developing countries like India. It is like power. So its sharing is necessary for National Development. Nowadays we transmit information through telephone and optical media, which is more cheaper than conventional form. It is important that all available information is fully and efficiently disseminated for avoiding costly and unnecessary duplication of resources. The telecommunication network is convenient if the telephone charges are moderate and telephone lines easily available. It requires little equipment like telephone, modem and one PC only. However, in India charges are very high and line is not always available. The optical media initially requires more investment like optical disc driver, CR Rom database, software, etc. This media is suitable if the organization is capable of expanding within the available resources. Each of the above media are capable of quick and fast information sharing.

All the infrastructural networks mentioned above are in initial stages of development in India. The experience gained by the libraries and software developers in these networks will undoubtedly be very valuable. In case we are able to negotiate the hurdels coming in the way of development of the system we shall certainly be able to provide better services to our nation.

REFERENCES

1. Prasher, R.G. 'Resource sharing among Libraries'. In *Lucknow Librarian*, 20 (3-4). pp. 90-96, 1988.
2. Sarma, T.R.B. Modern Trends in Library Resources Sharing Network, *In Herald of Library Science.* 33 (1-2) pp. 28-34, 1994.
3. *Ibid.*, pp. 28-34
4. *Ibid.*, pp. 28-34
5. Haravu L.J. Library Automation and Networking in India : An overview of recent development. In *Annals of Library Science and Documentation* 40(1-2) pp. 32-40, 1993.
6. Kasirao, V. On Line Information Technology in the field of Library and Information management environment: An overview. In *RILISAR Bulletin* 8 (1). pp. 3-41, 1993.
7. Relan, Sonia. Application of CD-ROM in Libraries. In *Herald of Library Science.* 33(1-2). pp. 35-42, 1994.
8. Meera, B.M. Advance in Library Network Technology for Resource Sharing Activities : From WAN to LAN. In *Library Science with a slant to Documentation and Information Studies.* 311(2) pp. 1-17, 1994.
9. Department of Telecommunication. *Telephone Directory*, p. 48, 1995.
10. *Op. cit.*, (5).

Fifteen

Retrieval of Documents in a University Library System: Problems and Prospects

DR. J. YADAGIRI REDDY

Introduction

University libraries play a vital role in furtherance of Academic and Research activities. The University Education Commission (1948-49) has rightly pointed out "the library is the heart of all the University's work, directly so, as regards to its research work and indirectly as regards its educational work, which derives its life from research .... Both for humanistic and Scientific studies, a first class library is essential in a university".[1] To meet the academic and research requirement entrusted upon them, the university libraries, acquire books journals and other reading material relevant to the academic and research needs. The materials are organised for effective retrieval. They also provide library and information services for optimum utilization of its graphic/document resources.

Despite the best efforts made by the University librarian and his able staff, in providing library service, it is a commonly held notion that the user quite often fails to get the desired documents to meet his academic/research needs.

This paper briefly analyses some of the errors that have crept into the organization of documents, whereby the retrieval of the desired documents has been greatly hampered.

Retrieval of Documents : Problems

The users of the university libraries viz. students, research scholars and staff in pursuit of academic advancement, desire to consult books and other documents. They visit the University Library in search of these documents and in the process (a) retrieve quite a good number of documents, (b) find that their desired documents are not held in their library collections, and (c) fail to retrieve the documents from the available stock. I present below some of the causes which prevent the reader from retrieving the documents from the available stock.

1. Important books are stolen away from the library, whereas the library catalogues reveal that such books are in the library stock. There are also cases, when important pages in books or journals are torn away.
2. A reader, who takes away book(s) from the shelf, replaces it at some point either not knowing its exact location or deliberately hiding in some other sequence in the racks. As a result books are misplaced and seemingly lost until they are recovered.
3. Call number means Greek and Latin to some of the library users. Instead of retrieving books using call number they try to identify particular shelf for a particular subject and restrict their search for documents to such shelves only.
4. Catalogue cards are at times found wrongly filed in the catalogue cabinets. The problem is more acute with the title cards. Quite related to this problem are spelling errors found in the entry element. Both the above cases mislead the readers.
5. (a) Wornout books are taken out for binding, (b) research scholars keep good number of books in their carrels/cubicles and (c) books are taken out of the library for home reading. Books taken away from the shelf on such occasions, are not recorded in a way that would help the reader to know the whereabouts of such books, when they are not found on the shelves.
6. Newly emerging disciplines, interdisciplinary subjects often make the job of classification and providing subject headings complicated. There are instances where books dealing with the same subject are assigned different class numbers and

subject headings. This in turn means, books with same subject are scattered at different places.

7. Library users, particularly the new entrants have little knowledge on (a) technicalities of cataloguing and classification, (b) arrangement of books on the shelf, and (c) various sections of library and nature of books possessed in each unit. The system of user education wherever existing, is carried out only in the beginning of the academic programme, afterwards the readers are left to use their own skills in locating their desired documents.
8. Newly acquired books often take several months to find their place on the stacks; so also filing of their catalogue cards in cabinets.
9. Analytical entries are more often not prepared for festschrift volumes/books brought out under editorial direction. This forces the readers to spend much time in the stack area looking for subjects of their interest and in the process they miss much of the information contained in these books.
10. Academic and research journals contain vast amounts of nascent and potential information. These journals are not indexed and also no efforts are made to maintain data banks of the information contained in these journals.

Solution

In an open access system, books are bound to be misplaced and lost, and hundred per cent retrieval of documents is not a pragmatic proposition. However, it is believed that with certain procedural changes, the ratio of retrieval of books can be improved considerably. I present below some such procedural changes for effective retrieval of documents.

1. "Reader Assistance function" needs to be strengthened. A separate section with some dedicated staff should be established and placed near the stack area, with the prime function to assist the readers in getting their desired books.
2. Security of books and other library materials needs to be improved. A section of the library staff should be entrusted with the job of going round the stack area at periodic intervals, and the security at check point needs to be strengthened. As

far as possible, the library counter should be placed near the exit point. Prompt xerox services also help in checking thefts and tearing of pages from the books.

3. Newark Charging System used for the issue of books, needs to be slightly modified. For each book, two book cards have to be prepared. Whenever a book is taken away for general issue, one book card gets filed behind the due date guide card and the other book card has to be arranged according to its accession number in a separate sequence called 'duplicate sequence'. One card of the books taken away for binding and books taken to the carrels/cubicles should be filed in this duplicate sequence with necessary remarks on it. This enables the reader to know the whereabouts of the book, not found on the shelf, by comparing the accession number of a book taken from the catalogues with the book cards in duplicate sequence.
4. The catalogue cards filed by one staff, should be rechecked by some senior staff.
5. Shelf reading at regular intervals has to be carried out to retrieve the wrongly filed books and to replace them in their proper places. Shelving of books as far as possible should be done atleast by the semi-professional staff.
6. Classification and subject indexing requires expertise on the part of the library professionals. It will be advantageous, if this function is entrusted to a person who has good understanding of Universe of subjects and who is good at classification and indexing work.
7. Suggestion/complaint register should be placed near the catalogues, to register any suggestion/difficulties. This helps in improving the reader's service. Complaints should be viewed constructively.
8. Each stack in the library should be numbered, and should have labels containing class numbers and subjects covered in each shelf. Guide cards containing stack number, and proportionate class number covered by them should be placed near the catalogues. This facilitates easy and quick location of documents in the library.
9. Academic and Research journals in important disciplines

have to be indexed, and the index cards should be filed subsequently in the data bank. This facilitates the user in retrieving the micro literature held in the library collection.

10. Automation of library services, naturally improves the quality of reader's service.

Conclusion

There is an urgent need to extend library function from mere document collection and organization to user/reader satisfaction service. It is suggested that with, (a) greater security of the library collections, (b) periodic shelf reading, (c) modification in the charging system, (d) establishment of reader assistance unit, and (e) highly motivated and committed library staff, a reader would be able to retrieve a great deal of his documents to his utmost satisfaction.

REFERENCES

1. India University Education Commission 1948-49. Report. Delhi : Manager of Publications, 1949, Vol. 1, p. 110.

Sixteen

Public Library Services in Madhya Pradesh

DR SURENDRA SINGH

Introduction

Public Libraries are considered an essential part of modern society. They provide information, education, recreation, entertainment and inspiration, to all members of our society without any distinction of caste, creed, sex or religion. Being democratic institutions, operated by the people, for the people they are the heart of the citizens. Their users are diversified and belong to varied fields like: engineering, law, science and technology, agriculture, medical science, etc. In addition to this students and community members of the society belonging to different vocations and professions, are also the users of the public library. The public libraries should become citizen - centered and there should be a close and willing partnership between libraries and public as a whole.

The State of Madhya Pradesh

As per its name, Madhya Pradesh lies in the very heart of India. It spreads mainly over the table land of Central India. It consists of the Gangetic Valley in the north and is bordered by the States of Maharashtra and Andhra Pradesh in the South. Towards east of Madhya Pradesh is Orissa and towards its west are Rajasthan and Gujarat States.

Areas which form part of this State are the seventeen districts of Mahakoshal, eight district of previous Vindhya Pradesh, sixteen districts of the east while Madhya Bharat, and the whole of Bhopal state consisting of two districts. The density of population in the State is 189 per square mile and the literacy percentage is 43.45. A great majority of the population understands and speaks Hindi or a related language.

The State has had a name and tradition of being a land of litterateurs since historical times. The names of some of the luminaries of this State who have attained an enviable place in the history of world literature are: Kalidas, Bhavabhuti, Gangadhar, Varahmihir, Acharya Keshavadas, Bihari, Bhushan, Padmakar, Vikramaditya, Beju, Tansen and Rupmati.

Public Library Services in Madhya Pradesh

The first recorded account of any library of this State is that of Bhoja, a twelfth century king of Dhar. On the conquest of his kingdom by the Chalukyan King Sidharaja, this library was removed to the famous city of Patan in the territory of His Highness, the Maharaja of Gaikwad and incorporated with the Royal Chalukyan library there. The Nawab of Bhopal also had a very rich collection of Urdu and Persian books and manuscripts in his Royal Library attached to the palace.

The credit of initiating the establishment of public libraries goes to the Princes of the State such as Maharajas of Gwalior and Indore. Under the patronage of Maharaja Tukojirao Holkar II, the Indore General Library was founded in 1854 at Indore. Some of the important public and institutional libraries, which are still giving services and were established by the close of 19th Century are: Municipal District Library, Jabalpur (1885); Mahakoshal Mahavidyala Library, Jabalpur (1873), Holkar College Library, Indore (1890) and Madhav College Library, Ujjain 1891.

Some of the important libraries, which have been established during this period, are : Madhav Pustakalaya, Gwalior (1903); Public Library, Sagar (1909); and Hamidia State Library, Bhopal (1911). These libraries are public in the sense that they are open to all. But, in the strict sense they are subscription libraries, and do not provide free service.

The notable landmark in the development of public libraries in the State is the establishment of the Central Library at Gwalior in the year 1928. This was followed by the establishment of museum-cum-libraries at the seats of the capital of the constituent States of old Vindhya Pradesh, viz Rewa, Panna, Nagod, Chhatarpur, Datia, Tikamgarh, Kothi and Maihar.

In order to organize rural library service, attempts were initiated by the rural development department of the defunct State of Madhya Bharat in 1948-49. This envisaged establishment of village libraries at every Panchayat centre. In 1950-51 a sum of Rs. 57,000 was granted for the Panchayat Centre Libraries.

The year 1952 is a significant date when the Madhya Bharat Government invited Mr Frank M. Gardner of England "to visit the State and inspect libraries, with a view to suggesting possible development and improvement". In this report, Mr Gardner pointed out the deficiencies of the existing libraries and suggested a scheme for development of library service over a period of five years with an annual State expenditure of Rs 6,00,000. Unfortunately, the recommendations made by Mr Gardner could not be implemented even in part.

In 1951-52 the old Madhya Pradesh Government launched a library scheme under the Directorate of Panchayats and Social Welfare. The purpose of the scheme was to provide a follow-up programme for neo-literates so as to prevent them from lapsing into illiteracy as well as to be a source of continued education to the rural literates. Under this scheme, many circulating libraries in the village of Madhya Bharat and Mahakoshal regions and one Central Library at Indore have been established.

A scheme for "Improvement of Library Service" was included in the First Five Year Plan of Educational Development 1951-56. It envisaged the establishment of district libraries with a network of circulating libraries in villages served through deposit stations, and to supplement and support the district libraries. It was proposed to have a central library for the whole State and linguistic region.

By the end of the First Five Year Plan this State established under this scheme three central libraries one each at Jabalpur, Rewa and Bhopal; 23 district libraries i.e. four in Mahakoshal

Region, seven in Vindhya Pradesh Region and two in Bhopal Region, and three Integrated Library Service Centres, one each at Jabalpur, Sanchi and Dabra.

During the Second Five Year Plan no appreciable Progress was made in the field of libraries. A notable event of this period was the founding in January, 1958 of the Madhya Pradesh Library Association which owes its existence to the initiative of Dr S.R. Ranganathan. Another significant landmark of this period is the Report of the Maulana Azad Library Development Committee (1958). The recommendations made by this committee covered a wider field and stressed the immediate need for the enactment of Library legislation. It put forth a scheme which envisaged an outlay of Rs 32 lacs for development of the Maulana Azad Central Library in seven progressive stages. The recommendations of this committee were practical and within the means of the State but were not somehow implemented.

No satisfactory provision has been made by the State in its Third and Fourth Five Year plans for the Development of Public library service. In 1961 the Government, however, established Shri Ahilya Central Library at Indore for which the H.H. Maharaja Yeshwant Rao Holkar, Indore donated a sum of Rs. 1,50,000.

Coverage

The Primary consideration is: How far is the State "covered" and how far are its people, wherever they reside, able to avail themselves of adequate library facilities?

Rural

Except in some of the villages of Mahakoshal and Madhya Bharat Regions, there is no public library service of any sort in most of the rural areas of this State. In Mahakoshal region there are about 800 so called "Book Deposit Centres" in the rural areas and they have been maintained by the respective district libraries of the education department. Under the social education scheme in Directorate of Panchayats and Social Welfare are running 1224 and 4239 circulating village libraries in Mahakoshal and Madhya Bharat region respectively. In addition there are village libraries run by the Janpad Sabha and Block Development and Tribal Welfare Department.

The book deposit centres and circulating village libraries are housed in village Panchayat centres or village schools and are under the charge of a teacher or a volunteer worker. Each centre has a collection of about 40 to 60 books, mostly fiction and religious books. The collection is exchanged from one centre to another with its region at a stipulated time interval.

The schemes of village library service have been started by several agencies of the Government without careful planning and consequently the development of rural library service has been sporadic and haphazard and no provision exists for any sort of library service to more than three fourth of the rural population.

Urban

The situation of Library service in the Urban areas is also not very satisfactory. As already stated, out of 43 districts only 23 districts have district libraries in their respective headquarters. There are five regional central libraries: one each at Jabalpur, Rewa, Bhopal, Indore and Gwalior. As per information supplied by the office of the Director Public Instruction, there are about 75 town libraries in the Mahakoshal Region, 39 in Madhya Bharat Region, 16 in Vindhya Pradesh region and only 1 in Bhopal Region, maintained and aided by the Government agencies. Besides the district, central and town libraries of the Government agencies, there are libraries run by the Municipalities, corporations and other local and private bodies and institutions in many cities and towns.

The regional central libraries are rendering good service to the community. The services of district libraries and the libraries of the corporation and municipalities, have also been more or less satisfactory.

The following account of four regional libraries illustrates the inadequacy of library provision in rural areas too.

(a) Jabalpur has a population of 3,67,215 but has no branch libraries while it requires 14 branch libraries, i.e. one for each 25,000 population;

(b) Bhopal has a population of 2,25,560 but has only one branch library while it requires seven more such branches;

(c) Gwalior has a population of 3,00,513 but has no branches while it needs eleven branch libraries;

(d) Indore has a population of 3,95,035 but has no branches while it needs 15 branch libraries.

Factors Responsible for Inadequate Coverage

Some of the important factors which have contributed to inadequate coverage are: lack of educational opportunities, difficulty of supporting adequate library service in rural areas which have greatly dispersed population and very poor financial support.

This has led to establishment of stray and un-coordinated libraries at scattered points rendering partial or unsatisfactory service.

Efficiency of Library Service

The main activity of the regional and district libraries is lending service on payment of nominal amount as deposit. Figures relating to registered borrowers and loan of books reveal that on the whole library service reaches students and adult males much more fully than the children and female adults. Reading room facilities are provided in all the libraries. Figures relating to use of books and number of visitors in the reading rooms of the central libraries reveal that people come mostly to read newspapers and magazines rather than for purposive reading. Attendance of female members in the reading rooms is almost nil and the provision for children has been awefully neglected. As regards reference and information service in the regional libraries, it is difficult to measure it either in quality or in quantity. However, in the light of observation and of such figures as are available, it may be said that the service is generally below the satisfactory level. Use of these libraries for fact finding and research purposes is handicapped by lack of necessary material and by lack of qualified library personnel.

Book Collection

The Maulana Azad Central Library Development Committee, 1958 states that "a library that expects to discharge its responsibilities must have a book collection equal to the demands made upon it". However, the strength of the book collection of the regional central libraries is very meagre and requires to be augmented ten times to reach the minimum standards. The stock comprises mainly Hindi and English books and a very small percentage in Urdu, Marathi and Bengali. The provision of technical, scientific and business books fitted to the community's interests is negligible. Further no attempt is made to keep the collection up-to-date. In some of the libraries, shabby, unattractive and out-moded books occupy shelf space at the cost of important recent books. Attempts are lacking to organize and arrange the material neatly to present a decent look to the readers. Non-book materials especially audiovisual materials do not find any place in the collections of the libraries. Periodicals which are being subscribed by these libraries are neither adequate nor representative.

Personnel

The authorities do not seem to be convinced that good services need adequate, qualified and better paid staff. The strength of Library staff in the State is not only utterly inadequate but also not properly trained. Amongst the whole of the staff working in the libraries run by the State, there are about a dozen members only who possess diploma or degree in Library Science. Most of the district libraries are manned by the Assistant District Inspectors of Schools or Assistant Masters. The salary scales of library personnel on the whole are poor and unattractive and vary from one region to another. Librarians especially district librarians, have no status or position comparable to their responsibility.

Training in Library Science

At present B. Lib. Science courses are being conducted at Ujjain, Gwalior, Sagar, Jabalpur, Indore, Bhopal, Raipur and Rewa by their respective Universities. M. Lib.Sc. Courses are being conducted at Ujjain, Gwalior and Sagar. No special emphasis is laid in the curriculum on problems connected with the organization and development of public libraries of the country or the State in particular. The public libraries should cover an important and compulsory place in the syllabi of library science courses, because these libraries play a very significant role in building a healthy and progressive community. Public libraries are an indispensable part of society and help in developing competent and responsible citizens. They are the real source of inspiration to the people at large and cater to the needs of the community—educational or recreational. A right type of public library can create and stimulate reading habits. It helps in providing balanced, integrated and satisfied individuals, useful and valuable citizens. Thus, Public libraries, their organization and management, importance and services, etc., should necessarily be the part of library science syllabi.

Premises

The Regional libraries are mostly housed in buildings which are completely outmoded and outgrown. Bad ventilation, poor lighting, dinginess, small and unsuitable premises, and an uninviting atmosphere prevail in the library buildings. In some of the regional and district library buildings there are cracks.

Owing to economic difficulties and, partly due to neglect by the Education Department, expenditure on public library buildings has been regarded as of no importance. Whatever little capital expenditure has been made available, is utilized for repair of most serious and alarming defects in the existing library building or/and to extend its premises. The Maulana Azad Central Library Development Committee, 1958 had prepared a plan for the extension and development of its present library building, but no action has been taken to implement it.

Furniture and Equipment

The Regional Central Libraries have more or less satisfactory equipment and furniture. But district libraries, barring a few, lack modern equipment and facilities like proper lighting, electric fans, etc. None of the regional or district libraries has a telephone connection.

Finance

The figures of expenditure incurred by the Regional Central Libraries of Jabalpur, Gwalior, Rewa and Bhopal of staff, books and periodicals, furniture and equipment, etc., during the last three years, point out serious deficiencies in finance. Further the allocation of finance is uncertain, and unevenly distributed. Figures of expenditure on development of public libraries for First Five year Plan could not be ascertained. Total expenditure incurred by the State on public libraries during the Second Five Year Plan was Rs 4.14 lacs. The amount proposed to be spent for libraries during the Third Five Year Plan was only Rs 3.50 lacs.

Problems

In the field of education Madhya Pradesh is one of the backward States in India. About 85 per cent of the people, mostly residing in rural areas, are illiterate. Hence both the State and Local Governments' first concern has been to remove illiteracy and for this many elementary and secondary educational institutions have been established and are being established all over the state. But it is hardly realized that public libraries are an important means of continual self education, and that without adequate provision of these illiteracy will replace neo-literacy.

The factor detrimental to growth of libraries in this State has been the absence of effective government policies and programmes. People in the State have barely begun to utilize the potential of an effective State library agency. There has been utter lack of clear thinking on library matters, and authorities at the helm of affairs have not given any thought to public library service. This has led them to under-rate librarians and libraries.

Linking of the public libraries to the educational responsibilities of the State has not helped growth of libraries. It would not be wrong to state that the State's responsibilities towards public library service have been thus minimized because of the confusion in the relationship between public education and public library service. At the same time the legislatures have not been conditioned to demand for separate public library service as an important obligation.

Librarians in this State have rarely assumed a strong role and pressed for the establishment of firm library policies. They have done little to drive home to the community and its leaders the library's potential. It is true that the librarians face difficult problems and all the blame for the malady should not be cast upon them. Most of the librarians are not professionally trained and are not able to mobilize professional opinion for the development of strong public library system.

The above factors throw a challenge before all those concerned with library development in this State. They must devise a public library policy and ensure its implementation. At the same time the library must be brought into a closer working relationship with the dominant governmental structure.

A Policy for Public Library Service

The first step towards providing better library facilities should be development of programme and setting up of goals for public library services. Once the goals are determined, the plan for securing acceptance and support could be developed. It is important to keep in mind that the public library should be designed to serve ultimately the broad cross-section of the population and that support for the library must correspondingly come from as great a variety of groups in the community as can possibly be mustered to promote the cause. Library planning should be a continuing and dynamic process and should be divided into programmes of shorter and intermediate durations.

Role of the State Government

The State Government has the primary responsibility for the establishment and development of public library service, and should play a more active role in the development of library service throughout the region by observing the principle that "Library is an educational concern of the State".

Conclusion

The credit of establishing public libraries in the State of Madhya Pradesh, no doubt, goes to the princes of States, local bodies and enlightened citizens in the past. But real progress could be made only since the advent of the First Five Year Plan, when the Union Ministry of Education started giving grants for—"Improvement of Library Services", in 1952-53. At present, there are 5 Regional Central Libraries, 23 District Libraries and 3 Integrated Library Service units, managed by the Education Departments. Besides there are libraries run by other Government Departments, of which the Directorate of Panchayats and Social Welfare claims a large number.

Any one who has inspected the public libraries of Madhya Pradesh is conscious of many depressing facts and of appalling deficiencies in books, staff, premises and equipment. It becomes apparent that the schemes of Public library service have been started by several Government agencies without giving sufficient thought over its purpose and problems and consequently sporadic, haphazard and un-coordinated development of library service has taken place. Taken as a whole, the public library service in the State is ill-supported, undernourished, unappreciated and under-staffed, struggling to provide minimal service. There has been some growth, no doubt and in some areas appreciable development too, but this is only a beginning and there is still a long way to go before the people are assured of satisfactory library service.

The challenge must be encountered at different levels. Firstly the State Government should ensure a strong legal foundation for its public libraries by constitutional or legislative provisions which recognize public library service as a State concern and make the establishment and maintenance of public library service mandatory throughout the State. Secondly , the State should establish a strong central library agency which will plan and promote the extension and more efficient organization of a State-wide, integrated library service. Thirdly, librarians and well wishers of libraries should bring to the attention of the community the library resources and services, by combination of methods such as persuasion, education and illustration. It is certain that only a unified, loyal and active association of these three elements can build a better foundation for library development.

It is highly desirable and essential for the Government of Madhya Pradesh to take the initiative in appointing a high power expert committee to comprehensively assess the existing situations and to suggest ways and means for a dynamic integrated State wide public library service.

REFERENCES

1. Bal Satya Narayan, L.K. *Law of Public Libraries in India*. Allahabad: Law Book, 1962.
2. Bhatia, Satwant Singh. *History of Library Legislation in India and UK*. Chandigarh: Punjab University, 1963.
3. Khanna, J.B. Library Legislation; A necessity. *Herald of Lib. Sc.* 2(2). April, 1963.
4. Mookherji, S.K. *Development of Libraries and Library Science in India*. Calcutta: World Press - 1969.
5. Ramakrishna Rao, K. Library Development in India. *Lib. Qrt*. Vol. XXI(2). 1961.
6. Sen, N.B. ed.: *Development of Libraries in New India*. New Delhi: New Book Depot. 1965.
7. Sharma, J.S.: *Fundamental of Library Science*. Delhi: McMillian, 1978.
8. Thillainayagam, V.: Library Movement in India. Yesterday, Today and Tomorrow. *Culture Forum*. Vol. 9(4). 1967.

Seventeen

Library Movement in Jammu & Kashmir

A.R. LATTOO

Historical Background of the State

The Jammu and Kashmir State occupies the northern most part of India and looks like a crown on the map of India. It is endowed with natures bounties and occupies a pride place in India. It is due to the benevolence of nature that the cultural heritage of Kashmir is so rich and varied. By virtue of the uniqueness of its situation, the valley has remained a sanctuary of a mixed and harmonized culture. The Kashmiris have derived full inspiration from their amiable surroundings and produced a galaxy of philosophers, scholars, poets and chroniclers. Not a single branch of literature has been left untouched by them and this mental exercise has never cooled down but continues till date.

Hiuen-Tsang, a Chinese traveller, who visited India in 629-645 AD after visiting Udayana, Bolar and Texila reached Kashmir. We have come to know from his life that on arrival in Kashmir, he spent one night at Jayendra Monastery. The next day he went to the palace on royal invitation and stayed there for two years. The king of Kashmir appointed scores of people with the illustrious Bhadanta at their head, to wait on him. The king also invited the pilgrim to read and expound the scriptures, gave him twenty clerks to copy out the manuscripts and five men to act as attendants. These details amply prove the existence of a splendid palace Library of Kashmir. Reading of manuscripts was a regular feature and there was provision for copying them.

It was again in the 6th or 7th century AD Kashmir produced the world famous historian poet Kalhana, the author of the famous book *Rajtarangini*; Patanjali, the immortal grammarian; Charka, the great physician, Abhinavagupta, the great philosopher and other famous philosophers. The technique of learning flourished during this period. During later years Kashmir passed into hands of Mughals, Afghans, Sikhs and lastly the British.

Sultan Zain-ul-Din, popularly known as Budshah, was a lover of learning and did much for the upliftment of education by providing library facilities to the scholars. There were famous collections of Persian and Sanskrit manuscripts in the libraries built by him. These libraries contained about 25,000 volumes. His interest towards the development of libraries can be assessed from the fact that for the first time in Northern India the paper industry was started by him at Nowshera about 10 Kms away from Srinagar sometime between 1420-70 AD. He got many books translated from Sanskrit and Arabic into Persian and Kashmiri.

"His activities in the domain of literature and scholarship were not confined to translating of books. He spent huge sums in collecting a Library which could favourably compare with the one collected by samavids. The Library remained intact for 100 years after his death when it was destroyed."[1]

Besides this, the great writers of this period like Sheikh Yaqub Sarfi, Baba Daud Khaki, Khwaja Habibullah Nowsheri, and poets like Habba Khatoon, Maqbool Shah Kralwari, Rasool Mir, Laxman Joo, Permanand, Krishna Dass, etc; had their own personal libraries. Lad Ded and her disciple Sheikh Noor-ud-Din popularly called Nund Reshi had also a good collection of their own. From this period to 1846, the State passed through many turmoils because of the change of rulers and their short lived rules over the State. This change of hands and political instability were impediments to the progress of learning and scholarship. It was, however, in the Dogra period (1846-1947) when the State became one of the largest princely States of India and rule of law was established.

Development of Education and Libraries During Pre-Independence Period

Jammu and Kashmir State as a single political entity, was founded by Maharaja Gulab Singh under the Amritsar Treaty signed by him with the British Government, in March 1846. Since this period, attention towards the development of education was given by Dogra rulers but the initiative to develop the libraries did not fetch any good results. However, the later links in the hierarchy of this dynasty, devoted some of their revenue towards the development of education and free book service. Accordingly, two major public libraries were established by Maharaja Ranbir Singh and Maharaja Pratap Singh in 1879 and 1898 respectively at Jammu and Srinagar respectively. The two libraries at Jammu and Srinagar are named after the two rulers i.e. Sri Ranbir Singh (SRS) Library and Sri Pratap Singh (SPS) Library.

As a result of this development though not a satisfactory one, the percentage of literacy rose up to 16 per cent in 1947.[2] This percentage of literacy was mainly due to the efforts of Maharaja Hari Singh who started 175 primary schools in the State. These schools provided free education and free book service to readers. Maharaja Hari Singh also paid due attention towards the development of libraries in Jammu and Kashmir. Besides his efforts, many organizational measures were taken towards this direction with the development of political consciousness among the people. Many book clubs were started at the important towns in the State by the young and progressive people. These clubs used to circulate books worth any cost among their members.

Development of Education and Libraries During Post-Independence Period

During post independence period, the State Government and many religious and social organizations played a prominent role in promoting the development of learning through a network of libraries. The Government provided sufficient funds for providing free education up to the postgraduate level from 1953 onwards. This caused revolution in education. The religious and social organizations also propagated education and their own ideas. In order to achieve this they established their libraries. The chief religious and social organizations were:

(1) Arya Samaj
(2) Vivekanand Society
(3) Ramakrishna Mission
(4) Samaj Sudhar Samiti
(5) Jamat-i-Islami and
(6) Rashtra Bhasha Prachar Samiti

Their efforts were first towards the direction of free book service to the people on organizational level. They established reading rooms at important towns and their service points were most popular with the public for they used to render service free of cost. These organizations have been very helpful for developing the library consciousness among the people.

Since Kashmir has a long tradition of culture and literature, there have been many movements for development of education and literacy, but it has, due to one or the other reason not progressed well. It was again in 1931 that the freedom loving intelligentia of Kashmir with the leadership of Sheikh Mohammad Abdullah established a reading room at Fateh Kadal in Srinagar which later on became a nuclues of Kashmir freedom movement.

Role of Government in Development of Education and Libraries

On the part of Government, free book service was extended to the villages under the National Extension Service Scheme. In every Panchayat Ghar small libraries were opened with the books mostly on agriculture. At the town level, the Town Area Committees established their own libraries to provide free book service to all. At the city level, Municipal Committees did this job by opening Municipal reading rooms.

Seeing that the public is becoming more and more library conscious, the Government tried to keep up and improve upon the literacy level, by setting up a separate Directorate of Libraries and Archives under the charge of the renowned librarian Prof. S. Bashir-u-Din in 1961. This directorate gave a new impetus to the library service in the state and devised a plan under which district and branch libraries, were established. These libraries provided free book service to respective areas and covered all the general subjects. The directorate also appointed two research officers as subject experts, one for classification and cataloguing of Hindi and Sanskrit manuscripts and the other for Persian and Arabic manuscripts.[3]

The Government also framed rules and regulations named as the Jammu and Kashmir library and reading room rules, 1963, for the guidance of public and the library personnel, in order to improve the harmonious relations between the two. These rules define the duties of the directorate and the librarian and clearly laid down the categories of persons who can become the members of such libraries.[4] The important features of these rules are that no security money is to be deposited by any category of members except, of course for a temporary membership where the security deposit has been fixed as rupees twenty. Under these rules the public libraries throughout the State function as the leading depots for the Central Public Libraries. The provision of inter-library loan has also been made at the Government cost.

Randhawa Commission

With a view to go into the working of the Department of Libraries, Research and Museums and also because of the keen interest of late Sheikh Mohammad Abdullah to improve and develop the conditions of the libraries the Government of Jammu and Kashmir vide Government order No. 1867 GD of 1975, dated: 18th September, 1975 appointed a Committee with Dr M.S. Randhawa the then Vice-Chancellor of Punjab Agriculture University, as Chairman and Prof. Noor-ul-Hassan Khan the then Head Department of Library and Information Science, University of Kashmir, Srinagar, he was Librarian Maulana Azad Library, Aligarh Muslim University, Aligarh as one of the members to go into the working of the Department of Libraries and also to recommend the improvements which were necessary to run the department on scientific lines. The Committee submitted its report on 10th August, 1976. Some of the recommendations of the Committee are given below.[5]

Library Legislation

Library legislation is the very basis for the development of a public library system. It alone can ensure free library service, adequate funds, and maintenance of proper library standards. A library legislation for the State, on the pattern of Tamil Nadu was recommended.

Funds

Funds for the continuing operation of library system should be provided through the library cess of five paisa per rupee on property tax, supported by regular Government grants, and from other donations without guaranteed funds and grants, the libraries can again become the same fossilized institutions as before.

Structure of Public Libraries

The following structure for the Public Library system was suggested.

(i) State Central Libraries at Jammu and Srinagar
(ii) District Libraries at Jammu and Srinagar
(iii) Tehsil Libraries
(iv) Block Libraries and
(v) Village Libraries

In addition to the above, there should be mobile library vans attached to each Central library to provide library service in remote areas.

Besides the above recommendations, the Committee also made various other recommendations such as: about the functions of the library department; who should be the head of library department; what should be the rights and duties of the head of the library department and other staff; the State Central Library Composition of the Library Committee, the District Libraries and what should be the staff strength and pattern of staffing for the State Central Library and other Libraries.

The above recommendations were submitted to the Chief Minister by Dr M.S. Randhawa, Chairman of the Committee. Due to one reason or other the Government has not been able to enact library legislation as yet.

Library Association: Efforts of Prof. P.N. Kaula

Prior to Independence, there was only one trained librarian in the State, viz; Prof. P.N. Kaula. He after passing his Diploma in Library Science creditably in 1946, wrote a series of articles in newspapers and journals of the State and published an outline scheme for the development of libraries. He also wrote a book *Kashmir Main Illimi Inqualab* with a forward by the then education secretary.[6] After representing the state at the 8th All India Library Conference at Nagpur in January, 1949. Prof. P.N. Kaula made several efforts for the formation of the Library association in the State. These efforts could not bear fruit because of political instability. He was invited to submit a plan for the development of libraries along with a draft Library Bill. This plan was submitted by him to the then Chief Minister Sheikh Mohammad Abdullah of the State in 1951. It bears an introduction by Dr S.R. Ranganathan, the then President, Indian Library Association.[7] Unfortunately, political developments changed the priorities in the State. The Sheikh Mohammad Abdullah had agreed to enact library law but before it could be done, his ministry was dismissed in 1953. At the invitation of Education Secretary Prof. Kaula examined the working of the SPS Library, Srinagar and submitted his scheme for its reorganization and development. A meeting of librarians was also convened by him in 1956.

Between 1951 and 1964 three attempts were made for the formation of a Library Association for the promotion of free book service in the State. But due to the lack of cooperation from the authorities and non-availability of sufficient funds there was no success. However, on 22nd April, 1964, a convention of Librarians in Kashmir was held.[8] It was presided over by Mr M.H. Razvi of J & K University Library. The ways and means of improving the library service in the State and the formation of library association to foster such activities were discussed. The main outcome of this convention was the formation of an *ad hoc* committee consisting of seven members. On 19th June, 1966 the librarians and other library staff of the State met together to lay the foundation of J & K Library Association under chairmanship of P.N. Kaula. The draft constitution prepared by the *ad hoc* committee, which was framed on the basis of the consensus arrived at the convention of 1964, after being scrutinized by Prof. Kaula, was approved. Prof. P.N. Pushp, Director of Libraries and Archives who was also present on this occasion gave a number of helpful suggestions.

Though this Association had the blessings of the Government and expert advice of the Director of Libraries and many philanthrophists, this could not achieve the high ideals for which it came into being.

In order to promote the library movement and improvement in library services in all its aspects in J & K State, a State level Library Association namely Jàmmu & Kashmir Library and Information Science Association (JAKLISA) was framed in 1991. The Association published *JAKLISA* newsletter (quarterly) highlighting the important events of librarianship.

Very recently, on 5th May, 1994 a meeting of Jammu and Kashmir Library and Information Science Association was held in the Deptt. of Library and Information Science, University of Kashmir under the Chairmanship of Prof. M.L. Wali.. Among other things members resolved to change the name of Association from JAKLISA to Jammu and Kashmir Library Association (JKLA) Prof. M.L. Qali Head, Department of Library and Information Science, University of Kashmir was elected as President. The executive of this association has framed a new Constitution and is contemplating to have a seminar on improving public library service in the State and refresher courses for working college and public library professionals for updating their technical skills and making aware of the latest concept and changes being introduced all over the country.

Library Seminar

A seminar on the Library services in the State was held on June 19, 1966.[9] It was inaugurated by the Chairman of the Legislative Council and presided over by Prof. Kaula. A number of librarians and educationists participated in it. Prof. Pushp, the Director of Libraries, invited the attention of Government for the provisions of better library accommodation, technical services, trained library personnel, right type of reading material and better emoluments for library staff in order to give improved library services. According to the statement of Prof. Pushp, Director of Libraries 3 per cent of literate population had enrolled itself as members of the public library in Srinagar. Though he mentioned that a children's library on open access system with separate accommodation was provided in Jammu and Kashmir (Srinagar), but it has not come to the set standards.

Existing Public Library Facilities in Jammu & Kashmir

Today we have 83 public libraries, throughout the entire State, besides one research and public library in Srinagar. The break-up of these libraries is given in Table 1 and Table 2.

TABLE - 1
PUBLIC LIBRARIES IN JAMMU PROVINCE

Name of the District	*Name of the Distt. Library*	*Name of the Tehsil Library*	*Name of the Block Library*
Jammu	1. S.R.S. Library	1. Bishnan	1. New Plots
	2. Gandhinagar	2. Samba	2. Talab Tilu
		3. R.S.Pura	
		4. Akhboor	
Udhampur	1. Udhampur	1. Gool	1. Reasi
		2. Chenane	2. Ram Nagar
		3. Mahors	
Kathua	1. Kathua	1. Bhaddu	1. Hiranagar
		2. Bilawar	2. Bani
		3. Basoli	
Doda	1. Doda	1. Ramban	1. Batote
		2. Bhaderwah	2. Padder
		3. Banihal	
		4. Thathri	
		5. Dachan	
		6. Kishtwar	
Poonch	1. Poonch	1. Surekote	
		2. Mendhar	
Rajouri	1. Rajouri	1. Sundirbani	1. Dudhal
		2. Nowshera	2. Kotranka
		3. Kalakote	
		4. Thanamandi	

TABLE - 2
PUBLIC LIBRARIES IN THE KASHMIR PROVINCE

Name of the District	*Name of the Distt. Library*	*Name of the Tehsil Library*	*Name of the Block Library*
1. Srinagar	1. S.P.S. Library 2. Habbakadal	1. Zadibal 2. Ganderbal 3. Kangan 4. Rajourikadal	1. Soura 2. Khanyar
2. Anantnag	1. Anantnag	1. Aishmuqam 2. Dooru 3. Bijbehara 4. Kulgam	1. Qazigund 2. Awantipor
3. Baramulla	1. Baramulla	1. Pattan 2. Uri 3. Bijhema 4. Keeri 5. Sumbal 6. Tangmarg 7. Bandipora 8. Sopore 9. Booniyar	1. Hajin
4. Badgam	1. Badgam	1. Chararisharief 2. Beerwah 3. Chadoora	1. Magam 2. Khansahib
5. Pulwama	1. Rulwama	1. Shopian 2. Tral 3. Pampore	
6. Kupwara	1. Kupwara	1. Handwara 2. Tangdar	
7. Kargil	1. Kargil	1. Zanskar 2. Drass	
8. Leh, Ladakh	1. Leh	1. Khaltsi	

Most of the libraries are housed in rented buildings comprising one or two rooms. The physical condition of most of these buildings is quite unsatisfactory. In 1994 the Government of Jammu and Kashmir opened 36 Border Block Libraries in the State, out of which 17 are in Jammu province and 19 in Kashmir valley.

In Jammu, the Border Block Libraries fall in the following border blocks:

1. R.S. Pora
2. Bishna
3. Samba
4. Khour
5. Satwari
6. Akhnoor
7. Marh
8. Manjkote
9. Rajouri
10. Nowshera
11. Kathua
12. Hiranagar
13. Bharnoti
14. Ghagwal
15. Poonch
16. Mandi
17. Marwah

In Kashmir Valley Border Block Libraries have been started in:

1. Delina (Baramulla)
2. Pahlipora (Uri)
3. Kunzer (Tangnarg)
4. Kharkot (Uri)
5. Guil (Maghgham)
6. Dangiwacha (Sopore)
7. Rehama (Baramulla)
8. Wagoora (Baramulla)
9. Dangher-pora (Baramulla)
10. Tangdar (Kupwara)
11. Tregam (Kupwara)

12. Kalamabad (Kupwara)
13. Kralpora (Kupwara)
14. Zachaldar (Rajwar)
15. Sogam (Kupwara)
16. Langate (Kupwara)
17. Vilgam (Kupwara)
18. Ramhal (Maghgam)
19. Khag (Budgam)

Conclusion

Libraries are an essential constituent of the society. They play an important role in the educational development of the society. They are the essential prerequisite of a social system. Recent developments in Jammu & Kashmir, show the interest of the present Government to develop library services by providing network of libraries all over the State. Yet the provision of funds to provide modern services are meagre and need additional funds by government and through library legislation to be enacted in the State.

REFERENCES

1. Bamzai, P.N.K. *History of Kashmir*. 2nd Revised Edition. New Delhi: Metropolitan. p. 329, 1973.
2. Wali, M.L. and Kaul, R.K. Library Development in Kashmir In *Herald of Library Science* V.B. (4). p. 300, 1969.
3. *Ibid.*, p. 302.
4. Jammu and Kashmir, Sectt.(Civil) (Education Branch). Jammu and Kashmir Library and Reading room rules, 1963.
5. Khan, Noorul Hassan. Public Libraries in Jammu and Kashmir : A review In 28th All India Library Conference, Seminar Papers, ILA. Delhi. pp. 134-35, 1982.
6. *Op. cit.*, (21; p. 302).
7. *Ibid.*, p. 302.
8. Ranganathan, S.R.; et. al., ed, Free Book Service for all, p. 88.
9. Kaula, P.N. The First Kashmir Library Conference In *Herald of Library Science*, V. 5, p. 230, 1966.

Eighteen

Criteria for Comparison of Library Classification Schemes

REKHA D. PAI

Introduction

Systematic grouping or classification lies at the base of every well-managed human activity. Classification involves putting together like entities and separating the unlike entities. The characteristics of entities are used as basis for determining the likeness or unlikeness between them. Library is a service oriented organization which must cater to the needs of all types of its users. For this, the documents in the library must be properly organised. Library classification helps in the proper arrangement of documents. The aim of library classification is to arrange the documents in a most helpful sequence. Because, a sytematic arrangement which breaks the entire collection into groups is always useful.

Classification has been defined variously by different authors.

According to Margaret Mann "Library classification is the arranging of things according to likeness and unlikeness. It is the sorting and grouping of things, but in addition classification of books is a knowledge classification with adjustments made necessary by the physical form of books."[1]

According to J.H. Shera: Library classification is - "a list of terms which are specifically different from each other, used to describe the subject content of graphic records inclusive of all knowledge, defined by the limits of the scheme, infinitely hospitable with regard to significant differences among the concepts with an arrangement that is linear, unique and meaningful to the user and which, when applied to graphic records, results in the arrangement of records themselves."[2]

According to A. Maltby: Classification is "the systematic arrangement of subject of books and other material on shelves or of a catalogue and index entries in the manner which is most useful to those who read or who seek a definite piece of information."[3]

S.R. Ranganathan has offered a classified definition for library classification. According to him, "it is the translation of the name of the subject of a book into preferred artificial language of ordinal numbers, and the individualization of several books dealing with the same specific subject by means of a further set of ordinal numbers which represent some features of books other than their thought content."[4]

Thus, library classification is a process which leads to systematic, mechanized and helpful arrangement of documents in libraries.

Classification Schemes

Classification Scheme is a scheme of classes fitted with terminology and notation. Many classification schemes have been developed for the purpose of library classification. The nature of universe of subjects is multidimensional. New developments in knowledge have to be incorporated in the classification scheme. Thus, a scheme has to keep pace with developments in the universe of subjects. The existing library classification schemes are categorized as enumerative classification schemes. Almost enumerative classification schemes; Almost faceted classification schemes; Rigidly faceted classification schemes; Freely faceted/ Analytico-synthetic schemes, etc. The selection of specific type for a particular library is very important. A comparative study of these schemes will enable one to get a proper perspective.

Comparison of Classification Schemes

Many schemes of classification are available for the classification of subjects/documents. Generally it is accepted that DDC, UDC, LC, CC & BC are the major general schemes of classification.

A comparative study of classification schemes would enable one to determine their strengths and weaknesses. At the beginning of prolegomena, a basic work in classification, Ranganathan says: "to compare the relative merits of two or more schemes it is necessary and helpful to enunciate a set of tests and to laydown some systematic procedure".[5]

Different persons have given varying views regarding the criterias for comparison of library classification schemes.

Criteria for Comparison of Classification Schemes

For comparing the schemes of library classification in a correct way, it is essential to derive a set of criterias, which makes the procedure a systematic one.

Dutta, D.N. (1962), has given the following criterias for a good classification:

"(a) A scheme should be comprehensive and reasonably minute;
(b) Systematic order should be there to bring together related subjects;
(c) Headings should be based on 'literary warrant;
(d) Should be flexible and expansive;
(e) Should have simple flexible notation and
(f) Should have good index"[6]

Gopinath (1975) quotes Ranganathan about his criterias for comparison of schemes for classification in the FID/CR report (No. 14);

According to Ranganathan, the following are the criterias for comparison:

(1) Scope of classification;
(2) Sequence of main subjects;
(3) Hospitality for new basic subjects;
(4) Crisp words to denote ideas;
(5) Sameness of patterns in the sequence of subjects going with different basic subject;
(6) Objectively used postulates and principles;
(7) Systematic procedure for practical classification;
(8) Avoidance of faults such as homonyms and synonyms in class number language;

(9) Inner mechanism to find a helpful place to a new compound basic subject;
(10) Length of base of notational system;
(11) Provision of indicator digits to indicate relations coextensively;
(12) Hospitality in chain;
(13) Hospitality in array;
(14) Agency for promoting use; and
(15) Permanent organization for development of the scheme."[7]

Susan Bury, (1980) has put forward certain basic criterias for comparison of classification schemes for libraries, they are: Intellectual basis, Order, Universality, Hospitality, Adaptability. Terminology, Relations Synthesis, Notation, Ease of use, Revision and Practical use."[8]

Totally, the following may be considered as the basic criterias for comparison of classification schemes:

1. Intellectual Basis

Different schemes of classification are based on different principles. But a scheme must be based on the patterns of human thought. Classification schemes should provide the provision for synthesis, so that they can accommodate the compound subjects.

2. Order/Sequence of Subjects

The most related subjects must be kept together in a classification scheme; main class order is an important feature of a classification scheme.

3. Universality

This may be taken as one of the criterias for comparison of classification schemes. A scheme should ideally include all subjects and be applicable in all types of libraries. A scheme must be convertible to mechanized system also.

4. Hospitality

This includes both hospitality in chain and hospitality in array. Newly emerged subjects must be readily accommodated, as and when they are developed. To achieve this, the classification schemes use many devices such as: Decimal fraction device; Facet device; Phase device, etc.

5. Adaptability

A classification scheme must be adaptable. It must satisfy alternative approach to subjects by readers. Alternative methods of classifying must be provided which is possible in case of synthetic schemes.

6. Terminology

The terminology used in a classification scheme must be clear, distinct, current and non-critical.

7. Postulational approach

A scheme which follows, the postulates and principles of classification is found to be more helpful.

8. Relations

A scheme of classification must give the scope for facet analysis. It must show clearly the hierarchical relationship between subjects, there must be a provision for phase relations also.

9. Synthesis

In case of composite subjects to indicate accurately and closely all the aspects and relationships manifested, it is essential that a scheme must provide for synthesis.

10. Notation

As far as notation is concerned it must be hospitable, simple, brief, mnemomic expressive, specific, flexible and correlative.

11. Ease of Use

A scheme should be easy to use with simple notation, index, instructions, rules and layout.

12. Revision

A constant study and revision is very essential to keep pace with the fast developing subjects/information.

13. Practical Use

It is generally agreed that the highly used scheme is most useful. But practical testing of schemes needs to be done before conclusions can be reached on this criterion.

14. Permanent Organization

It is very essential that there must be a permanent organization to look after, update and revise the scheme. Such a scheme will live for a long time.

Thus, schemes of library classification may be compared on the basis of above criterias.

Conclusion

From above discussions, it may be concluded that it is feasible to study the classification schemes by comparative analysis. This also shows that a technical subject like classification can be included in comparative librarianship. The criterias set out for the purpose of comparison are not equally important. Anyhow, these fourteen criterias may be used for comparison. This study helps in finding out the strengths and weaknesses of the schemes. This also helps in selection of suitable scheme for the library.

REFERENCES

1. Margaret, Mann. *Introduction to Cataloguing & Classification of books*, Chicago, ALA, 1943, p. 33.
2. Shera, J.H. *Libraries & Organization of knowledge*, London, Crossby Lockwood, 1966, p. 135.
3. Maltby, Arthur Sayers. *Mannul of Classification for librarians*, 5th ed. London. Andre Deutsh, 1978, p. 15.
4. Ranganathan S.R. *Elements of Library Classification*, 3rd ed. Bombay, Asia Pub. House, 1962. p. 10.
5. Ranganathan S.R. *Prolegomena to library classification*, 3rd ed. Bombay, 1967: p. 47.
6. Dutta, D.N. *Library Classification: Theory & Practice*, Nagpur Western Book Depot, 1962 p. 48.
7. Gopinath, M.A. Classification Research (India) : 1968 - 1973, FID/ CR Report No. 14, Bangalore, DRTC FID Pub. No. 405, 1975.
8. Burry. Susan. *Comparison of classification schemes for libraries*. Library Science with a siant to documentation V 17)3), 1980. p. 73-82.

Nineteen

Organization of Research in Biological Sciences

DR SURENDRA SINGH *and* DR SONAL SINGH

Introduction

The importance of research in modern world of knowledge explosion cannot be over emphasized. Research is the basis of knowledge explosion and a process and means to acquire knowledge. It helps in discovery, development and verification of knowledge. It is the interpretation of old theories, principles and ideas in the light of new circumstances. It is performed in every field of human activity. Research means continuous search for knowledge. Through research, new ideas are created in different disciplines of knowledge as well as the horizons and frontiers of existing knowledge are also expanded. Men's desire to know more about their world has led them from primitive superstition to modern scientific knowledge. There is a history of continuous struggle between man and nature. The history of man on earth is the history of knowledge. Knowledge is the result of human needs, human desire and human achievements.

Man examines nature self and society. The study of nature results in natural sciences, study of man in relation to man results in humanities and study of man in relation to society results in Social Sciences.

Natural Sciences may be defined as "a branch of study which is concerned either with a connected body of demonstrated truth or with observed facts systematically classified and more or less collected by being brought under general laws and which includes trustworthy methods for the discovery of new truth within its domain".[1]

Natural Sciences may be divided mainly into biological sciences, physical sciences, mathematical sciences and chemical sciences. This study is only limited to Biological Sciences.

Biological Sciences

Biological Sciences means Sciences of life. It is the study of life in all its manifestations. It concerns itself, on a scientific level, with their structure and form, their function and behaviour, their reproduction, growth and development, and with their relationship to their physical environment and to other similar and dissimilar organisms, both modern and extinct. The biological sciences can be divided into Botany and Zoology.

Botany is the science which deals with the study of plants. The science of botany includes various main subdivisions : taxonomy, or systematic botany, morphology, physiology, genetics, ecology, other branches of botanical science including pathology, paleobotany, bactereology, algology, mycology, embryology and pteridology.[2]

Zoology is the science which deals with the study of animals. Because of its vast scope, zoology is usually broken up into several subsidiary branches of which the chief ones are - morphology, histology, embryology, palaentology, taxonomy, genetics, and evolution, ecology and physiology.[3]

The approaches to modern biology have been along several different lines. The interest in systematic zoology and botany, was the dominant one in the nineteenth century, and still continues so. Three other social influences have become much more potent, those from medicine, from agriculture, and from the new biological industry.

The two great World Wars and the depression that fell in between, suffice to divide up the fifty years into five periods of unequal length. The first period upto 1914 was the period of the first great triumphs of medicine against malaria and yellow fever, and marked the new turn in animal and plant breeding. The major branches of biology that have shown the greatest advances in the last fifty years are: biochemistry, molecular biology, microbiology, cytology, embryology, organism and its control mechanism and studies in heridity and evolution.

Biochemistry

The science of biochemistry is far more than the application of chemistry to biological problems. Its object is not only to probe into the structures of the molecules that are to be found in living organisms but also into their overall mode of reaction, both separately and in combination. For this purpose it has developed a number of approaches in which whole organisms or organs are studied or broken down to different degrees. This specific biochemical approach goes on developing more refined methods of measurement, bringing in physical methods such as tracers, chemical methods such as various types of molecular separation processes, and more immunological analysis.

It was to take some forty years, however, even to begin to understand the nature of enzymes and mechanism of their action. First of all the co-enzymes - cozymase were detected by Harden in 1865-1940 and Young in 1906. The linking of a protein enzyme with a small and active molecule brings out the close parallelism between enzyme action and that of the so-called respiratory pigments like haemoglobin of the blood or cytochrome of the cell. These consists of a protein globuline.

It was the genius of Hopkins that first drew attention to the presence in full diet of small quantities of substances in the absence of which growth did not occur and degenerative symptoms appeared. These accessory factors, later came to be known as vitamins. Other researches showing that many bodily conditions were dependent on the existence of minute quantities of substances produced inside the body itself, usually in special places, the so-called ductless glands. Thus, a new group of substances was discovered, the hormones or messengers as E.H. Starling (1866-1927) first called them in 1905.

Molecular Biology

The essential feature of molecular biology is that, it is concerned with the structure and functions of entities of dimensions below those of the cells studied by biological methods, and above those of the molecules studied by normal chemical methods, in particular, with the molecules of proteins and of nucleic acids. It is now one of the most exciting and rapidly growing branches of biological science. It might be said to begin with the early studies of W.T. Abstury (1898-1961). The whole of biomolecular studies represent an extremely fast and coherent body of research carried by an informal and somewhat casually organised operation of different fields of work.

Microbiology

Biochemistry in the twentieth century is at last beginning to unravel the secrets of the life of the smallest of organisms like of bacteria, yeasts, and moulds, and of the simplest of animals, the single-celled protozoa. Bio-chemically, they are atleast as complex; if not more so, than the higher organisms. Their contribution to agriculture is now also beginning to be studied, for on them depends in large measure the fertility of the soil.

Cytology and Embryology

The microscopic study of the structures of cells long anticipated those of cell-biochemistry and still longer that of molecular biology. Nevertheless, it is on the lines of molecular biology that we can now interpret and extend the observations of cells as a whole, either isolated in monocellular animals or tissue culture or together in a living higher organism. The new interpretation does not in any way diminish the value of the old but rather, extends it through new and refined methods of cytology, particularly in the study of hereditary material in chromosomes. In the last fifty years, through the study of enzymes, chemistry has begun to be an effective way of approaching biological problems. The earlier contacts between biology and chemistry were invaluable aids to the progress of chemistry but made little contribution to biology. The arguments used in Darwin's *Origin of species* did not depend on any chemical knowledge. The methods of observation and dissection have also, in the twentieth century, made enormous advances, putting forward step by step the limits of microscopic vision. First by observation alone and later by observation combined with experiments, the inner structure of cells was gradually elucidated. The nucleus with its chromozomes, and the cytoplasmic inclusions such as the mitochondria and plastids, were also studied, both in the resting centrozome and more fully in the dividing cell. Interest in them was enormously increased in 1910, when Morgan showed that the chromozomes of the cell were connected with the inheritance of specific characters already forecast in Mendel's Theory of Heredity.

The interest in the growth of an animal from the egg has gone right back to the origins of science itself. Loeb (1859-1924) showed in 1900 that it was possible to induce an unfertilized egg to produce a complete organism by subjecting it to chemical treatment. Some of these contradictions were removed when Spemann (1869-1941), Holtfreter, and Mangold demonstrated in 1931 that certain chemical stimuli, when applied to an undifferentiated egg, were capable of including the formation of the organism as a whole, others, acting only at a later stage when the organism had begun to grow, were capable of producing various parts of it, such as an eye or a limb. The nature of these organizers is still obscure.

These studies of chemical embryology seem to show that the general development of organisms must be controlled as much as, is their normal and abnormal metabolism, by chemical factors.

The Organism as a Whole and its Control Mechanisms

One of the major struggles between the mechanists and the vitalists was the concept of an organism as a whole. The phythagorean-Platonic view was that each organism, as an individual, must have something corresponding to an individuality, a soul, psyche or breath of life.

The limits of resistance of the body to the pressure of deep living and the anoxia of high flying or mountain climbing led to intensive research on the function of respiration. J.S. Haldane (1860-1936) and his son J.B.S. Haldane (1892-1964), by quantitative measurements and heroic experiments in which they were their own subjects, explored the limits of human tolerance of different gas concentrations and provided a rational picture of how the body coped with considerable variations which were tolerated. It proved to be so complex, involving lungs, heart, nerves, and brain, that J.S. Haldane was driven to accept a supernatural explanation.

The study of digestion carried on over the centuries, received two new impulses - one of them from experimental physiology. Biochemical methods resolved the successive breakdown of food materials by the enzymes of Ptyalin, pepsin and trypsin, the absorption of the products by the intestinal mucosa, and their later transformation and storage in the liver. These all are detailed chemical activities.

The most significant of all the recent advances has been the study of the action of the endocrine organs - the ductless glands which produce the hormones. They are the chemical regulators of the whole body. One of the first of such actions to be observed was that of the hormone adrenalin, which stimulates the whole body to an effective response. Further research, particularly on the sex hormones, shows that the chemical control mechanisms are far more complicated.

The nature of animal memory is now being studied by a variety of experimental methods. More recent experiments on mice give some indication that the memory may be actually stored in altered varieties of nucleic acids in the sense organs possibly also in the brains.

Heredity and Evolution

At the turn of the century, with the Darwinian controversy dying down, came a new need for science in practical breeding and a corresponding interest in heredity. On the scientific side, the main lines of evolution having been laid down. The laws of inheritance began to acquire a new importance.

Devries was already experimenting on variation and in 1890 William Bateson (1861-1926) criticised the logical basis at the evidence of Haeckel. Bateson pointed out that every breeder of plants or animals knows that while small variations from the normal do occur, large variations also are common.

Simultaneously, with the later work of Darwin (1865), a series of researches was being carried out, which might have modified the history of Darwin's hypothesis.

The essence of Mendel's discovery consists that: in heredity certain characters may be treated as indivisible and apparently unalterable units. The presence or absence of an organism is a sharply contrasted pair of qualities. Thus, the tall and dwarf varieties of the common edible pea, when self fertilized, each breed true to type. When crossed with each other, all hybrids are tall, and outwardly resemble the tall parent. Tallness is therefore said to be dominant over dwarfness, which is called 'recessive'. But when these tall hybrids are allowed to fertilize themselves they are found to be different in genetic properties from the parent whom they resemble outwardly. Many Mendalian characters have been traced in plants and animals.

When Mendel's work was rediscovered, investigation into cell structure had revealed the fact that within each cell nucleus is a definite number of thread like bodies called chromozomes.

The theory of evolution has become more and more firmly established as palaentological evidence has accumulated. For example, there were no angiosperms, higher plants with protected seeds, in carboniferous times, new orders and new species must therefore have arisen somehow.

Some biologists still hold that natural selection acting on small variations is enough when long continued to explain evolution. Others think that, in Mendalian mutations we see species in the making.

Since the earlier discoveries on cytology and chromozomes, much new work has been done, which has helped forward the science of genetics and begun to affect the practical art of the plant and animal breeders. Progress has been made in solving the question of sex determination, in which two factors, heredity and development are involved.

Dr Hargobind Khurana, announced that he has accomplished the first successful total synthesis of a genetic basic hereditary unit of life.

The scientific breakthrough by the noted molecular biologist who won the 1968 Nobel Prize for deciphering the genetic code, and his teams of associates would mean the production of a gene by artificial means by combining simple organic chemicals in a test tube. Dr Khurana is the first to show that genes can be synthesized from atoms of simple chemical building blocks with no natural gene required as model in the reaction mixture.

About his discovery Dr Khurana said ; "In the long distant future the knowledge might allow for genetic planning of individuals - tailoring people to fit patterns, turn out athletes or intellectuals." He said he started with the four nucleotides that are basic building blocks of genes and which can be synthesized easily from atoms. He joined the nucleotides into a number of single-stranded segments with the nucleotides in proper sequence and later jointed those fragments into a complete, double-stranded 77 nucleotide gene.

The single stranded fragments were designed by Dr Khurana, so they would spontaneously line up in proper sequence for the double strands, exactly as happens in natural deoxyribonucleic acid (DNA). The gene is a molecule of DNA.

Dr Khurana said the ends of the fragments were joined by the enzymes DNA ligase, which is purified from living cells.

Ever since the time of Lamarck, it has been felt that environment must in some way direct the course of changed inheritance to such obvious advantage of the organism. Yet every effort to prove inheritance of acquired characteristics has failed. We now see why in the case of higher animals and plants with their long reproductive period and mechanisms, this should be so difficult. When we come to the lower organisms, such as bacteria, with life cycle measured in minutes, it is possible to observe changes in response to chemical environment which are definitely adaptive, in the sense of being able to grow in new media. It would appear that here direct effects on the nucleoprotein hereditary materials are possible, when Ovary produced a change from one type of pneumococcus to another by addition of nucleic acids of the second type. We know very similar effects produced by virus infections.[4]

This, however is still a long way from adaptive inheritance connected with general environmental stimuli. One type of this has been discovered by Waddington.

Even more striking cases are reported where habits and not structures are inherited.

Biological Sciences in Library Classification Scheme

In the modern times biology is used for the common works related to all living organisms. Example - Man and Plant. The main study of biology is now cell and its functions.

The main subdivisions of biological sciences in different schemes are shown in Table 1.

The detailed division of biological sciences started with the Dewey Decimal Classification, by which time many scientists recognized different divisions and subdivisions in each discipline. Leonordo da Vinci, Linnaeous and others were the systematic botanists and zoologists who classified zoology and botany on the basis of morphological and anatomical structures. On the basis of these knowledge divisions biological sciences are mapped in the different library classification schemes.

In Dewey Decimal classification, biological sciences are included in 570, 580 and 590 and their applications in 610 and 630. The actual division of general class for biology starts with 574 to 579. Botanical sciences and their divisions are included in 580-589 and zoological sciences and their sub-divisions in 590-599. Dewey first arranged seed bearing plants in 582-584 and then proceeded to Gymnosperms, pteridophyta, bryophyta and thallophyta. This is against the evolutionary tendencies and will not bring helpful sequence in the shelf arrangement. On the other hand, arrangement of zoological science is according to the evolutionary sequence.

In Universal Decimal classification and Colon classification, the arrangement of botanical and zoological sciences is in the evolutionary sequence. The main drawback of UDC is that all such divisions are incorporated in main class 582 only. This has made 582 a very compact class.

Colon has superseded all other schemes of classification in the sense that energy isolates of main class I and K are common to those in main class G, while in DC and UDC they have been re-enumerated in 581 and 591 respectively.

In Colon classification main class G biology is very much elaborated and can accommodate all the general works in biological sciences but not related to any specific field.

TABLE - 1: MAIN SUB-DIVISIONS OF BIOLOGICAL SCIENCES IN DIFFERENT SCHEMES OF LIBRARY CLASSIFICATION

DEWEY DECIMAL CLASSIFICATION[1]	UNIVERSAL DECIMAL CLASSIFICATION[2]	COLON CLASSIFICATION [3]		
		G Biology (E)	I Botany (P)	J Agriculture (E)
570 Life Sciences	57 Biological Sciences	1 Preliminaries	1 Cryptogamia	1 Soil
571 Unassigned		2 Morphology	2 Thallophyta	2 Manure
572 Human races	571 Archaeology	3 Physiology	3 Bryophyta	3 Propagation
573 Physical Anthropology	574 General biology	4 Pathology	4 Pteridophyta	4 Disease
574 Biology	575 Evolution	5 Ecology	5 Phenerogamia	5 Development
575 Organic evolution and genetics	576 Morphology, Physiology, cytology, symbiosis, bacteriology, microbiology.	6 Phylogeny	6 Gymnosperms	6 Breeding
576 Micro Biology		7 Development	7 Monocotyledons	7 Harvesting
577 General Nature of life		8 Manipulations	8 Dicotyledons	91-95 Nomenclature classification morphology, physiology, Ecology.
578 Microscopy in Biology			95 Ecological groups	
579 Collection and preservation of biological specimens				
580 Botanical Sciences	577 General properties of life			
581 Botany				
582 Spermat opyat a	578 Biological techniques	K Zoology (P)	KZ Animal Husbandry (E)	L Medicine (P)
583 Dico tyledons				
584 Monocotyledons.	579 Collection			
585 Gymnospermae	58 Botany	1 Invertebrata	1 Feeding	1 Basic & regional
586 Cryptogamia	581 Plant biology	2 Protozoa	2 Morphology	2 Digestive system
587 Pteridophyta	582 Plant taxonomy			
588 Bryophyta	59 Zoology	3 Porifera	3 Physiology	3 Circulatory system
589 Thallophyta	591 Animal biology			
590 Zoological Sciences	592 Invertebrates	4 Coelentrata	4 Disease	4 Respiratory system
591 Zoology	593 Protozoa porifera Coelentrata, Echinodermata			
592 Invertebrates		5 Echinodermata	5 Hygiene	5 Geneto-urinary system
593 Protozao, Parazoa, Metazoa				
594 Mollusca and Mollusco idea	594 Mollusca			

595	Other invertebrates	595	Arthropoda and Helminthes	6 Vermes	6 Breeding	6 Ductless gland
596	Chordata (vertebrates)	596	Vertebrata	7 Mollusca	7 Produce	7 Nervous system
597	Anamnia Fishes	598	Reptiles, birds			
598	Reptiles and birds	599	Mammalia	8 Arthropoda	8 Training	8 Other systems
599	Mammalia (Mammals)	6	Applied sciences			
610	Medical Sciences Medicine	61	Medical sciences	9 Vertebrata	91 Nomeclature	
611	Human anatomy, cytology, tissue, biology	611	Anatomy	92 Pisces	96 Pharmacognosy	(E)
612	Human physiology	612	Physiology	93 Amphibia		1 Preliminaries
613	General and personal hygiene	613	Hygiene	94 Reptilia		2 Morphology
614	Public Health	614	Public Health	96 Aves		3 Physiology
615	Pharmacology and Therapeutics treatment	615	Pharmacy	97 Mammalia		4 Disease
616	Diseases	616	Pathology	995 Ecological groups		5 Public Health and Hygiene
617	Surgery and related topics	617	Surgery			6 Development and ontogency
618	Other branches of medicine Gynaecology and obstetrics	618	Gynaecology and obstetrics			
619	Experimental medicine	63	Agriculture			
630	Agriculture and related technologies	631	Agronomy			
631	General agricultural techniques, apparatus, equipment, materials	632	Plant injuries			
632	Plant injuries, diseases, pests	633	Field crops			
633	Field crops	634	Arboxyculture			
634	Orchards, fruits, forestry	635	Horticulture			
635	Garden crops (Horticulture) vegetables	636	Livestock			
636	Animal husbandry	637	Dairy			
637	Dairy and related technology	638	Insect and reptile			
638	Insect culture	639	Marine husbandry			
639	Nondomesticated animals and plants					

1. Dewey, Melwil : Dewey Decimal Classification. Ed. 18 New York : Forest Press, 1971, p. 970.
2. Universal Decimal Classification. Ed 3. British Standards, 1961, p. 73.
3. Ranganathan, S.R.: Colon Classification Ed. 6 Bombay, Asia Publishing, 1966, p. 2.51.

Applied Sciences

The applied sciences of biology, zoology and botany are accommodated in separate main classes in the three schemes of classifications.

In DDC, medical sciences are grouped from 610 to 619 and agriculture 603-609. In UDC 61-619 and 63-639 respectively. In Colon classification J represents agriculture and L medicine. Colon classification recognizes Animal Husbandry KX and pharmacognosy LX as separate classes. These two classes are not recognized as main classes in DDC and UDC. They are treated as part of medical science and agriculture. In Colon classification, applied sciences are mapped just after their immediate theoretical main classes. So agriculture is interpolated between botany and zoology, animal husbandry, between zoology and useful arts and medicine just after zoology.

In edition 7 of Colon classification, several new main classes and partial comprehensive classes have been recognized in biological sciences. Biological science FZ is a comprehensive main class of the comprehensive class natural science A. The partial comprehensive class 'Biological Science' comprises biology G, microbiology GT, molecular biology GUA, bio-mechanics GUB, biophysics GUC, and biochemistry GUE. Forestry JX is the new main class and a partial comprehension of agriculture, forestry and animal husbandry has been recognized as IZ. Several new main classes have been recognized in the medical sciences KZ. These were previously treated as parts of main class medicine. They are medical technology LT, public health LUS, hospital and sanitorium LU5Z, hospital LU5, sanitorium LU7, pharmacognosy LZ, nursing LYI, and medical jurisprudence LYX. These main classes are still isolates or subisolates of the other main classes in DDC and UDC.

Organization of Research in Biological Sciences

'Biology' is a young science. As a real science it came into existence only in the nineteenth century. Yet, there have been fantastic advances, and now we have many fundamentally different ways of viewing at the biological objects. We know that the knowledge consists of hierarchy or organizational levels - atomic, molecular, cellular, organizational, and populational, each interacting with one another and the environment.

A little more than hundred years ago, biology was merely a hobby. The origin of biology is lost in antiquity. Ever since man came into existence, he had to possess a differentiating knowledge between plants and animals. An error in identifying a poisonous plant or a deadly animal might well prove fatal. Thus, it may seem that biological knowledge is much older than recorded history. Modern methods of research have uncovered a great deal of reliable information that bears upon the prehistoric period of biology.

With the passage of time, the accumulation of acquired knowledge became unmanageable and needed systematization. It was the organization of this knowledge that brought the science of biology into being.

Small and big discoveries of the past led to the subsequent advances. Every little finding is significant for the progress of science.

The ancient science of biology gained its name in 1802 from Chevalier de Lamarck, soon after the explosion of knowledge necessitated the birth of different branches of biology, example, taxonomy, anatomy, histology, embryology, ecology, cytology, physiology, etc. Four periods as advancement in the study of biology after 1802 can be easily recognized. First, about 75 years in marked advanced in morphology and physiology; second, the period of renaissance (1875-1920); third, the recent period (1920-1950), and finally the period from 1950 onwards which can be called the modern period. The first period was characterized by a quest for a natural system of classification, the emergence of morphology from taxonomy and the beginning of physiology. During the second period, more stress was on structural (anatomical) and functional aspects of biology. During this period, the foundations of microbiology and genetics were laid down. Then followed the recent period with dramatic developments in physiology, genetics, tissue culture and biochemistry.

Terms like molecular biology, cell biology, etc., have been coined to embrace the interdisciplinary approaches to biology. History tells us that at various times during the life of biology, different sub-branches have originated, flourished and attained maturity. Cell biology and molecular biology are of comparatively recent origin and are continuing to explore the fundamentals of life. Cell and molecular biology have become the fashion of the day. As the fan spreads there will be an evergrowing risk of marginal disintegration of the flocks, extreme branches of specialization tending to lose touch with one another, and even with the central science itself. Let us take the example of taxonomy - one of the first branches of biology to develop. If at all we were to distinguish between classical and nonclassical (modern) branches of biology, taxonomy is certainly classical. Nucleic acid hybridization technique is no more a monopoly of nonclassical biologists. It is being used to analyse the extent of terminology between different ecotypes, species, general and so on. Various sub-branches like numeral taxonomy, chemotaxonomy, macrotazonomy, etc., have sprouted off from this branch of biology. Not only that, even Darwin's theories are strengthened by the studies on the molecular organization of DNA.

Research in India

Science and Technology today have revolutionized thought and action in every sphere of human activity. The all-pervasive impact of science and technology demands more than ever before, a bigger emphasis on research and development. This is particularly true of a country like India which, has not only to catch up with the developed countries but also has to march in steps with them. But what is our present investment in science and technology?

According to the report of the Committee on Science and Technology of the Cabinet Secretariat (COST), India is estimated to have spent about Rs 168.69 crores on Research and Development, during 1970-71. This includes expenditure by the Centre, State and the Private sector, their share being 85.9 per cent, 7.5 per cent and 6.6 per cent respectively.

The major organizations in India doing Research and Development work are, Department of Atomic Energy (DAE), Council of Scientific and Industrial Research (CSIR), Defence Research and Development Organization (DRDO), Indian Council of Agricultural Research (ICAR) and Indian Council of Medical Research (ICMR). They together consume 66 per cent of the total expenditure.

Pre-Independence

An important landmark in the scientific activity in India is the establishment of Royal Asiatic Society of Bengal in 1784. The Botanical Survey was founded in 1889 and the Zoological Survey was established in 1841. Medical research was initiated in India during the close of the nineteenth century. In the first decade of this century, the Imperial Agricultural Research Institute, now known as Indian Agricultural Research Institute, was established.

Post-Independence

After Independence, scientific activities got a further impetus. Medical and agriculture research was organized by Indian Council of Medical Research (ICMR) and Indian Council of Agricultural Research (ICAR). The ICAR, though it is being recognized along with State Governments, heads about 117 veterinary and fisheries institutes and about 700 agricultural centres. Medical research is being conducted by about 40 medical research institutes.

History of Developments

(i) The ancient developments in medicine and biology have occurred in third century BC.

(ii) In the twelfth century AD during the Buddhist period, the study of science and medicine was at its climax.

(iii) From about the middle of the nineteenth century, during 1851, the Biological society published a paper on positive science - zoology and botany.

(iv) Agricultural society of India in Calcutta was renamed Agricultural and Historical Society of India, and published 'transactions' in 1820.

(v) In the year 1841, research in zoology was initiated in the museum of Asiatic Society.

(vi) Anthropology was encouraged by the Indian Museum in 1856 and changed to zoological survey of India in 1916.

(vii) In 1951, Cancer Research Institute was founded at Calcutta and Bombay.

(viii) Specially in Medicine and Agriculture, government sponsored in 1899, Hoffkine Institute, Bombay on plague research, but now this works as an important centre of preventive medicine.

(ix) Nutrition Research Institute was organised at Coonoor.

(x) All India Institute of Public Health and Hygiene and other Medical Institutes, like Kings Institute of Preventive Medicine at Madras were started by State Governments in 1903.

(xi) Medical Research Institute at Shillong and School of Tropical Medicine at Calcutta were started in 1917 and 1927 respectively.

(xii) In agriculture the following institutes were started:
- (a) In 1906 Forest Research Institute at Dehradun.
- (b) In 1911 Tocklai Experimental Station at Assam.
- (c) In 1920 Dairy Institute at Bangalore.
- (d) In 1924 Institute of Plant Industry at Indore.
- (e) In 1925 Institute of Veterinary Research.
- (f) In 1926 Lac Research Institute at Ranchi.
- (g) In 1934 Agriculture Research Institute at Delhi.
- (h) In 1936 Institute of Sugar Technology at Kanpur.
- (i) In 1939 Jute Research Institute at Calcutta.

A Bi-national Conference by the University Grants Commission, in collaboration with the National Council of Science Education and National Science Foundation of USA was held at Bangalore in June 1971, in which scientists, educationists, and administrators from India, UK and USA engaged in different spheres of the life sciences, participated. Of the various recommendations, quite a number apply to biological sciences as well as areas of research to suit our national needs. Shifting of emphasis towards genetics, microbiology, ecology, environmental studies from a purely organismic level has been recommended.

Biological Research in India

Let us consider the state of biological research in India. Ours is a developing country and we cannot afford to go molecular at this stage. This should not be a cause for concern because there are many other biological problems facing us like food scarcity, population explosion and conservation of the environment. These are not merely national but international problems.

First, a word about the food problem. We are about to be self sufficient in wheat and rice. This is due to major leap in production during the last few years, and it has resulted from concentrated and combined efforts in plant breeding and pathology, and by the application of knowledge of soils, fertilizers and irrigation. This is an example of an excellent interplay between various branches of biology.

Control of population is as important as the increase in food production. The discovery of steroids is sure to work wonders. The usual starting point for such steroid production (it can not be produced by complete synthesis) is the plant period diosgenin, extracted from discorea. Subsequent modification of the molecule is brought about partly by the technique of organic chemistry and partly by stereo specific microbiological transformation, using suitable strains of fungi and bacteria. Thus, biology is concerned with atleast two important stages of the production of "the pill".

These are some of the areas which need proper appreciation, evaluation and investigation. We in India can help in the integration of knowledge from various fields of biology and can do more research in the applied aspects. It may not be out of place to point out that applied and fundamental aspects of biology are inseparable. Knowledge gained from fundamental research is a prerequisite of its application in agriculture or industry.

In a developing country like India, applied aspects of a science are more important than fundamentals. The application of tried methods of the use of scientific knowledge for hitherto unknown effects will pay quicker dividends. This does not mean that we should lose sight of the fundamental aspects of biology. The country has some very good laboratories, they should be encouraged to do fundamental research. There is a two-way relationship between fundamental and applied research. Observations made in the course of applied research can form the basis for completion of new fundamental investigations.

Biology faculties of the universities in collaboration with other faculties may meet the challenge with participation from the industries for which certain proper research and development allocation is essential. The biologists role in pollution control is reflected in the fact that leaving aside the sources of pollution from industrial waste, fumes, noise, etc., the wide use of radiation, detergents, insecticides, drugs resulting in chromozomal and genetic damage including the use of contraceptives and sedatives contribute in a much more serious way to pollution. Effective participation of biologists can be secured by setting up acrobiological sampling units, based on ecological study centres, chromozomal and genetic research centres on action of drugs, adulterants and other products which are widely used in a civilized society. Researches on soil binders, soil analysis and preservation of flora to check pollution are also significant areas of study. Investigations on the impact of pollution on the natural eco system is highly desirable. The effective way of tackling these problems is to direct research and development efforts towards establishing research units on a regional basis in suitable areas having strong faculties in the universities on the one hand and location of industries on the other.

The area of population control is one in which the significant contribution from biological science is imperative. Studies in different drugs as well as biological, genetic, chemical and pharmaceutical investigations on different plant species are necessary. Such projects should also include within their scope, exploration of species hitherto unknown, for an adequate and more effective substitute. This sector demands a considerable share of Research and Development allocation.

The other areas where Research and Development efforts need to be concentrated through scientists engaged in biological, researches are on commercial and medicinal products for domestic consumption as well as those serving as sources of foreign exchange. Unfortunately even though genetic engineering and other technical advancements have paid high dividends in crop species with the ushering of an era of green revolution, no serious effort has been made to achieve a breakthrough in these directions. Mention may be made of tea, species yielding paper pulp as well as Rauwolfia, Cinchona, digitalis and so on. Significant R and D efforts in this sector involving the universities are essential as more government laboratories and agencies in these areas have so far failed to create any impact in this country.

Similar attention is also desired to be directed towards problems of cancer therapy involving genetics and chromozome researches, microbiology and immunology. Researches on population level and various issues of population biology involving concentrated R and D effort are desired to solve certain biological problems effecting the country as a whole. Emphasis is also necessary towards researches in cell biology, implying a synthetic and coherent approach from organismic to molecular level.

In order to achieve these objectives, it would be preferable to set up multidisciplinary research units specially in the universities which may run in collaboration with local industries, the operational procedure ensuring coordinated functioning.

In addition to the fact, that such research projects should have multiple funding facilities, considerable R and D efforts need to be directed towards establishing marine biological and high altitude research units in east, west and south and the high altitude units in Eastern and Northern Himalayas are extremely essential. The marine biological wealth of this country which may even serve as sources for different industries have been really neglected for long. Well equipped high altitude units are also essential not only for the utilization of our high altitude flora but for the different multidisciplinary research projects of the physical and earth sciences as well. Such marine and high altitude research units can also be effectively utilized by multidisciplinary units located at the universities. There is no reason why India which has already passed through a successful revolution in agriculture, should not utilize its biological potential through judicious utilization of Research and Development allocation.

Problems in India

Because India has limited resources, therefore it is essential to identify the lines of researches to be conducted. There has been much debate as to whether only applied research should be supported or both applied and fundamental researches should be encouraged. It is true that applied researches will go a long way in satisfying immediate national needs, but we have to plan for the posterity too. Universities are the only places where fundamental researches can be carried out. Such researches are expensive, therefore, our universities need large financial support. Now, the question arises whether all the universities should be allowed to develop fundamental research facilities or only a few. The latter seems to be a more practical alternative.

In order to have an allround growth of biology, faculties of theoretical biology, molecular biology, microbiology, genetics, and microbiological, photobiology, marine and environmental biology and similar branches which hold promise for the future of mankind and which have hitherto been neglected in Indian universities, should be opened. An interaction between biological and social sciences is badly needed. These call upon the government, industry, and private agencies for liberal support, encouragement and organization. With rapid industrialization and marked technological change, it becomes imperative for our scientists to develop endemic processes and to organize fundamental researches.

The quality and quantity of research can be stepped up by giving incentives for research and by international cooperation. There should be a proper machinery for evaluating research proposals. There is a striking correlation between growth and vigour of scientific research and the progress of a nation. Rapid development of science in the right direction needs implementation of ingenious recommendations of expressed bodies. Much can be achieved in this direction by a coordinated action by the governmental agencies, universities, individual communities and biologists.

India is almost alone among the developing countries in possessing the cultural, educational and industrial infrastructure in which major research and development effort is practicable. Not only has the government taken the lead by establishing a cadre of research scientists in the Central Government Research Institutions, but the educational machinery of India is producing highly trained scientists, many of whom are adding to their individual knowledge and experience by training abroad.

There is, however, a growing anxiety among both scientists and others that scientific development has not been integrated into the economy as it should. It is in the development of this all important innovation chain that the larger multinational enterprises can contribute most effectively and directly to the growth of a strong Indian economy.

There is no scope for collaboration between government research centres and industrial units. On the contrary, an industrial unit with its own research and development facilities is much better equipped to establish fruitful relationship with independent research centres. If the wealth of talent is to be rapidly used, the only way to achieve this is, firstly, to have in industry itself, research and development skills developed to a stage which allow scientists from the two groups to effectively communicate with one another. Secondly, both industry and research laboratories have to develop a new and scarce skill - the ability to direct research effort and manage a group of highly talented and individualistic scientists, so that they all work towards common goals and yet are not so cramped in their style.

All this has clearly shown that research must necessarily be a fairly expensive, activity, if it has to have any real chance of success. It is therefore of vital importance that organizations which have invested large sums in invaluable scientific talent and research equipment should not be forced by controls on prices and output, to slacken or reduce their effort beyond a certain minimum level. Likewise, rigid licensing rules should not come in the way of putting their discoveries into practice.

Biology education and research in India needs a thorough overall and proper reorientation. In order to upgrade the standards of teaching and research in biology, there is an urgent need for recognizing newer areas of biological sciences relevant to the pressing needs of our country. Emphasis has gradually been shifted towards meaningful projects suitable to Indian conditions. India notwithstanding its potential, is playing mostly the role of a mute spectator in several fields of biological sciences.

Conclusion

The universe of knowledge is an infinite, evergrowing, multidimensional and continuum. It may develop in any direction along the lines of research. For the development of a subject, the organization of research is an essential phenomenon. The research activities in a developing country like India, may be organized at national, international and regional levels to solve the problems of our limited resources. Universities are the proper places where fundamental research may be carried out. Such researches are expensive, therefore, our universities need a large financial support.

A few selected universities should be allowed to develop fundamental research facilities. For satisfying immediate needs, applied researches are useful. But, for future plans, fundamental researches are useful. In order to have an increasing area of biological research, different branches of lesser importance which have been neglected hitherto in Indian universities, should be opened.

The development of a subject may be described on the basis of spiral or scientific method. Biology has already passed through one cycle of the spiral and entered the second cycle. Biological sciences are progressive in verification stage and show the developments especially in the field of genetics and heredity. Empirical stage is characterized by the classification of plants and animals. And the hypothesizing phase and fundamental laws show the revolutionary ideas according to different scientists. One of the important landmarks of this stage is the embryology of plants and animals.

Thus, the growth of a subject depends upon the speed of research. In Biology, the research potential is increasing continuously. Improvements in previous researches are also done as in evolution, genetics, biochemistry, etc. The discovery of Hargovind Khurana is also a striking example of this change.

The universe of knowledge being multi directional, ever turbulent, ever changing is throwing forth new cascades giving rise to new subjects. The formation of sections and cross sections in the universe of knowledge is a continued process. As we move towards the present day along the lines of research, we find new disciplines.

REFERENCES

1. Singh, Sonal, *Universe of Knowledge: Structure and Development*, p. 128, Jaipur, Raj, 1998.
2. Ranganathan, S.R. *Five Laws of Library Science*. Ed. 2. Bombay, Asia Publishing, p. 356, 1957.
3. *Encyclopaedia Americana*, p. 307, 1957, V. 4.
4. *Encyclopaedia Britanica*, p. 976, 1959, V. 23.
5. Bernal, J.D. *Science in History*, Ed. 4, p. 867, V. 3, London, 1969.

Twenty

Internal Aspects of Current Awareness Bulletins Issued by the Science Libraries in Karnataka

DR BARADOL A.K.

Introduction

The current awareness bulletin is known as information bulletin, library bulletin, documentation bulletin, documentation list and local documentation list, etc. Henceforth, the term bulletins is used here to represent these.

These bulletins are meant for keeping the clients of the library alert about the latest information in the field. Some libraries systematically scan the information and note the references and mimeograph the same and circulate them to the users of the library regularly. Primarily the information in such bulletins include articles from periodicals. In some cases the information about books is also included. Such bulletins also include the other primary sources of information viz. standards, patents, trade catalogues, etc. These are the publications of the libraries and information centres. Some libraries prepare the photocopies of the bulletins. A few libraries print the bulletins. There is no definite rule or pattern regarding this. The mimeographing, photocopying or printing depends on the availability of the resources and the number of copies of bulletins required for the distribution. Such bulletins vary in internal structure. Hence the study of internal aspects of bulletins was carried out.

Objectives

The study was conducted with the following objectives:

(a) To know whether the bulletins have introduction in the beginning.

(b) To know the types of documents included in the bulletins.

(c) To know whether the entries in the bulletins have an identification number.

(d) To know the arrangement of entries.

(e) To know whether the abstracts are included in the entries.

(f) To know the language of the bulletins.

Methodology

The current awareness bulletins published from science libraries and information centres in Karnataka were studied. The industrial libraries were also covered in the study. A suitable questionnaire was circulated to the libraries of 150 organizations. Out of this 105 organizations responded to the questionnaire. This was considered as a satisfactory sample. Most of the libraries publish a single bulletin. There are instances of one library publishing two or three bulletins. Altogether 48 information bulletins are being published by 105 libraries and information centres.

Introduction to the Information Bulletins

An introduction to any document would in general inform about the scope of the document, its coverage, aims, the group of persons to whom it is meant, etc. The information bulletins are not an exception to this. The users of the bulletins need to be told regarding the basis of selection, the sources of items, the kind of abstracts provided, etc. In large organizations, there is a constant turnover of personnel and the current awareness services should be explained to them as early as possible. Hence, there has to be an introduction in the information bulletins. When once the introduction is written and produced it can be reproduced without any extra time spent on it.

Among the samples studied 10 bulletins have an introduction.

Some have provided it with a heading and some have provided such information without any specific heading for the same. The introduction has to be very brief. Generally a page long introduction appears; or the aims of the bulletin are highlighted on the back of the front covers.

Types of Documents Included

Different types of documents were listed in the bulletin by both research organizations and industries. The bulletins specially meant for new additions to the libraries had this type of mixing. The main reason for this is the low acquisitions. The policy of some libraries is to acquire what is essential for their organization.

The Mangalore Chemicals and Fertilizers Ltd does not specify about the inclusion of the new additions in its bulletin. Different types of documents acquired are included. Though the title of the bulletin is "Journal Abstract Service", it includes the list of other types of documents like books, etc.

Information from 48 bulletin samples was collected to know whether various types of documents are included in bulletins or whether the bulletins are exclusively meant for specific category of documents.

Table 1 shows that as many as 12 organizations (5 research organizations and 7 industries) include the different types of documents like standards, books, periodicals, etc.

TABLE - 1
TYPES OF DOCUMENTS INCLUDED

Organizations	*Meant for Different Types of Documents*	*Meant for Exclusively One Type of Document*	*Total*
Research Organizations	05	21	26
Industries	07	15	22
Total	12	36	48

Identification Numbers

The bulletins would generate a number of requests for the full text of the documents listed. The compilation of the bulletins is done by the compilers, i.e., the library staff. The users of bulletins make their requests to the staff of the library for the text of the items. The requests have to be perfect, otherwise the library staff might give an irrelevant document. The procedure of request poses some problems. They are:

(a) how should the user notify the requirements to the library;

(b) what details the users are expected to provide to the library;

The library generally wishes the number(s) of item(s) to be mentioned in the request slip or letter or proforma. Only the entry identification number and volume number of the bulletin or year is enough, if each volume of the bulletin provides fresh series of numbers of items. There are instances where fresh series of numbers are provided in each issue of the bulletin. This makes it difficuilt for library staff to provide correct document. The user has to add the volume number, issue number, month, year, etc., along with entry identification number.

Among the 48 bulletins studied, the latest additions lists of the research organizations, especially universities provide fresh series of identification numbers to the entries in each issue. The bulletins produced by industries assign continuous numbers. The continuous numbering has advantages over assigning fresh series of numbers in each issue.

The item number is to be translated into the citation before it is located. This will lead to additional work by the library staff. Contrary to this, if the full bibliographical details are provided, it is easy for the library staff. The fourth law of library science enunciated by Dr S.R. Ranganathan viz. 'save the time of the reader' has to be borne in mind here. The highly paid scientific staff should not be forced to write more details.

The bulletins also can be used for complying with requests. If bulletins are printed on one side and if each entry is perforated it will be a great help. The scientists and technologists in this case need only tear off the particular item and send it to the library. Among the sample bulletin studies, no such thing was found. The printing in such cases has to be done on one side only. The verso of the sheet of the bulletin has to be kept blank. This procedure has one serious disadvantage; the user no longer has a complete copy of the bulletin. This is considered a disadvantage because the bulletins may have to be referred to later.

There is a counter argument for the view expressed above. Some people feel that the bulletin is a perishable product. The current awareness bulletin necessarily is a product which has a very limited value. As Strauss and others observe: "it is a throw-away product".[1] It is true that it can be discarded after certain days. The scientists need not preserve them.

Arrangement of Entries

The presentation of entries or internal arrangement of bulletins is perhaps difficult to study. There are a number of options available to the compilers of the bulletins. It is a controversial point in decision-making regarding 'the format' of entries and their arrangement. The controversies are very clearly shown in the divergent practices of arrangements in the Indian current awareness bulletins and especially from the samples collected from the libraries of Karnataka State. The arrangement of entries is shown in the Table 2.

TABLE - 2
ARRANGEMENT OF ENTRIES

Organization	*Classified (Library Classification)*				*Not Classified*	*Total*
	UDC	*DC*	*CC*	*Total*		
Research organization	3	7	4	14	12	26
Industries	5	--	--	5	17	22
Total	8	7	4	19	29	48

From the above table it is clear that in as many as 29 bulletins, the entries are not classified and are arranged according to the subject headings or by the title of periodicals or by patent numbers, etc. Of the 19 (Nineteen) bulletins which have adopted library classification schemes, the Universal Decimal Classification (UDC) is used in 8 which shows the popularity of UDC. Some bulletins follow the different schemes viz. Decimal Classification (DC) and Colon Classification (CC) to suit their subjects.

Subject Headings

The subject headings are known by many names as 'keywords', 'descriptors', etc. Some bulletins provide the subject headings to the articles covered. Among the sample studied, providing the subject headings is a common practice.

Guha found that "the largest number of current awareness bulletins are arranged by some chosen subject headings".[2] The present study also supplements this view. This shows that there is a continuity in the pattern of internal arrangement of bulletins.

Presence of Abstracts

Among the 48 samples, only 15 bulletins (5 bulletins from research organizations and 10 bulletins from industries) provide the abstracts/extracts. Table 3 shows the presence/absence of abstracts in the bulletins.

TABLE - 3

PRESENCE/ABSENCE OF ABSTRACTS IN THE BULLETIN

Organizations	*Bulletin with Abstract*	*Bulletins without Abstract*	*Total*
Research organization	05	21	26
Industries	10	12	22
Total	15	33	48

The libraries which publish the bulletins without abstracts have given the lack of time as the reason for not giving an abstract. As one of the documentation officers says "Only bibliographical details are provided in such lists in order to avoid likely delay in giving abstracts of articles for which separate abstracting/indexing services are available".[3] It is true that if the libraries provide abstracts in the bulletins, it will take longer time for preparation and thus defeat the very purpose of a bulletin.

The user is not concerned with the source of an item until he has read the title and abstract; and the citation is better placed after the abstract than before it.

Use of Published Abstracts

The bulletins if designed to have the abstracts they may be prepared by the staff or copied from an abstracting journal. Of course, it needs the negotiation for permission to use the abstracts.

The payment may be made to the agencies who publish the abstracting journals for using the abstracts, but it may result in an inordinate delay. The very purpose of current awareness bulletin to inform about the current information as quickly as possible is defeated in such a case. Hence, it is better to avoid the practice. The samples studied show that the published abstracts are not used from abstracting periodicals. However, the author abstracts, if available with the article are used for inclusion in the bulletins.

Request Form

The request form is a printed/mimeographed proforma for requesting for documents from the library and its address. It carries the full address, if the bulletins are circulated to other libraries outside the organization. The forms also contain space for the name and address of the requester. The main items are the bibliographical details of the documents requested for. It is a practice to provide request form for copies of documents in some bulletins. Table 4 shows the same.

TABLE - 4
FORM FOR COPIES OF ARTICLES

Organizations	*Bulletin Which have Forms*	*Bulletins Which have no Forms*	*Total*
Research organizations	01	25	26
Industries	01	21	22
Total	02	46	48

It is interesting to know from Table 4 that only 2 bulletins have the forms printed with the bulletins. The bulletins will have added attraction if the form is provided. When librarians were asked regarding forms they said that the forms have been provided to the scientists/section heads for the same purpose well in advance in bulk. This also should serve the purpose.

Language

Language plays an important role in scientific communication. A good amount of information is being published in various languages in the world such as French, German, English, Russian, Chinese and Japanese. A number of scientific information services have been started to cover the information published in various languages. The moment the information is published in any language, its coverage in current awareness publications viz. bulletins becomes essential. Such publications are either in the same language in which the information is published originally, or else are covered in the language which is more in use. This depends on the need of the scientific community.

A good amount of information is being published in the language of the nation i.e. Hindi and an equal amount of information is also being published in the regional languages of the States in India. Of course, the trend of scientific publication in regional language has a history of only four decades. Earlier, there was not much scientific information published in Hindi or in any other regional language. It is only after India's independence that the scientific information is found in languages other than English. The scientific periodicals of the universities in Karnataka State publish articles on scientific subjects in Kannada language.

This study revealed that there is a uniformity as regards the use of language in the information bulletins. It is only the English language which has been enjoying the monopoly. Not even one organization publishes the information bulletin in the language of the Karnataka State, i.e., Kannada. Table 5 reveals the fact. The lists of latest additions published by Karnataka University, Mangalore University and Gulbarga University included the scientific books in Kannada added to their libraries.

TABLE - 5

LANGUAGE OF THE BULLETINS

Organizations	*Bulletin in English Language*	*Bulletins other than English Language*	*Total No. of Bulletins*
Research organization	26	--	26
Industries	22	--	22
Total	48	--	48

The utility of the products or publications of information service in the language of the nation or regional languages is beyond doubt. These will be very useful if published in regional languages along with English. To quote Voigt: "Services issued in the local language are most successful, particularly for engineers, medical practitioners, agriculturists and the like".[4] Although there is enough information published in the Kannada language, there are no current awareness publications published in Kannada either in sciences or in applied sciences.

Conclusion

The current awareness bulletins in Karnataka differ from each other in their internal aspects. There is no uniformity as regards the presence of introduction to the bulletins, types of documents included, identification numbers, arrangement of entries, subject heading and inclusion of abstracts. There is uniformity in one aspect i.e. language of the bulletins. All the bulletins published by science libraries in Karnataka State are published in English language only. It is quite likely that more and more scientific information will be published in the regional language of the State, i.e., Kannada. The science libraries will naturally acquire the literature in Kannada language. Things are likely to change in future and bulletins may be published in the regional language of the Karnataka State i.e. Kannada.

REFERENCES

1. Strauss, L.J. Striby I.M. and Brown, A.L.: *Scientific and Technical Libraries;* Their Organization and Management. 2nd ed. p. 246, New York: Becker and Haves, 1972.
2. Guha, B. "Indian Current awareness services", UNESCO Bulletin for Libraries. Vol. 22, p. 74, 1968.
3. Patil, Y.M. Evaluation of soil science information service Current Awareness Bulletin. Soil Science information Service CA bulletin. Vol. 1 (8 & 9), p. 5, 1980.
4. Voigt Melvin J. Scientists Approach to Information. Chicago, American Library Association, p. 77, 1961.

Twenty One

A Treatise on Fundamental Theories in Abstracting A *sine-qua non* for Research and Development

(World's First Abstracting Theories Based on Experiment)

PARAM BHUSHAN DR B.B. SHUKLA

The Necessity of an Abstract

With the phenomenal increase in the production of literature, research activity was and even now is being given topmost priority because it is research that could foster for new knowledge producing more refined and sophisticated products for the economic and cultural advancement of the people of the world. It is therefore, that, developed and developing countries of the world spend billions and billions dollars/pounds/rupees/sterlings/yens, etc., in research in all fields of human activity and more precisely in the field of Science and Technology, thereby generating new knowledge and information in the form of research articles, reports, etc., in published form for the furtherance of research and development. It is surprising enough to note that the volume, variety and size of literature output, more particularly the output of literature in Science and technology is becoming very vaste, for example, in case of biomedical literature, the number of research papers published in 70 languages of the World is 2.6 million papers per annum (as per an estimation of Dr Shukla in 1994). If a research scholar in biomedicine having knowledge in 70 languages, has all the documents in his/her hand, will devote, 3 hours per day in reading regularly for 365 days in a year, he/she would take 2374.4292 years or 23.744292 (more than 23.74 centuries) centuries to complete the reading of one year' technical literature in biomedicine. In case of production of one years literature in chemistry of the whole world, it would take about 2 centuries (approx) for a research scholar to complete reading at the same rate. So also in the field of humanities and social sciences, the production of micro thought literature is surprisingly very vaste. Moreover, the life span of a normal human being is 70-80 years. It is, therefore, humanly impossible and very difficult on the part of the researchers/ scientists/other groups of readers in any discipline to keep them update with the production of literature in their respective subject fields. They, thus, want the second hand literature of their own interest in the form of abstract of the original documents for use by which they could save their valuable time needed to read the original document and secondly they could come to know the comprehensive coverage of data/ information of their own subject fields, if the original documents are properly abstracted on grouping techniques. If we can not read the total textual matters of the original document, we must read a few selected ones, and the selection of words, phrases, sentences must be geared up and organized comprehensively in a condensed form with the repackage of data and to pour these data into the abstract in such a manner that not a single vital item of the information or data of the original document will go out of the sight of the researcher who will use abstract in latter's absence. Thus, the abstract should be comprehensive, in detail touching the vital elements of the original research paper or article or report so that the researcher may not desire to consult the original document and in hard cases of controversy dispute or conflicting opinion he/she may read the original one. Therefore the coverage of subject matters in an abstract is extremely essential and besides other formalities of procedure adopted in abstracting, careful attention must also be paid in scanning or selecting the vital elements of subject matter from the original documents, comprehensively by the application of certain principles, canons, instructions, theories, standards and the data so obtained should be converted to form a stable abstract. No doubt, certain abstracting agencies, Government Departments and individuals have prepared certain rules, criterias, instructions in the form of canons and also standards in abstracting by the application of which the comprehensiveness of an abstract can be confirmed.

Borko and Chatman's Study

In 1962, H. Borko and S. Chatman had surveyed a set of criteria for acceptable abstract used by the abstractors of 130 scientific publications. The purpose of this study was to formulate a set of principles by the application of which the adequacy of computer generated abstract could be prepared and to instruct the computer to extract certain sentences from the original document in developing new programmes which was done, but the study did not do much in formulating certain principles to improve upon the quality of writing an abstract.[1]

Published Instructions issued by Abstracting Agencies

Apart from this, the abstracting and indexing agencies too published their own instructions for the preparation of abstracts to meet the specific requirement of their users. The notable among them are:

(1) Direction for abstractors by the Chemical Abstracts Service (CAS), 1971.

(2) Policy and procedure in Abstracting of the American Bibliographical Centre, 1973.

(3) Applied Mechanics Reviews (AMR) Guidelines for Review (n.d.)

Formulation of Standards in Abstracting

Standardization in Abstracting Services was also done by the technical information agencies with the publication of guidelines in abstracting. A few noteworthy attempts are:

(1) Armed Services Technical Information Agency (ASTIA)

USA, Guidelines for cataloguing and Abstracting, 1962.

(2) Defence Documentation Centre (DDC) standards, 1968, Rules for preparing abstracts, (the changed name of ASTIA, USA).

(3) International Standard Organization (ISO) Guide to Abstractor, 1961.

(4) UNESCO Guide for the preparation of Authors Abstracts, UNESCO, 1968.

(5) Compilation of World Inventory of Indexing and Abstracting Services, 1972.
- a joint venture of US National Science Foundation and UNESCO carried out by National Federation of Abstracting and Indexing Services (NFAIS), USA and FID. It is a developed planning venture launched in 1972 in abstracting and indexing services of the World Science information system.

(6) Bureau of Indian Standard (previously as ISI) has laid down certain standards in abstracting vide No. 795 (1966). So also standards institutions in other countries of the world have formulated certain standards in Abstracting for adoption by the specialist users in the preparation of Abstracts from the original research articles, etc.

(7) Dr S.R. Ranganathan, the father of the Library Science in India has also formulated certain Canons in Abstracting.

While examining the above instructions, criteria, principles, guidelines and standards, etc., of the International and National Abstracting Services, Divisions, Agencies, Government Departments, etc., it is found that the above instructions in some way or other are not comprehensive in detail in fulfilling the requirements of the researchers, scientists or other groups of users, and that a lot of differences are noticed in coverage of subject matters between the original documents and abstracts. It is, therefore important that a thorough investigation into the abstracting principles should be undertaken in order to prepare stable abstracts free from error from the original documents.

Dr Shukla's Theories in Abstracting: A New Venture in Abstracting Service

Abstracts are being prepared from the original document since long, but the items which are extremely useful for the general as well as special types of readers are often not found in the abstract although the original document is fortified with the above elements. It is therefore, considered essential to have certain Fundamental Theories in Abstracting in order to prepare a stable abstract from the original document. Moreover, it is not possible on the part of every library to procure all the micro thought publications which are emerging in terrific rate in the world. Thus, the abstracts of such publications should be secured from the documentation centres or libraries should prepare accurate abstracts for those documents. Further, it would be difficult on the part of the readers, especially the scientists, research scholars, other categories of educationists and authorities in most fields of specialization to go through the contents of the original micro documents, especially the pages of articles appearing in various journals of their own interest. The alternative solution would be to prepare an accurate abstract from the original document with related information on contextual basis so that abstracting professionals shall use them for the preparation of an accurate abstract from the original document. The abstracting theories deduced in this paper are the explanatory theories which uses simple class lists bifurcating the original documents on readers' requirement.

Background of the Study of the Theories in Abstracting and the Experiment with Revisions

This paper discusses the background of the project, i.e. the reason why I began to work on getting some concrete theories in abstracting. I became interested to study the theories in Abstracting in 1970 when I was a College Librarian at the Government Training College, Bolangir (Orissa). I was thinking as to how a librarian or a documentalist shall provide its users exhaustive information on current topics which is emerging so quickly in the world in an accelerating rate with the pace of knowledge explosion. I was thinking that dissemination of information in original form to the users is a matter of total impossibility on the part of a librarian or a documentalist. Neither a librarian nor a documentalist can provide its users all the information in original form, nor do the educationists, research scholars, scientists and other authorities have time to go through it. I wanted to save the time of the modern man, to properly guide the scientists, research scholars, educationists and authorities in most fields of specialization to contribute more and more for the prosperity of the nation through research by providing them pin-pointed, exhaustive, nascent information at the quickest possible time. The alternative solution to me on this vaste launch was to prepare an accurate abstract from the original document or an article. But to my great surprise, I did, not find the exact theories on abstracting excepting certain criteria, instructions, canons, or standards, etc., as discussed earlier. When I enquired about the abstracting periodicals, to my great surprise, I noticed a gulf of difference in facts between the original publication and the abstract which made me think about such a research project which took me years and years of investigation, inquiry, and deep thinking resulting in the promulgation of the theories in abstracting.

It was in January 1971 that I began to send questionnaires of my theories to many experienced librarians, library science professors, educationist in the country, notable among them were Dr S.R. Ranganathan, Prof. P.N. Kaula, Prof. V.V. Kulkarni, Prof. M.R. Kumbhar, and many others. The response was very cordial. Many professors felt the need of such a vast project and they have given their opinion to widen the scope of the project to "Experimental analysis on the theories in abstracting". Eleven Theories covered in this paper were highly welcomed from all quarters. Dr S.R. Ranganathan, the National Research Professor in Library Science and father of Library Science in India referred this work as "The Most valuable, precise, original and masterly which could provide new light to documentation work specially for the researchers engaged in research work and educationists in most fields of specialisation".[2] To quote Prof. P.N. Kaula, the father of library movement in India, a renowned professor of library and information science of Banaras Hindu University and an international authority in library and information science, welcoming this work as "Unique and perhaps no one else has been able to do so in this way"[3] Prof. Kaula further states that "Dr. Banabihari Shukla has been engaged in formulating certain fundamental and original theories in abstracting. He has stated this theory even before he joined M.Lib. Sc. course in the Deptt. of Library and Information Science of Banaras Hindu University. I had, therefore, the opportunity to watch his way of thinking and analysis on this issue. In fact I got a seminar conducted by Dr Shukla on his theory of abstracting. He also published an extract of his theory before he qualified with M.Lib. Science. Dr Shukla has now brought out his whole study and the theory in print. The work will certainly attract specialists, thinkers and practitioners who are deeply involved in the study and development of abstracting work. Abstracting has become an important product of the information industry and the theory advocated by Dr Shukla will be of great help in producing quality work in abstracting. It will also stimulate those engaged in the field to have a new approach in abstracting work".[4]

Prof. V.V. Kulkarni commenting on the theories in abstracting, states that "the theories in abstracting brought out by you is a commendable achievement and I have always high regards for such students".[5] According to Prof. M.R. Kumbhar late Professor of Library and Information Science, Karnataka University, Dharwad, "I am very much pleased that your theorisation of the abstracting service is a commendable job, and with much appreciation you have theorised the abstracting service entirely satisfactory. To my mind, I have not come across such theorisation of abstracting work so far. I, simply congratulate you upon this unique achievement and pray God to give you more and more strength to bring out such pieces of theories, which could be propagated in later times and keep your name alive".[6] "Fundamental theories of Abstracting promulgated by Dr Banbihari Shukla is of great help in producing quality work in abstracting and will attract, specialists, thinkers and practitioners who are deeply, involved in the study and development of abstracting works. It will also stimulate those who are engaged in the field to have a new approach in abstracting work. The theories promulgated by Dr Shukla, are the product of high intensive research carried out to facilitate quick and exhaustive information retrieval and dissemination".[7]

Though my theories were experimented and published in 1974, due to financial difficulties, comprehensive experiment of this project was delayed. In 1977, I had the opportunity of getting an international assignment from UNESCO, Paris, through the Government of India to write a learned work on the theories that I have promulgated entitled "Experimental analysis on the theories of abstract-A new methodical dimension on documentation." Many learned journals, newspapers and authorities had highly praised my theories and the review appeared in many papers and journals highly welcoming this work as the most original and valuable in the field of library and information science. However, my theories got the concurrence of the UGC and finally approved as a research project. Financial assistance to this effect was made available to me by the UGC New Delhi in 1986-87., It was, therefore, that my eleven theories got the channel for further experimentation. The validity and authenticity of my theories, having been tested at the national level, due to their pervasive influence and wide coverage required to be experimented internationally, which was done.

Finally in 1988 my Eleven theories were again published in the form of an article under the title "Experimental analysis on the theories of abstracts: New Methodical dimension on Documentation".[8] The product of experiments conducted during the preceeding years was the theories that could able to construct a comprehensive and mature abstract, free from friction with the original document. By the application of the theories, significant information required for the specialized readers on given theme(s) or experiment(s) of the subject field are being scanned on grouping techniques, with quite different property specifications which would provide direct access to information and serves as a substitute of the original document though in a lesser degree. The abstracts so prepared with the aid of the theories would help the specialized readers to get all the information of the original document in a compact form and utilize the same in his/her research work. In hard cases of controversy, the researcher may consult the original article in order to confirm the correctness of the statement(s) enlisted in the abstract or otherwise not.

Purpose of the Study

The institutionally based original and pure theories under study of Abstracting are my own invention, empirically verified and deducted for practical documentation work. The theories have been broken into mutually exclusive groups, considering the components which are essential for scientific reader's research purposes. The steps necessarily required to particularize, the mode of applying it and the device that the intellectual methods require for information retrieval are the modes of mechanized transformation of knowledge in place of an original document. Concurrently a detailed analysis was made on the issue and how far the process could be freed to computers will be the next stage of development on the theories of abstracting. Despite the experimental and specialized character of the study, the preliminary requirement is to present the study a comprehensive scheme for the interconnection of tasks which could be generally applicable by the scientists, research scholars and other groups of educationists in saving their valuable time depending on the quality of the research articles. Secondly the entire library profession could use these theories in planning their practical work to help the specialist readers through abstract. The study seeks to describe the comprehensive account of the theories of abstracts, necessarily conforming to the original plan of the issue. It has been seen that the process of experimentation and differentiation with reference to distinct transformation of the groups are in general commutative to each other. In fact, the difference as derived is the result of experiments, group tests, proportional scores and derivation of object under consideration with respect to another infinitesimal transformation.

Objective of the Study

It is necessary to study the techniques involved in this part of experimentation and the important factors that are necessary for the development of the Theories of Abstracts. The various objectives that hinders round this scientific information processing are:

(1) The data of all kinds of document of any description, in a particular field of scientific research, carried out to facilitate retrieval of information and consultation through stable abstract.

(2) Working from these data, the final process of operation in deriving important documentary products in the shape of abstract to the specialist readers and to facilitate consultation of scientific materials.

(3) In accordance with the term, scientific information processing, document distribution to scientists and specialists readers are of vital significance which covers :

   (i) To help the development of a subject consisting of an area of knowledge.

   (ii) Development of an area of knowledge other than that of the subject.

   (iii) Update, new and comprehensive ideas of a subject field including important facts and figures.

   (iv) Inclusion of Important charts, illustrations, graphs, diagrams and formulas of most original nature.

   (v) Comprehensive assessment of coordinating factors and techniques from original documents which could with advantage be utilized for developing newer channels for augmenting resourceful material for research.

(4) To automatically classify important items of information from the original document.

(5) To obtain sets of inter substitutable vital elements from the original document which would extend the range of retrieval of information as per the requirement of the users on the assumption that such identical elements would be derived from co-occurrence information. The identical elements had stronger relations from the abstracting point of view, which could permit an abstract to have loosely organized sets of information from the original document rather than tightly connected information from the retrieval point of view.

(6) To comprehensively select items necessary to retrieve in clear terms as primary requirement on different aspects on view point of search element that will automatically be adhered to.

(7) To promulgate a set of theories in Abstracting that would comprehensively classify the host document on grouping techniques as per the requirements of the users and secondly the classificatory data so segregated be converted to form a

suitable abstract in which case the abstract must accompany all the vital segments of the original document including incorporation of references to all studies undertaken previously on the particular concept.

Dr Shukla's Theories in Abstracting: As Promulgated after Experimentation

In this paper definitions of the theories with their short analysis have been given excepting the major experiments, research plan evaluation and programme, commutation formulas and Mathematical deductions in order to make the paper comprehensively brief and scientific.

As per the empirical verification, the theories of Abstracting can be analysed under the following major heads:

(1) Theory of Search Value;
(2) Theory of Methodical Variation of Contraction and
(3) Theory of Quantum Analysis of Abstract.

Theory of Search Value

"The mode of contraction of an article/scientific or research paper (herein referred as original document) in any subject field either scientific or technical, humanities or social sciences, relates to the totalization of valid facts of the original document and is equivalent to the abstract in an indirect way when vital themes from the original document are scanned segregated and incorporated into an abstract comprehensively in a condensed form fulfilling all the requirement of scientist or researcher or any intendant pursuing in any subject(s) through an abstract in later's absence." No doubt, the abstract will not be exactly identical with that of an original document in the coverage of contents, analysis, interpretation of data information, significance or importance and findings, but will be the carrier of all vital elements of the original document and therefore, the abstracts need to be prepared on stable scientific lines.

"The theory of Search value relates that an abstract is the sum and substance of the original document or an article accompanied with adequate informative or indicative description of the original one to enable the reader to know the original publication in which it is written in latter's absence. In other words, the theory of search value relates that comprehensive searching of vital elements from the original document is essentially a prerequisite that will fulfil the major goals of the researcher who could use an abstract in absence of the original document."

"Under the theory of search value, contraction is made in all direction of the original document and all relevant information or data from it are scanned so as to enable the abstract to be free from friction or we may say that the abstract is equivalent to the totalization of the valid facts of the original document or an article though less in degree considering the utility of it for a researcher/ scientist or any user of any subject field who wants to use it in absence of the original document."

"The residual information/data after scanning of core information from the Original Document is termed as the residue or Surplus which is otherwise known as the surplus value. The sum and substance of the valid facts of the original document is equivalent to abstract plus (+) surplus value or in other words, the original document minus (-) abstract is the surplus value".

While contracting vital information from the original document, the contracting elements are decreased chronologically thereby adding frequency to the abstract. Thus it is the mode of contraction, and surplus value at different stages that add frequency to the abstract (the 8 theories vide No. 3.1 to 3.8) while contracting forceful information from the original document into it. Therefore, the abstract so prepared must be fortified with such elements as are required by the researcher/scientist/ or any user and not with the fabricated information which are incorporated into an abstract by various agencies/firms/industries, etc.

Theory of Methodical Variation of Contraction

"As the mode of contraction in an original document changes, the productive forces of the valid facts come into conflict with the latter, i.e., with the abstract and thus it turns into fetters on the forces of production. Thus, there is a clash in the mechanism of contraction and the substantive power of the original one. This power is generally reduced in case of the original document while contracting it in all directions. This clash between the original document and the abstract is destablized as to the value of both while contracting the former to the latter. On this analysis, the theory of methodical variation of contraction comes into being".

The theory relates that the brief and informative substance of the original content and conclusion of the article or the original publication is equivalent to the abstract in a direct way but less in degree to the sum total value of the former.

The quantitative transformation of the use value is replaced here by the quantitative expansion of the exchange value, i.e. the abstract as to the objective of the production of the original one. The difference between the original document and the abstract is the surplus value which is left surplus after the last level of contraction is made from the original document.

Through the theory of search value, the value of the abstract is equivalent to the sum total of the value of the original document minus surplus value but in case of the latter, i.e. in the theory of methodical variation of contraction, the value of the abstract also remaines the same when compared with the original document whose value is taken as one unit, or "the theory constitutes the analytico contracting qualities of the theory of contraction. Thus the important factor in case of variation of contraction is determined by the magnitude of the surplus value and the contraction of it in all directions. Hence the rate of surplus value and the component parts of contraction can be accelerated when the surplus value is co-adjusted with the abstract in order to equalize it with the power of the original document, though less in degree."

Thus the rate of contraction of the surplus value is determined as the sum total value of the original document minus the abstract. In other words, "The surplus value of an abstract can be analysed as such value which denotes to the frequency of conversion of an abstract from the original document. In determining the rate of surplus value, the identical qualities/units of the quantitative analysis of the abstract is equalised when frequency is added to it. To equalize or balance the power of both the original publication and the abstract, the surplus value is added to the abstract."

Theory of Quantum Analysis of Abstract

"The theory relates to the inner qualities of the publication of the totalization of the valid facts of the original document and consists of the accumulation of the total value. The abstract contains all the essential aspects of the original document in a concise but precise form and is distinguished from the original document by hierarchy when it is presented briefly but intelligently adding to it all the identical aspects and component parts of the original document. The theory states that the original document and the abstract have something common spread over the whole gamut of the document that differ from one another by sequence of arrangement."

"By the application of the theories as per the quantum analysis, the abstractor can choose how far he goes on in searching with the relevant items of information from the original document in successive degree of likeness and attempts to obtain further information from the original document. When all the theories are applied to the original document and the shifted information so obtained are taken into the abstract, the scale of relevance of the matching information so derived in the latter case is said to be the substitute of the original document. The theory of quantum analysis further states that while transforming appropriate ideas and co-occurrence information describing denser areas on a subject, discussed in an article or the original document, the theories should be carefully memorized and set into the abstract intelligently in order not leave any identifying key information from the original documents."

The theories solicit all but conveying the maximum information contained in the original document in a minimum number of words deducting from it the surplus value.

The abstract prepared as per the theory of quantum analysis can serve the purpose best in order to transmit important information to the readers accurately and quickly.

The quantum analysis of abstract comprises of the eight theories of noteworthy significance which are as follows:

1. Theory of Objectivity;
2. Theory of Recrimination;
3. Theory of Generalization;

4. Theory of Technical Treatment;
5. Theory of Concentration;
6. Theory of Identical units;
7. Theory of Fundamental Inheritance; and
8. Theory of compact value;

Theory of Objectivity

"The inner feeling or the action of the original document directed in a line aiming at the indifferent subject describing the primary aims, objective and purpose and governed by the introduction when controlled by the mode of transition of the subject matter is called the theory of objectivity of an abstract and is equivalent to 1/20th part of value of the original document minus the surplus value (the value remained surplus up to the last level of contraction of the original document is taken as the surplus value.)

"The theory of objectivity states that while preparing an abstract, the abstractor should see that the primary objectives of the paper should in no way be left over unassessed since such information has its own significance and control over the whole document". Thus such information should positively be included in the abstract in the desired form while scanning information/ data from the original document.

Theory of Recrimination

Every action has its equal and opposite reaction. On this analysis, the theory of Recrimination lays the basic factor of an abstract.

"The theory states that, while framing counter charges to an original document indulged in mutual reciprocity or retort accusation of discontentment, the abstract seems to be in a breaking point and has the reversible attachment with the original one. The theory of Recrimination says that the point (s) where requirements that go counter to the inclination for one which has not been scanned from the original document for inclusion into an abstract should not be detached even though disputed. Such items if any should positively be included in the abstract."

The main intention of giving weightage to this theory is that if such disputed items become controversial and it is nor known where to keep the information then these types of information should be placed under the purview of the theory of Recrimination and must be scanned accordingly from the original paper in desired form of inclusion into an abstract.

Theory of Generalization

"The theory of Generalization has a special significance and control over whole document. The theory says that the distribution of the individual power of the original document when taken into the abstract form, the general characteristics or the inborn qualities should in no way be left over. Thus, in this aspect the theory of Generalization has overall control on the original document and such items which are coming under its purview should positively be included into an abstract".

Theory of Technical Treatment

"The theory of Technical Treatment is by far an important theory in abstract writing and as such the text should be scanned for information on the technical treatment or vital core formula and on the range of operation of the original document.

The theory of Technical Treatment is the productive force of an abstract and remains aloof from the clash with the theoretic exaggeration of the original document and the abstract while contracting it to the later. And as such to avoid conflict, the important formula which describes the core of the topic should positively be included in the abstract.

The theory relates that an important part of the original document, the data of investigation, the technical aspects and the formulas are invariably important in abstract writing and as such the vital powers of the original document as per the theory should positively be included in the abstract."

Thus, the theory of technical treatment is the vital power and such information coming under its purview should positively be included in the abstract while taking it from the original document.

Theory of Concentration

"The most valuable and potential findings that describe the result of investigation of the authors should in no way be left over while preparing an abstract. Besides, the points of information on which more stress and concentration is given should also be included. On this context, the theory of concentration is important in abstract writing.

The theory of concentration says that the authors potential findings that describe accurately any experimental or theoretical results concerning the project must be included in the abstract and soon after these data are exhausted leaving thereby some valuable information of importance to effect the memory or concentrate the attention of the individual to lay stress thereon should be included in the abstract."

For systematic development of an abstract, the theory of concentration plays a vital role in the abstract writing and therefore, the elements coming under its purview should not go away of the sight of the user.

Theory of Identical Units

"The theory of Identical Unit has special significance in abstract writing and as such while preparing an abstract, the aspects of the original document that describe the treatise and declaration of significant importance of important person(s) or body(s) etc., reproduction in the original form of the original document must positively be included in the abstract and on such aspects identify between the original document and the abstract must be restored.

That means there must be identity between the original publication and the abstract in respect of treatise, discussion of significant importance and declaration of important matters of important personalities or bodies, etc., and while preparing an abstract such matters since been vital must be included."

Theory of Fundamental Inheritance

"The theory says that if a collection of the source of the original document is generally known by the readers and is mostly not useful for higher study and research, the qualities of the quantitative discipline of the inherited matters which are fundamental or basic in its approach and are the negation for inclusion in an abstract are not to be taken into the abstract in detail. Only important outlines of it are to be taken down. In this aspect the theory plays the part of a mediator to settle the matters as intended to do."

Theory of Compact Value

"The theory of compact value is the overall modified indicative or informative qualities of the original document classified under sequence as per their value and should carefully be included in the abstract in the desired form wherever necessary as per the mode of approach and inner qualities basically useful for the intendants. The theory is by far an inborn necessity of a successful abstract."

"The theory says that after completion of the abstract, careful attention must be paid not to omit relapsible inborn qualities from the original document and should be rectified again under classified sequence to make the abstract free from error without omission. The theory of compact value is by far a theory without any specific power but overall majesty on all theories generally adding frequency to the abstract from the original document."

Suppose after completion of the abstract, the value of the abstract in comparison to the original document is lowered adding thereby some hints of specific qualities. The theory of compact value therefore, guides an abstractor as to whether any omission is noticed in the abstract so constructed from the original document or not. Hence, he is guided to check again to both the original document and the abstract, as to the authenticity of incorporating valuable matters in the abstract and hence in order not to leave such information, he adds qualitative substantive information or deductive facts to the abstract.

The theory of compact value is by far an important theory and the matters which are coming under its purview must be included into an abstract.

Assigning a Supplementary Title to the Original Document

Another important matter to be kept in mind is that in case of preparing an abstract from the original document, "if the title of the original document does not represent the subject matter in complete detail, the article may go out of the sight of the reader.

Hence the abstractor is advised to write this misleading textual title at the top of the abstract and juxtapose a suitable alternative title of the original document below and index it and place it at appropriate place to facilitate the reader to consult the misleading original document in absence of the misleading original title which may be termed as law of juxtaposition."

Conclusion

An abstract should be the replica of the original document so that specialized readers shall use it in absence of the original one. Such an abstract must include the specialized information or data (as detailed under the theories of abstracting) from the original article including diagnostic approach of the project, significance of the result, interpretation of data, its application to any object or sophisticated requirement for use, formulas if any, etc. No doubt, while preparing an abstract, the formalities such as abstract designation, code number, the author (surname followed by forename) of the work or the institution of work or affiliation; title of the article; reference if any from other text (either translation or original text, etc); year of publication; volumes (in capital letters); serial number(s); page(s) (conversation of the original article into the abstract proper with the aid of theories of abstracting); document availability on the concerned aspect; signature of the abstractor; chronological period, number and office of the origin are vital for incorporation. However, the subject proper of the original article being extremely important forming the core for specialized readers, must be included in an abstract properly and accurately while scanning informative facts from the original document. In case of an informative abstract, it should be written in the past-tense with active voice and in case of indicative abstract it should be written in present tense with passive voice.

Thus, the theories in abstracting would tend to comprehensively classify the host document on grouping techniques involving quite different property specifications and intended as a recall device in enlarging the scope of an abstract. The theories of abstracting, therefore, would tend to construct a mature abstract free from error by which specialized readers could be able to save 9/10th to 19/20th part of their valuable time by referring to the abstract of an original document pertaining to their field of knowledge.

REFERENCES

1. Borko, and Bernier C. *Abstracting Concepts and Methods*, New York: Academic Press. p. 36, 1975.
2. Ranganathan, S.R. Letter dt. 12.04.1971 of Dr. Ranganathan to Dr. Shukla.
3. Kaula, P.N. Letter dt. 19.04.1974 of Prof. Kaula to Dr. Shukla.
4. Kaula, P.N. *Fundamental Theories in Abstracting*. Cuttack: Bharti Publication, 1984 (Foreword).
5. Kulkarni V.V. Letter dt. 14.08.1974 of Prof. Kulkarni to Dr.Shukla.
6. Kumbhar, M.R. Letter dt. 25.-07.1979 of Prof. Kumbhar to Dr. Shukla.
7. Shukla, B.B. *Fundamental Theories in Abstracting and Fundamental Laws in Library Science*. Cuttack, Bharati Publication, pp. 15-38, 1983. and *Herald of Library Science*. V. 22 No. 1-2, 1984 (Review)
8. Shukla, B.B. Experimental analysis on the theories of Abstract: A New Methodical Dimension of Documentation, *Indian Journal of Inf. Lib. & Soc.* VI, NI. pp. 18-57, 1986.

Twenty Two

Role of Information Technology in Indian Libraries

K.T. DILLI

Introduction

We are living in an age of 'information explosion'. And it is expected from the library managers that the required information must be gushed out without delay and in accuracy. The 'information technology' comprising computers with telecommunication technology, satellite technology, reprographic technology, printing technology and CD-ROM technology comes to the rescue of the librarian in satisfying the needs of the present users. With the onslaught of micro computers the library managers could solve the traditional methods of handling information such as storage, processing, retrieval and dissemination mechanically.

Role of Information Technology in Libraries

According to ALA glossary, "Information Technology" is the application of computers and other telecommunication technologies to the acquisition, organization, storage, retrieval and dissemination of information".

UNESCO defines Information Technology as, "Scientific, technological and engineering disciplines and management techniques used in information handling and processing, their applications, computers and their interaction with man machines, and associated social, economic and cultural matters".

With the introduction of new Information Technology, libraries are now expected to make use of those technologies to provide nascent information quickly and in great volume which is globally available than before. In this context it would be apt to refer to the fourth law of library science - To save the time of reader/staff.

On account of exponential growth of information and information sources, the print media is becoming obsolete and the storage media is also fast changing in a dramatic manner. Following are some of the novel methods of storage media available:

(a) Print media (papers, metal sheets etc.)
(b) Film Media (microfilm, micro-fische, etc.)
(c) Magnetic media (Magnetic tapes, drums, etc.)
(d) Electronic media (floppy and Hard discs, microchips, etc.)
(e) Optical media (CD-Rom, Video disc, CD-WORM, CD-I, etc.)

Emergence of Information Society

In the age of science, the computers can make the libraries and society paperless in future. The world famous futurist, Alvin Tofler predicts the 21st century 'Space age', 'Computer age', 'Information age' and 'electronic era'. Blaise Cronin calls' the future society as "Information Society" and predicts the emergence of information workers.

The developing countries have reached a stage where the communication technology threatens the very existence of traditional libraries and it is true with the fact that libraries are being digitalized and traditional libraries are slowly waning and give place to emergence of a new type of library known as digital library in other words 'virtual library'.

A developing country like India with sparse resources needs to educate millions of its library users in conceptualizing their information needs and matching them with the resources of the library by comprehensing the methodology of the library. It is generally felt that any invention which does not reach the last man would die a natural death. But in the case of information technology the impact of computer and telecommunication technologies have already become one with the people.

The problem we face today is not of dearth of information, but of excessive information. Almost in all the fields, abstracts are available but even these have become so numerous that abstracts of various abstracting services are necessary. With the deluge of information, the traditional library with its system can not process, store and distribute to the users. Hence there is a need for introduction of microcomputers in the library. The microcomputers have revolutionized the management of information in relation to speed, accuracy, efficiency and effectiveness which was not possible otherwise. The microcomputers with telecommunication technologies have enabled the users to have instant access to digitized information and also provide services like paper to paperless forms including multimedia.

India and Information Technology

With the advent of information technology, information programme like NISSAT, NICNET, INDONET, VIKRAM, INSDOC AND SENDOC are being evolved and generated successfully in India. There are about 20 organizations in India which offer computerized bibliographical information services. Among them, INDONET has an integrated information management and distributed data processing facility spanning the entire country. A new attempt has been made to get database from various national and international organizations and make them accessible on-line through INDONET. And also an international gateway in Bombay is set up with the cooperation of 'Videsh Sanchar Nigam Ltd.' (VSNL) to enable Indian users to access international databases available from LOCKHEED/ DIALOG, SDC/ORBIT ESANT etc.

All is well with the special libraries in India, where the maximum harnessing of information is taking place with the help of information technology. In the case of academic libraries the condition is reversed. The UGC the apex body of universities and colleges in India has financed, only a few universities for implementation of computerization, rest of them are only in infant stage. INFIBNET, a part of UGC is financially assisting only university librarians to automate their library operations. But such facilities are not extended to the college libraries. Though there is a provision of getting Rs one lakh to purchase PCs. from the UGC.

In spite of that, there seems to be very little efforts in the direction of introducing the technological developments in the academic and public libraries in India. This may be due to:

(i) Non - availability of skilled personnel.
(ii) Lack of training opportunities to handle sophisticated tools and machineries.
(iii) Lack of motivation and awareness on the part of the library managers.
(iv) Financial crunch.

Digital Libraries

The digital library concept has emerged very recently and is getting deeply rooted in the field of library and information science. Organizations where information is being handled are increasingly replacing conventional storage, process and retrieval systems with digital systems. On account of discrete analysis of documents, the conversion from manual to digital is inevitable. Hence the digital medium is fast replacing paper in a dramatic revolution.

Digital libraries aim to provide ready access to the store-house of information. Generally the digital libraries specialize in storing a particular subject field of information which will be inter-woven together with the other participating libraries. Digital libraries combine communication technology and information source and allow remote access of its resources to other libraries, by breaking down the physical barriers through national and international computer networks. The suitable example of this is Internet.

Conclusion

In the age of information, easy access to information is an essential prerequisite for the development of a country and access to information is also a hallmark of democracy. Hence, the developing countries like India should make an earnest effort to concentrate more on developing and using new electronic gadgets that provide better access to information.

Twenty Three

Indian Literature on Information Technology: A Bibliometric Study

B. BHAGAVATHI SUDHA *and* DR B. RAMESH BABU

Introduction

Bibliometrics and the application of its laws has been on the increase over the past two decades to highlight the growth of literature in a particular field of knowledge quantitatively. In the recent years the field of information technology is marching ahead with tremendous growth and development. This in turn resulted in the publication of literature on the IT applications to the field of Library and Information Services (LIS). The proliferation of literature has been accommodated in a number of bibliographic forms which calls for the bibliographic organization and control of information.

The literature published by the Indian contributors in a variety of bibliographic forms have been recorded in the "Indian Library and Information Science Literature".[1] The same source has been considered for the purpose of this paper.

Scope and Objectives of this Paper

The major objectives of this paper are as follows:

(i) To assess the extent of literary contribution in the application of Information Technology (IT) on LIS activities.

(ii) To find out the quantum of Indian contributions on this area during the period of 1990-93.

(iii) To study the authorship pattern, collaborative research, nature of and status of the contributors, etc.
(iv) To identify the length of contributions.
(v) To identify the distribution of literature in different forms of publications.

Information Technology: An Overview

Information Technology (IT) is a comprehensive term which describes the whole range of processes for acquisition, storage, transmission, retrieval and processing of documents. It is a combination of several components of technologies, systems which may be grouped as follows:

Computer Technology
Telecommunication systems and services
Micrographics and reprographic technology
Information storage technology

In recent years, the field of IT is marching ahead with tremendous and fast growth and development. The emergence of IT has made various difficult tasks in the field of LIS much easier and faster. Further, the development of microcomputers coupled with telecommunication technology has helped in compact and portable development of software systems.

Analysis and Interpretation of Data

Year-Wise Break-up of Contributions

Table 1 presents the distribution of contributions by year.

TABLE 1
YEAR-WISE BREAK-UP OF CONTRIBUTION

Sl.No.	*Year*	*Number of Contributions*	*Percentage*	*Cumulative Total*	*Cumulative Percentage*
1.	1990	221	23.46	221	23.46
2.	1991	199	21	420	44.59
3.	1992	289	30.68	709	75.27
4.	1993	233	24.73	942	100.00
	Total	942	100.00		

Average number of contributions = 235.5

From Table 1, it is seen that the highest number of contributions of Information Technology and its applications in LIS were published during 1992 (289) and the lowest during 1991 (199). Thus, an average of 235.2 contributions per year were noticed for the period under study. However, there is no significant year-wise growth of publications. There is a slight fluctuation from year to year as seen in Table 1.

Gender of The Contributors

Table 2 presents the gender of contributors or who have published articles in the volumes under study.

TABLE 2
GENDER OF THE CONTRIBUTORS

Sl. No.	*Category*	*Number of Contri-butions*	*Percen-tage*	*Cumulative Total*	*Cumulative Percentage*
1.	Male	1007	83.92	1007	83.92
2.	Female	154	12.83	1161	96.75
3.	Unidentified	39	3.25	1200	100.00
	Total	942	100.00		

On the whole, there were 1200 contributors for 942 contributions. Out of 1200 contributors it becomes difficult for the investigation to judge the gender of 39 persons (3.25%) due to the complexity of the structure of the personal names. From the remaining data, the majority (1007) of the contributors were overwhelmingly by male (i.e. 83.92) females 154 constituting only 12.83%. So this analysis shows that a majority of the Indian literature on Information Technology has been contributed by male professionals in the field of Library and Information Science.

Affiliation of the Contributors

Table 3 presents the affiliation of the contributors as teachers in Library and Information Science or practising librarians. As seen in Table 2 which shows a total of 1200 contributors were scrutinized and it was found that there are 780 individual authors. It means an individual author might have contributed more than once. Thus, the total number of contributors were arrived at 780 for the period under study. These contributors were further classified whether they belong to teachers in Library and Information Science or practising librarian as shown in Table 3.

TABLE 3
AFFILIATION OF THE CONTRIBUTORS

S.No.	*Type of Affiliation*	*No. of Authors*	*Percentage*
1.	Teachers of Library & Information Science	143	18.33
2.	Practising Librarians and others	637	81.67
	Total	780	100.00

From Table 3 it was found that the majority (637) of the contributors (81.67%) are working librarians and other categories. Whereas only 143 (18.33%) belong to teaching community. However, the classification of contributors as teaching and practising librarians is relative. The analysis may be further interpreted that it is the practising librarians who made more contributions in the application of Information Technology to Library and Information Science services and naturally they come to the larger segment of contributors.

Authorship pattern

There were 942 contributions identified in the study on application of Information Technology in Library and Information Science. These were further classified by authorship patterns and the data has been presented in Table 4.

TABLE 4
AUTHORSHIP PATTERN

Sl. No.	*Type of Authorship*	*No. of Contributors*	*Percentage*
1.	Single Author	596	63.27
2.	Two Authors	212	22.51
3.	Three Authors	44	4.67
4.	Four Authors	12	1.27
5.	Corporate Authors	29	3.08
6.	Anonymous	49	5.20
	Total	942	100.00

It is interesting to note from Table 4 that the solo research (single authorship pattern) is in higher degree (596) out of 942 contributors, though collaborative research is dominating in the field of science. A similar finding of solo research is noticed in the analysis of the articles in *JLIS*[1] ILR[2] and Library Science.[3] Further it is also seen that 49 contributions (5.2%) has no authorship details and it is presumed that they may constitute editorials or similar other information where authorship will not be mentioned.

Degree of Collaboration

Table 5 presents the year wise distribution of contributions according to single, double, triple authorship pattern. In Table 4 it was stated that out of 942 contributions, 49 were anonymous. Therefore, in Tables 5 & 6 the data is confined to 864 contributions by single or multiple authorship pattern.

TABLE 5
DEGREE OF COLLABORATION

Sl. No.	*Year*	*No. of Authors*				*Total of Authors in a year*	*Average No. of Auth. per Paper*	*Degree of Collabo-ration*	*Total No. of Contri-bution*
		1	*2*	*3*	*4*				
1.	1990	130	60	14	3	304	1.47	0.37	207
		62.80	28.99	6.79	1.45				
2.	1991	132	23	9	2	233	1.32	0.25	176
		75	18.75	5.11	1.14				
3.	1992	189	65	11	3	364	1.36	0.29	268
		70.52	24.25	4.11	1.12				
4.	1993	145	54	10	4	299	1.40	0.32	213
		68.08	25.35	4.69	1.88				
	Total	596	212	44	12	1200			864

TABLE 6
SINGLE VS. MULTIPLE AUTHORS

Sl. No.	*Year*	*Number of Contribution*	*Single Authors*		*Multiple Authors*	
1.	1990	207	130	21.81	77	28.73
2.	1991	176	132	22.15	44	16.42
3.	1992	268	189	31.71	79	29.48
4.	1993	213	145	24.33	68	25.37
	Total	864	596		268	

The extent of degree of collaboration in research is measured with the help of formula derived by K. Subramanian which reads as follows:

$$C = \frac{Nm}{Nm + Ns}$$

Where C = Degree of collaboration in a discipline
Nm = No. of Multiauthored Research Papers in the discipline published during a certain period.
Ns = No. of single authors research papers in the discipline published during the same period.

The degree of collaboration from the data given in Table 5 is calculated as follows:

$$C = \frac{268}{268 + 596} = 0.310$$

Further the yearwise degree of collaboration in this study is ranging from 0.25 to 0.37

Indian Vs. Foreign Authors

Table 7 provides details about the contributions by Indian authors and foreign authors.

TABLE 7
INDIAN VS. FOREIGN AUTHORS

S.No.	*Type of Authorship*	*No. of Contribution*	*Percentage*
1.	Indian Authors	681	87.31
2.	Foreign Authors	99	12.69
	Total	780	100.00

It is seen that the majority of (681) contributions (87.33%) work by Indian authors. Further it is also interesting to note that 99 contributions (12.69%) are from foreign authors published in Indian sources.

Author vs. No. of Contributions

Table 8 presents the quantum of contributions by an author. It is seen from the Table 8 that the maximum number of contributions (10) were made by one author. Two authors have contributed 9 contributions each. It is further seen that as the number of contributions increases, the number of authors are decreasing and vice versa. Further, it is seen that there are 159 contributions by different authors. In other words, 159 authors produced single contribution.

TABLE 8
AUTHOR VS. NO. OF CONTRIBUTIONS

Sl No.	*Number of Contribution*	*Number of Authors*	*Number of Contribution*	*Percentage*	*Cumulative Total*	*Cumulative Percentage*
1.	10	1	10	1.28	10	1.28
2.	9	2	18	2.31	28	3.59
3.	8	3	24	3.08	52	6.67
4.	7	6	42	5.38	94	12.05
5.	6	6	36	4.62	130	16.67
6.	5	16	80	10.26	210	26.93
7.	4	15	60	7.69	270	34.62
8.	3	47	141	18.08	411	52.70
9.	2	105	210	26.92	521	79.62
10.	1	159	159	20.38	780	100.00
		Total	780	100.00		

Ranking of Authors

Table 9 presents the ranking of authors of the contributions shown is Table 8.

From Table 9 it is seen that the highest number (10) contributions on IT in the period of survey were produced by I.K. Ravichandra Rao and contributed as core author followed by T. Viswanathan and S. Seetharaman with 9 contributions each. By looking at the ranking order first rank was cited to one person and second rank to two persons, third rank to 3 persons and fourth and fifth ranks to 6 persons.

Distribution of Literature in Different Bibliographic Forms

The literature under study has been classified according to the form of publication in which they were published. Accordingly the analysis was presented in Table 10.

TABLE 9
RANKING OF AUTHORS

Sl. No.	*Name of the Authors*	*No. of Contributions*	*CT*	*Rank*
1.	Ravichandra Rao, I.K.	10	10	1
2.	Viswanathan, T	9	19	2
3.	Seetharama, S.	9	28	2
4.	Sewa Singh	8	36	3
5.	Kuldip Chand	8	44	3
6.	Kaul, H.K.	8	52	3
7.	Tejomurthy, A.	7	59	4
8.	Ramaiah, L.S.	7	66	4
9.	Rajasekaran, K.	7	73	4
10.	Laxman Rao, N.	7	80	4
11.	Lahari, A.	7	87	4
12.	Gopinath, M.A.	7	94	4
13.	Vyasamurthy, P	6	100	5
14.	Sen, B.K.	6	106	5
15.	Neelameghan, A.	6	112	5
16.	Mohandas, M.K.	6	118	5
17.	Krishan Kumar	6	124	5
18.	Chowdhury G G	6	130	5
19.	Vaishnav A.A.	5	135	6
20.	Swaroop Rani, B S	5	159	6
21.	Shet. K C	5	145	6
22.	Raman Nair, R	5	150	6
23.	Ramaiah, C.K.	5	155	6
24.	Rama Reddy, E	5	160	6
25.	Prasad, A R D	5	165	6
26.	Prafulla Chandra, T V	5	170	6
27.	Panda Krushna C	5	175	6
28.	Kumar, R P	5	180	6
29.	Kaula, R.P.	5	185	6
30.	Kanakacharya M	5	190	6
31.	Harinarayan, N S	5	195	6
32.	Gupta S.P.	5	200	6
33.	Bose, Kaushik	5	205	6
34.	Ashok Kumar	5	210	6
35.	Others (4 to 1)	570	780	
	Total	780		

TABLE 10
DISTRIBUTION OF LITERATURE IN DIFFERENT BIBLIOGRAPHIC FORMS

Sl. No.	*Form of Publication*	*Number of Contribution*	*Percentage*	*Cumulative Total*	*Cumulative Percentage*
1.	Journals	429	45.54	429	45.54
2.	Conference proceedings	262	27.81	691	73.35
3.	Edited Books	236	25.06	927	98.41
4.	Souvenirs	10	1.06	937	99.47
5.	Newspapers	5	0.53	942	100.00
	Total	942	100.00		

It is seen from Table 10 that journals consist of half of the (429) contributions (45.54%) followed by conference proceedings (262) and in books (236). Thus, literature has mostly been published in journals, conference proceedings and edited books.

Year-wise Break-up of Journal Articles

Table 11 presents the year-wise break-up of journal articles published in the period under survey.

TABLE 11
YEAR-WISE BREAK UP OF JOURNAL ARTICLES

Sl.	*Year*	*Number of Contributions*	*Percentage*	*Cumulative Total*	*Cumulative Percentage*
1.	1990	95	22.14	95	22.14
2.	1991	103	24.01	198	46.15
3.	1992	115	26.81	313	72.96
4.	1993	116	27.04	429	100.00
	Total	429	100.00		

It is seen from Table 11 that there is an increasing trend in the number of contributions published in the journal.

Ranking of Journals

Table 12 presents the ranking of journals which published literature on Information Technology.

The highest (60) number of contributions published in

"International Information Communication and Education" followed by *"NISSAT News letter"* (50) and *"Library Science with a Slant to Documentation and Information Studies"* (44).

TABLE 12
RANKING OF JOURNALS

Sl. No.	*Name of Journal*	*No. of Contributions*	*Ranking*	*Percentage*
1.	International Information Communication and Education	60	1	13.99
2.	NISSAT News letter	50	2	11.65
3.	Library Science with a Slant to Documentation and Information Studies			
4.	Annals of Library Science & Documentation	44	3	7.23
5.	IASLIC Bulletin	27	5	6.29
6.	Indian Journal of Information Science	20	6	4.66
7.	AGLIS Journal	20	6	4.66
8.	University News	19	7	4.43
9.	Herald of Library Science	16	8	3.73
10.	ILA Bulletin	15	9	3.50
11.	Lucknow Librarian	14	10	3.26
12.	Others (from 13 to a Single Contribution)	113	11	26.34
	Total	429		100.00

On the whole about 75 per cent of the literature in periodicals were published in 11 journals ranging from 14 contributions to the maximum of 60 contributions.

Subject Analysis of the Contributions

The field of IT and application of library and information services were broadly grouped into 7 categories for the purpose of study. The contributions were grouped by the subject matter of the contributions and analysed in Table 13.

It is seen from Table 13 that about one-fourth (238) of the total contribution (942) were published, on the subject of

"Networks". This is followed by the publication on "Information Technology - general concepts" has been much favoured by the Contributors.

TABLE 13
SUBJECT ANALYSIS OF THE CONTRIBUTIONS

Sl. No.	*Subject Category*	*No. of Contribution*	*Percentage*	*Rank*
1.	Network	238	25.27	1
2.	Information Technology-General Concepts	207	21.97	2
3.	Database	169	17.94	3
4.	Library Automation	161	17.09	4
5.	Computerised Library Service	97	10.30	5
6.	Software Packages	38	4.03	6
7.	Artificial Intelligence	32	2.40	7
	Total	942	100.00	

Subject-wise Distribution of Literature in Journal

The literature published in journals were analysed subject-wise and data has been presented in Table 14

TABLE 14
SUBJECTWISE DISTRIBUTION OF LITERATURE IN JOURNALS

Sl. No.	*Subject Category*	*No. of Contribution*	*Percentage*	*Rank*
1.	Network	109	25.41	1
2.	Information Technology-General Concepts	103	24.00	2
3.	Database	63	14.69	3
4.	Computerised Library Services	61	14.22	4
5.	Library Automation	49	11.42	5
6.	Software Package	24	5.59	6
7.	Artificial Intelligence	20	4.67	7
	Total	429	100.00	

It is seen from Table 14 that the contributions in journals on Networks (109) has been ranked first followed by Information Technology General concepts (103).

Subject-wise Distribution of Literature in Conference Proceedings

Table 15 presents the subject-wise distribution of literature in conference proceedings.

TABLE 15
SUBJECT-WISE DISTRIBUTION OF LITERATURE IN CONFERENCE PROCEEDINGS

Sl. No.	*Subject Category*	*No. of Contribution*	*Percentage*	*Rank*
1.	Database	65	24.81	1
2.	Network	65	24.81	1
3.	Library automation	52	19.85	2
4.	Information Technology-General concepts	42	16.03	3
5.	Computerised Library Services	21	8.02	4
6	Software Package	9	3.44	5
7.	Artificial Intelligence	8	3.05	6
	Total	262	100.00	

It is seen from Table 15 that literature on 'Data-bases' and on 'Networks' have been ranked first, publishing nearly one-fourth each of the total publications in conference proceedings. This is followed by "Library Automation" with 52 contributions (19.85%). This analysis may be further interpreted that more conferences have been held on Databases, Networks and Library Automation in the period of survey which shows an increasing trends towards the application of IT in Library Information Science.

Subject-wise Distribution of Literature in Edited Books

Table 16 presents subject wise distribution of literature in edited books.

It is seen from Table 16 that the highest number of contributions (54) were published in edited books on "Library Automation" followed by on "Information Technology-general concepts" (48) and on 'Databases' (46)

This analysis further reveals that the publication of edited volumes are mainly concentrated on subjects like 'Library Automation' with second rank, "Information Technology- general concepts" with second rank and 'Databases' with third rank and 'Networks' with fourth rank.

TABLE 16
SUBJECT-WISE DISTRIBUTION OF LITERATURE IN EDITED BOOKS

Sl. No.	*Subject Category*	*No. of Contribution*	*Percentage*	*Rank*
1.	Library automation	54	22.88	1
2.	Information technology-General concepts	48	20.34	2
3.	Database	46	19.49	
4.	Networks	40	16.95	4
5.	Computerised Library Services	25	10.59	5
6.	Software Package	18	7.63	6
7.	Artificial Intelligence	5	2.12	7
	Total	236	100.00	

Conclusion

"Indian Library and Information Science Literature" holds a significant position among the bibliographical tools in Library and Information Science from India. This consolidated analysis of contributions reported in this bibliographical tool over a period of four years (1990-93) throws light on the nature, and quantum of literature generated on Information Technology and its applications in Library and Information Science.

The subject of Information Technology has grown in its strength by publishing large number of contributions in a variety of bibliographical forms. It has now acquired a greater interest to Library and Information Science profession and its growth and development indicates that Information Technology has carved a niche for itself in the field of Library and Information Science discipline.

On the whole, study of this nature presents a scenario before the Library and Information Science professionals for the selection of documents in the field of Information Technology. This will pave the way to conduct similar studies on various branches of

Library and Information Science. Probably a large project can be attempted at doctoral level to analyse the contribution of India Literature on Information Technology from the first volume to the latest volume.

REFERENCES

1. Anand, J.K. Journal of Library and Information Science. 1976-81 : An Analytical study. *Journal of Library and Information Science.* 15 (2) pp. 101-27.
2. Nandini Muthuswamy. International Library Review 1987-1991 : A Bibliometric Study. M.Sc. Dissertation, University of Madras, May 1995 (Unpublished).
3. Prasher, R.G. Library Science with a slant to Documentation and Information Studies; A Bibliometric Study: In *Library and Information Science: Parameters and Perspectives* V2/edited by R.G. Prasher. New Delhi: Concept Publishing Company. pp. 297-313, 1997.

Twenty Four

Multimedia and its Application

M. VIJAYA KUMAR

Introduction

The term multimedia is relatively a new technology concept both in art and technology. Multimedia is truly the fruit of this decade. This word was unheard of by most of us in the last decade and before. The term Multimedia has been used within the computer industry since mid 1980's.

Definitions

Generally multimedia is the fusion of computing with audio-video technology. In other words, computer software which includes the following:

Text	: May be table of contents of entire novels.
Data	: May be statistics, tables, charts, graphs.
Spread Sheets	: Ledgers and others.
Audio	: May be human voice, music, sound effects, etc.,
Graphics	: May be drawings, paintings, prints, maps, blue prints etc.,
Still pictures	: Slides, Transparencies, negatives and others.
Animation	: Covers a vaste range of creative technology and Media from Three-dimensional figures to computer-generated figures.
Moving Pictures	: Moving photographic images.

"We define multimedia as any thing that requires more than two trips to the Car"

Robert May, President of IKNOIC

"Talking about multimedia is a lot like talking about love. Every body agrees that it's a good thing every body wants it, wants to participate in it, but every body has a different idea of what it really is. Right now, the industry reminds me of a bunch of tea bags dubbling in something that instinctively feels right all the while, wondering how and when they will know for sure if they are really in it, and what to do about it if they are.

Georgia Mc Cabe

Hardware and Standards

There is a wide range of technologies from different manufacturers. Actually the word multimedia hardware has no meaning.

CD-ROM

8X speed, 16X with remote with installation diskettes.

"CD-ROM holds six hundred digitised colour photographs, which itself are inadequate for storing moving images. [It will hold a mere fourty eight seconds of video]. Actually it has a capacity to hold two lakhs fifty thousands pages of machine-readable text."

CD-Interactive Titles

Compact disc-interactive scheduled in 1992. It is delayed because of failure to implement full motion. Software may be game to self instruction programmes.

CD-Writer

Through this we can write the information from the CD's to another, i.e., duplication of CD's.

CD-Extended Architecture

It is a bridge media for CD-I and CD-ROM.

Commodore Dynamic Total Vision

It is strong competitor of CD-I. It came to existence to the market in April, 1991. Here audio CD drive is attached to the television set.

Digital Video Interactive

Digital video interactive technology will run initially under DOS, OS/2 and Unix and Win-95 according to microsoft. It has net working capabilities.

Configuration

A full multimedia PC level 2 system requires the following elements and components, all of which must meet the full functional specifications.

CPU	:	100 MHZ, Pentium 133 MHZ
RAM	:	8 MB of RAM [16 MB recommended]
Magnetic Storage	:	Floppy drive, hard drive [540 MB minimum] 8 MB RAM
Optical Storage	:	CD-ROM double speed with CD-DA out puts, XA ready, multi sections capable.
Audio	:	16 bit ADC music synthesizer on board analog audio mixing.
Video	:	Display resolution of at least 640*480 with 65,536 [64K] colours.
Input	:	101/104 key boards [or functional equivalent]; two button mouse.
I/O	:	Serial port, parallel port, MIDI I/O port, Joystic port
System Soft ware	:	Binary compatibility with windows 3.0 plus multimedia extension or windows 3.1.

Applications

Multimedia's services are utilized in multifields. It is suitable for whenever and wherever people need access to electronic information of any type. Most commonly multimedia is used in:

Business
Schools/Colleges
Houses
Public Places
Libraries
Sports and Entertainment

Multimedia in Business

The application of multimedia in business are in the fields of marketing, advertising, presentations, training, product demonstrations, databases, catalogues, network communications, voice mail, conference, (conference is provide through local area net work and wide area network).

Multimedia in training has become common. The manager can describe the process of making the product, used in making the badging and identity card database. A new generation of interactive television and networked multimedia on line business to business services is evolving. These services delivered through interactive television and networked multimedia. These cases are much easier to construct, have short payback periods and require less investment than residential service proposal.

Multimedia in Houses

Television/VCR are platform for multimedia project at home, because currently television enjoys much higher penetration than home computers. The multimedia viewed on these sets will likely arrive on a pay-and-use basis. However, a computer with an attached CD-ROM drive can become a platform for multimedia projects.

Home computers are rapidly emerging as multimedia platform because of:

— Present users/people are becoming familiar with computer.
— Marketing of home computers reach saturation point.
— Game software developers are not far behind.
— The incremental cost of adding CD-ROM drive and sound board to a home computer is now almost marginal.

Multimedia in Schools/Colleges

Multimedia has made a great change in the traditional teaching methods. In present times, the teachers have become just guides or supervisors. In laboratory the students can do experiments themselves through multimedia. The teacher is merely a supervisor to explain the process.

Multimedia in Public Places

Multimedia provides information and helps the people/ tourists in hotels, railway stations, bus stations, shopping complex, museums, etc. This installation may replace the traditional information booths and personnel soon. The user/people can access it any time round the clock whenever he wants information or help.

Multimedia in Sports

Multimedia plays a dominant role in training sportsmen. Through this we can train the sports man all the traditional methods. The wrestler can learn how to use the techniques in the matches. He can see the great matches through which he can understand what precautions are to be taken. The training may be given through slides or transparency.

Multimedia for Entertainment

We can use multimedia like the radio/tape recorder to listen the news, song, it can be used as a newspaper to know the current awareness (through internet), it can be used as a television for entertainment. Through this we can see games as well as play the games. Cartoon films can also be viewed.

Multimedia in Library

Present multimedia applications can be categorized into computer aided learning and computer base training. Through computer-aided learning the doors of information are opened to the user. Information is provided on various subjects like: What are the information sources available and what are the information services provided to the user. How to use the catalogue in searching the information, which issue system classifies the documents in library and which are the rules and regulations to be followed. We can get information about the library without actually visiting it.

Conclusion

Multimedia is revolutionary and will change our lifestyle. A revolution is taking place today in the way humans access, learn and interact with information, simple multimedia applications will soon become standard items of stock in libraries. More complex systems will require serious resourcing financial managerial and technical.

REFERENCES

1. Ayre, J (et. al.): *Multimedia Year Book 1995*. Interactive media publications, 1995.
2. Grimshaw, A.: Multimedia - The Midas Touch. *Information Management and Technology*, Vol. 128. No. 2, March, 1995.
3. Martin, G.: Multimedia; technology, looking for an application. *ASLIB*. Vol. 20 No. 4, Apr. 1992.
4. Ozer, J.: *Video Compression for Multimedia*, Academic Press Professional, 1995.
5. Tay V.: *Multimedia Making it Work*. 2nd ed. New York, McGraw Hill, 1994.

Twenty Five

Internet: The Network of Networks

DR B.K. CHOUDHARY *and* B.B.CHAND

Introduction

Today, communication technology is rapidly playing a vital role in the development of society. In earlier days vocal and pictorial methods were mainly used for communication. But nowadays these primitive methods have given way to electronic pulses. Using computer, telephone links and microwave radio transmission, a vast amount of data is being transmitted within a few seconds. Speedy access to information is now being possible through computer networks. Internet is also a network of computers which provides information in the fields of business, education, military science, governmental and non-governmental organizations. Internet is now developing as the major way of communication media in the present society. So before going to Internet, let us discuss what actually is meant by Computer Network?

Computer Network

The old model of a single computer serving all the organizational computational needs is rapidly being replaced by one in which a large number of separate but interconnected computers do this job. These systems are called computer networks. Thus a computer network is:

— a system of interconnected computer based telecommunication systems and terminals.

— a system in which one mode is connected to another mode.

The main aim of computer network is the easy and quick communication of information. Through computer network it is possible to send information and receive feedback from the other one. Also we can say networking is a system with predominant flow of service and reverse flow of demand.

Types of Computer Network

A network can mean a small group of ten to twenty PCs that have been linked together in a small office, or a few hundred computers of different types spread around the world which have been linked together for exchange of information. Thus, networks vary widely in their size, complexity and geographical spread. On this basis, network can be classified as follows:

Local Area Networks (LANs)

LANs are computer networks connected to localised areas in an office, an office complex or factory. They connect computers and allow exchange of data. The work station in LAN are connected with each other through cables.

Metropolitan Area Networks (MANs)

MANs are computer networks that link computer facilities within a city or a metropolitan city. In MANs, the work stations are connected through microwaves or radio waves.

Wide Area Networks (WANs)

WANs are spread over countries and even across the seas. They are characterized by the long distance over which they operate. WANs, by definition involves electronic communication among remote users, some of whom may be hundreds of kilometres away from the central host. In WANs, the computers are connected through satellite communications

Need of Computer Network

The first and foremost advantage of computer network is resource sharing and its aim is to make all programs, data, equipment, and information available to any one on the network irrespective of either the physical location of the resource or the users.

The next goal is to provide high reliability by having alternative resources of supply. For instance, all the files could be replicated on two or more machines. So if one of them is unavailable, the other copies could be used.

The other goal is to save money. Small computers have a much better price performance ratio than larger ones.

The last goal of computer network is to provide a powerful communication medium among widely separated people. A network can communicate people remaining far away from each other quickly.

Internet

Internet is the network which is being developed by the cooperative interconnection of thousands of computer.networks. Internet is the jargon which was being coined from the word 'interconnection' and 'network'. Hence Internet can be defined as network of computers, usually made up of different kinds and varied technologies are put together in such a way that they appear as a single network. It is the global computer and communication system linking millions of businesses, organizations and private users. A user having Internet access can communicate to another user on the Internet anywhere in the world just like one communicates with the help of ISD telephone call. A huge amount of information can be accessed through the Internet from any where in the world, that is why Internet is also known as 'Internet Super Highway'.

Genesis of Internet

In the year 1957, Department of Defence (DoD) of the United States formed the Advanced Research Projects Agency (ARPA) to look after all the R & D projects going around the US. In the year 1969, the DoD moved a step forward to develop a network to make connection with all the R & D organizations, institutions and universities which are engaged in research funded by Ministry of Defence through the Computer Media. This network was known as ARPA net (Advanced Research Projects Administration

Network). The main aim behind the development of this network is the sharing of information between the agencies and the software and hardware that they could not afford. After getting huge success, the network was broken into two parts. One is the MILNET which manages all the Military Affairs and the new and smaller ARPANET manages all other affairs. During the 1970's other networks like BITNET, and the USENET came into being. In the year 1986, a network called the NSFNET (National Science Foundation Network) was formed which constitutes all the works. At that time, the backbone speed of NSFNET was 56 Kbps only. The NSFNET allows all the universities and research institutions to link up with its super computer. In 1992, WWW (World Wide Web) was released and NSFNET upgrades its backbone to 44736 Mbps. This growing web proves the birth of Internet.

Who Governs Internet

There is no permanent governing body to look after the functioning of the Internet. But there is an authority which is known as "Internet Society" or "ISOC" which takes the charge of the maintenance of Internet. ISOC is a voluntary membership organization whose purpose is to promote global information exchange through Internet technology. It appoints a council of invited volunteers called the Internet Architecture Board, or the IAB which has the responsibility for the technical management and direction of Internet. The IAB meets regularly to formulate standard which is required, it considers the problem, adopts a standard, and announces it via the network. Internet users express their options through meeting of the Internet Engineering Task Force (IETF). The IETF is also a voluntary organization and meets regularly to discuss operational and technical problems of the Internet. IETF can only recommend the solution to the problem and the final decisions are being taken by IAB.

Internet Users

The majority of Internet users are the students, other users being teachers, scientists, executives, corporate employees, government employees, businessmen, librarians and researchers. It is of immense help to researchers, because by sitting at one place they can make connection with other scientists about problems in their field, if any, and may get information about the earlier research that has been made in that field. Government officials and business men can contact officials or partners who are abroad and can have meetings with them. That is why it is now frequently being used by such types of users.

Hardware and Software Requirements

The hardware required to access the Internet are a PC, for using graphic user interface, the hardware should be PCAT-486 or higher with SVGA monitor. The hard disk should also have large capacity to down load files. The modem which is a mediator should be a good one having the capacity of at least 9600 bps. The communication software are Telix, Procomm Plus or PC Plus to access the service provided. In the windows environment Terminal Program can be used.

Ways to Access the Internet

Because the internet was not being maintained by a particular body, there is no standardized way to connect to it. Each network is responsible for providing easy access to their users. The two ways of accessing internet are :

Dedicated Access

In this type of accessing, the computer is linked directly to the internet and connected to it for 24 hours a day. Usually large companies which are mainly meant for commercial purpose have such connection. Dedicated lines are more expensive because it needs special hardwares.

Dial-Up Access

There are two methods for accessing internet through a service provider.

IP Accounts (SLIP or PPP Account)

SLIP stands for Serial Line Internet Protocol and PPP stands for Point to Point Protocol. PPP connections are faster than SLIP. A SLIP or a PPP connection is similar to a dedicated line, the only difference is that they have to access through a service provider.

Shell Accounts

Shell Accounts are another access method through which the service providers offer internet access gateway through their own system. With this type of system, a fixed hour of service is provided to a particular user and the user has to pay an annual charge for the service.

Cost of Accessing

Rs 5000 has been charged per annum to each professional who wants to access the Internet and the limit of using the Internet is 250 hours in a year. He can access it through 9.6 Kb Dial-up method. For commercial and non-commercial (Colleges, Universities and Non-Governmental Organizations) the cost is little higher and they can also access in both the access methods, i.e., Dedicated and Dial-Up. There is also a nominal charge for students of Rs 500 for 250 hours per annum. The price table is mentioned as under:

TABLE 1
PRICE TABLE OF INTERNET CONNECTIONS

Category	*Dial Up*		*Leased line*		
	9.6 KB	*24 KB*	*9.6 KB*	*64 KB*	*128 KB*
Professional	5,000	—	—	—	—
Commercial	25,000	1,50,000	6,00,000	15,00,000	25,00,000
Non-Commercial	15,000	60,000	2,40,000	6,00,000	10,00,000

Internet Address

Because millions of computers are attached to each other through internet to keep track with individual senders and receivers, internet protocol addressing system is used. Each computer on the network is called a host and has a name and number. The address is a series of words separated by dots.

The example cited below is for better clarity and understanding of the addressing system :

Pratap @ Ayurbedic. Org.

The word before the symbol '@' is meant for user known as Account field. The last word which constitute three characters is most important and is known as domain field. The rest words are known as sub domain field. Thus the naming structure is:

account @ subdomain domain

In our example

account → Pratap
subdomain → ayurbedic
domain → org.

The domain field is divided into seven major categories. These are as follows:

Abbreviation	*Represents*
edu	Educational Institution
mil	Military sites
gov	Government departments
net	Networking Organizations
com	Commercial Organizations
int	International Organizations
org	Professional Organizations

This addressing system also uses country codes which consists of two first letters of that country. For example, In for 'India', Ar for for 'Argentina' etc. This naming system is known as Domain Naming System (DNS).

There is also another addressing system where numbers are used instead of words. This series of numbers are known as dotted quad and are separated by dots. The number in between two dots is known as octate and cannot exceed 256. Example 212. 157. 168.

Services Provided on Internet

In the last two decades, Internet has grown enormously and every year new and easier methods for accessing information are being developed. The services which are generally provided by internet are:

E-mail

E-mail stands for electronic mail. This service is frequently being used by the Internet users. This service is just like a regular mail service. Whenever any person accesses internet, he is also provided with an E-mail address. Through this address he can be contacted by any of the other internet user.

FTP (File Transfer Protocol)

This application is used to transfer files between hosts. The files which are being created by other internet users can down load to his server by another Internet user through the FTP, but there should be an account with them. Several FTP sites permit the users to access their required file without establishing an account with them. These sites are known as anonymous sites. We can log in to such a machine by entering "anonymous". While login it will ask for password, and the password is the E-mail address.

Telnet

Through telnet remote login is possible, anybody can connect to a network of which he may not be a user. Telnet allows to communicate with a wide variety of remote system. Telnet is mainly used to access databases. This service is mostly used by the libraries for searching the resources of other libraries for the documents needed by their clienteles.

News groups

Through news group, it is possible to make group discussions on any topic that might be a general problem. A scientific research problem; or problems relating to political and social crisis about a particular country. There are some news groups which can be accessed by any Internet server whereas for others, we have to subscribe which cannot be forwarded to others.

Other Tools Through which Internet Services are Provided

Gophers

Gopher is an Internet based system through which retrieval of documents is possible. It was developed by University of Minnesota. Gophers allow the hosts to access information in the form of text, images, sound from any part of the world which are connected through Internet. It is a menu driven software tool which is quite easy to operate also.

Veronica

VERONICA is the abbreviated form of Very Easy Rodent Oriented Network wide Index to Computer Archives. It was developed by University of Nevada by Steve Foster and Fred Barrie. It is an index to titles and Internet Gopher items. It provides Keyward search to these titles. A VERONICA search typically searches all the gopher services and once the file is located, it allows to browse through them. It is being updated fortnightly. It is also a menudriven software tool.

Archie

Archie is another tool which allows the user to locate their required files and directories on anonymous FTP. The user has no enter the file name or partial file name and Archie will search the file which may be in the form of text, graphics or sound. The Archie database can be accessed through a local client, telnet or through E-mail.

Wais

Through Wais (Wide Area Information System), textual information can be collected from any database. The search is being carried out through the indexed keywords. WAIS does not respond to the and/or/not operators. It gives the information only if the required file perfectly matches.

World Wide Web (WWW)

The World Wide Web is a series of servers which are interconnected through hypertext. Indexed information are presented through the hypertext. By selecting any one indexed topic, it is easy to get more information about that particular topic. We can access the web through the web browser softwares like Mosaic, Netscap or Microsoft Internet Explorer. Home page which is the indexed page of any organization or information resource helps to extract the required information. Web not only stores the textual information but also high quality of graphics, sound and video are embedded within it. Web also offers another service - a URL or Uniform Resource Locator which defines a universal locator mechanism for data resident anywhere on the "Net".

Finger

It is a command which allows any one to find out others login name if he knows the computer he uses.

Mosaic

It is a primary means of window-shopping for net-surfing on the Net. It also supports Gopher, FTP, Telnet, and WAIS, and is one of the primary reasons for the increasing use and popularity of the Internet for business and commercial purpose.

Internet in India

In India, Internet access is made available by Videsh Sanchar Nigam Limited (VSNL), through its Gateway Internet Access Service (GIAS) on 15th August, 1995. Subscribers can access Internet by making contact in VSNL offices. Leased lines can be accessed directly from VSNL whereas dial up access can be available by INET a pack switched data network of DoT. Those who do not have INET also access the Internet through nearest INET via a special, low tariff long distance number (099). VSNL is accessing Internet through 2x64 Kbps lines. In Bombay there are 32 dial up lines whereas in all other metros and in Bangalore and Pune there is a 6 dial up line with 64 kbps backbone. The Computer Society of India urges upon the Department of Telecommunication to link up all villages with INTERNET.

Internet and Libraries

The main motto of modern libraries is to provide better information resources and quicker answers to the users. This is not possible without an efficient network to meet the present needs of the users. To meet the research function of the academic and research libraries, the librarian has to go to the doors of other libraries for the required document or information. Internet is the network which can meet the needs of the libraries.

The traditional library services which waste a lot of time of the users are now being replaced by the electronic or computer based services. Through Internet, we can provide the traditional library services in a new way i.e. electronically within a very short time. The communication service and current awareness service which are provided through telephone and exchange of memo traditionally now these services are provided on Internet through E-mail and FTP. The answers to reference service which was taking much time earlier, can be provided within few seconds. Maximum reference queries can be answered by using WAIS (Wide Area

Information Network) or Internet. Through telnet one library can also search the collection of other libraries. The inter-library loan facility becomes easier with the help of Internet. Most of the R & D resources are now available on the superweb. The two important organizations which are providing R&D resources are DIALOG's WWW and Silver Platter. OCLC/Forest Press has created a home page named "Dewey Home Page" which contains OCLC Forest Press Catalogue, Dewey News and Dewey ALA Report as well as 'hot' classification topics and Internet address of on-line catalogues using Dewey. The address of the home page is URL:http/ www.oclc.org/fp). The Classification and Cataloguing Quarterly which is published by Haworth Press Inc. is also now available on WWW's home page.

Conclusion

To conclude, it is evident from the above discussion how the Internet is having a profound impact on library services and what the people can achieve through it. If we have an Internet connection, the information is on our finger tips. We may call the Internet as the information market. When we go to the market for buying things by placing orders we get it. Likewise, by writing few commands or clicking options we can collect information. Now each and every library is interested in accessing the Internet because none other network can provide so much information. The virtual libraries in the Internet is the main resource of the modern libraries now. The librarian can also create their own virtual libraries on Internet. But in the context of Indian libraries, the scenario is quite different. As we know, in the developing countries, like India, the main problem lies with the inadequacy of funds. Though there are nearly 35,000 Internet users in India, there are very few libraries which are having the facility of Internet connection. Hence, it is the responsibility of the librarians and the authorities to take interest and initiative for providing quicker information and reference services through Internet.

REFERENCES

1. Asano, Shochiro. Operation of the Interest backbone. *INCEA*. 12(1) pp. 82-85, 1993.

2. The Asian Age. p. 13, 24, Nov. 1996.
3. Atul, Chitnis. The Interest is here. *PC Quest*. p. 59-64, Sept. 1995.
4. Dutta, Subrat and Dutta, Namita. Internet: A Virtual Library: An Indian Perspective. Information Technology Products of 1990s and Library and Information Centres. XX IASLIC Conference. Lucknow, 1995. Calcutta. pp. 81-87.
5. *Employment News*. pp. 1-2, 16-22 Nov. 1996.
6. *The Hindu*. p. 1, 15 August, 1995.
7. *ILA News letter*. 12(3). p. 7., 1996.
8. Reid (Edna O.F.). Exploiting Internet as an Enabler for Transforming Library Services. *IFLA Journal*. 22(1). pp. 18-26, 1996.
9. *The Telegraph*. p. 9, 15 August, 1995.

Twenty Six

Internet for Academic Libraries: Need of the Hour

K.C.DABAS *and* SHEELA DABAS

Introduction

With the world heading towards the 21st century the Internet is the biggest thing to have happened in the world of computing. Internet is the best flower gifted by Information Technology. It is the latest buzz word among the computer users and users of the information centres nowadays. Everyone, whether he is working in the field of IT (Information Technology) or not, is very anxious to know about it and use it. The Internet revolution reached India two years ago. There are already more than 60,000 Internet connections in India. Apart from accessing information you can also provide information about your library and university on the Internet. The information on the Internet is stored on computers that are called web servers. The Web refers to the World Wide Web (WWW) another name for this seamless 'web of' computer networks. On these web servers of computers are websites, i.e., sites of information. In the websites are home pages of information. A library home page may contain general description of a library. We can think of a home page as a book; a web site a book shelf; a web server as a library and the Internet as library of millions of libraries. Information Super Highway is the global information infrastructure and Internet is the via media to travel that information highway or visit that supermarket of global information. Internet is a world wide computer network that contains a large collection of information which could be made available to you on your computer. The person having Internet connection can retrieve any information of individual interest. Internet does not have any comprehensive index or catalogue to reflect what is contained where. It have software programs called search engines to help in locating the desired information.

What is Internet

Internet the network of networks or global network was established as ARPANET (Advanced Research Project Agency Network) almost three decades ago to meet the research needs of US defence industry. Now it is growing, at a very fast rate of 15% every month and is connected with more than 60,000 networks. Approximately 6 millions computer Hosts are interlinked and about 80 million users are making use of it. No one person runs the Internet and no single organization pays all the costs. There is no Internet corporation. It exists as a result of the cooperation of thousands of people all over the world. It never closes down because of its decentralized structure. It is based on the theory that any computer on the network should be able to talk to any other computer. The computer that requests the document is known as 'client' and the computer that makes the document available is known as a 'server'. Fault tolerance was designed so that a message from one computer to another could travel by any one of the many routes. Internet has a common and standard communication protocol known as Transmission Control Protocol of Internet Protocol TCPIP. It is the most complete learning tool for a group of people with varied educational backgrounds and interests. Teachers, students, business men and other educators can share ideas instantly across vast distances. For scientific and research community, Internet is an essential and indispensable tool. Through internet, scientists can gain and enjoy instant access to the World's most advanced research facilities and discuss their research problems with others working in the same field. For business community internet is the common place where they can discuss and set the business deals without moving from their place.

History of Internet

ARPANET (Advanced Research Projects Agency Network) laid the foundation of today's Internet almost three decades ago. It was established to test the security of a network. In 1982 TCP IP became the protocol suite for ARPANET and led to one of the first references to an "Internet" of connected networks. NSFNET (National Science Foundation Network), known as the backbone of Internet came into existence in 1986 and until 1995 NSFNET was operated by ANS (Advanced Network & Services) a research oriented non-profit company set up by Merit Network, IBM and MCI in 1990 under a cooperative agreement between NSF and Merit. When this contract ended after 1995, the running and maintaining of NSFNET has been taken over by Internet service providers like America On-line MCP and sprint in the United States. On an overall basis II of Internet Engineering Task Forces represented by the government and academic organizations largely governs the Internet.

Hardware and Software Required to Get an Internet Connection

The minimum hardware and software required to get the Internet Connection is as follows:

(a) *Computer:* All types of computers right from PC having DOS or Windows to pentium and the mainframes are suitable for Internet. If one intended to use the Internet for E-mail and transferring files, a text based terminal or a slow or outdated PC will serve the purpose. If one intends to explore World Wide Web (WWW) or play interactive graphic games, it requires fast machines that can handle high resolution graphics.

(b) *Modem:* It is a device that converts the digital signal from a computer into an analog one which is suitable for transmission over the telephone line or other continent communication channels. Every modem is characterized by the speed with which data can be transferred. The faster the modem, the lower the telephone bill will be, and its speed mainly depends on - Baud rate and date compression.

(c) *Telephone:* A dial-up telephone connection STD is needed for the purpose.

(d) *Communication Software:* These days, modems come with

all types of communication software. And if these are not supplied as a part of modem delivery, then it is either exclusively requested from the vendor or Internet is loaded with all kinds freeware and shareware.

(e) *HTML and HTTP:* Hypertext is a way of presenting the information so that you can get it in a non sequential way. It was designed to allow the computer to respond to the nonlinear way that humans think and access information. Hypertext mark up language for formatting the document and hypertext transfer protocol (HTTP) for transmitting the document from one computer to another. A universal resource locator URL is a basic HTML and when embedded in an HTML document, it points directly to another document on the Internet that can be retrieved by HTTP.

Benefits of Internet for Academic Libraries

The main objectives of academic libraries is to promote study, teaching, and learning so that higher educational institutions may be able to produce professionals for all walks of life of a nation. In this direction Internet is playing a very important role in the National Development by extending the following major benefits to the academic community.

- Education: Internet has made geographic distances time zones and language barrier insignificant for academic discussion, group research work, distance education and made the world a global village for all purposes. One could provide the OPACs of Library of Congress and Library on Campus on the same terminal with slight difference and you can be able to search as many sites as possible in a single query.
- Publishing: Internet offers a great bonanza for creative authorship. Internet has brought electronic publishing within the reach of any one with an Internet access or account. It has made convenient for the libraries to publish their home page, information services, sources, in house publications. OPACs databases, announcements on the seminars so that it may be accessible to infinite audience. It helps in upgrading the information.
- Acquisition: Internet helps in acquiring digital material rightly published over Internet.

- Advertising the services and programs of HRD, UGC, universities and academic libraries to community at large.
- Careers: Electronic discussion groups help in professional development and carrier advancement of professionals.
- At the touch of a key one can access a whole range of subjects and can become an expert in self learning.
- World Wide Web has made the librarians navigators to global intellectual resources as well as facilitators, instructors, evaluators, consultants, communicators, managers, researchers and has improved the image of librarians. The universities are trying to be compatible with Internet by amplifying their resources.
- Internet has brought about a new academic culture of understanding and cooperation that PCs alone could not have facilitated before networking.
- Internet is truly a network of best brains which helps in promoting the quality of life of this global village.

Who Maintains Internet?

It would be surprising to know that there is no regular maintenance body for Internet. Instead, there is an organization of Internet users called the Internet Society (ISOC). This organization is completely voluntary and their goal is to promote global information exchange through Internet. This group is responsible for standardizing the technology used to connect, to communicate with, and work with the Internet.

What Can We Do on the Internet?

Believe it, you can perform any task related to the computing or IT. Some of the few topics available on Internet are arts and culture, space and astronomy, travel and geography, international affairs, environment and nature, science and technology, and so on. Using the Internet's vast resources, one can communicate with people from all over the world and about any desired subject of choice. Files can easily be transferred from any remote computer to your computer system. You can get information on virtually any topic imaginable.

Why Internet for Academic Libraries?

In addition to exponential growth of information, financial shortage of staff and varying complex and increasing demand and expectations of users; Information Technology (IT) has completely changed the scenario of global information society. Information sector in general and university libraries in particular are under pressure to provide right information to the right user at right time and also at the right cost. In this environment, networking has become essential for sharing local as well as global informations. To make university truly universal in character NICKNET, ERNET, SIRNET, INDONET, INFLIBNET, etc., and various local area networks are right steps in preparing the ground and stressing the need for global network for academic libraries. Moreover this is more opportune by making it a historic occasion for university libraries to be ready for their entry into 21st century.

Internet and university libraries are not mutually exclusive. Just as library is important for learning, research, teaching and for generation, preservation and transmission of knowledge, so too is Internet. University libraries must be library without walls. Any move to drive a wedge between the Internet and academic libraries would be disastrous.

Major portion of the current information is being produced right over Internet in digital form instead of print or other traditional form. Moreover, many information providers have started to provide information to end users from single workstations. In such environment, university libraries have an onerous responsibility to collate, distribute and be a depository of local information, talent and research to the world community and global information to the local academic community.

For internationalization of higher education, scholarship, and globalisation of knowledge and information, Internet is the need of the hour. Every member of the academic community and every citizen who pays taxes and fees has every right to know about the latest development in his field of study or for the university going member of his family.

Moreover, academic libraries are under an obligation to go for Internet for the following reasons:

- How to provide a piece of information on a given topic to the right scholar or faculty at the right time and also at the right cost?

- How could convenient linkages be created among books and articles in different but related field.
- How should books be arranged for optimal use?
- House should library books be integrated into the university's programs of instruction?
- What kind of catalogue system could be invented to allow rapid access to the collection.
- How to help the researchers in reducing the duplication of efforts by providing the current details. For doing more with less access to Internet must be there to supplement local collection.
- The quality movement in the commercial sector has also started making inroads in information sector. For the satisfaction of all the fundamental laws and philosophies of library science and also for the satisfaction that every author has his contribution to the library and every reader must have his library.

Internet Resources for libraries

On-line library catalogue

A Gopher offers access to the libraries with library catalogues in different countries. The Internet gives access to the bibliographic records of millions of books, and details on the holdings of academic and research libraries around the world. One can also check on new and interesting titles and even order them form a number of libraries.

Electronic Journals and Newsletters

There are hundreds of electronic journals and newsletters on the Internet. These journals are like printed counterparts in that they appear on a regular schedule, have a team of editors and reviewers and focus on a specific topic. Many publish original research, some electronic journals appear in both paper and electronic editions including the bi-weekly newspaper, *The Scientist* and the journal, *Post-Modern Culture*. Traditional newspapers are becoming available on certain networks but they are not yet accessible on the layer network.

Discussion Lists

There are hundreds of electronic discussion lists and conference proceedings available over the Internet. They give users direct access to scholars in disciplines they are interested. Discussion lists give users an opportunity to ask or offer help.

Internet Library Services Through NICNET

In India, access to Internet for libraries is possible through NICNET, a National Informatics Centre Network. With more than 700 MES (micro earth stations) nodes have been spread all over the country. The following are Internet connectivity's through NICNET.

RENNIC

NICNET offers E-mail to researchers and educational networks with a nominal annual subscription fee of Rs 2700 and Rs 1000 for registration. Now for the universities the registration is limited to Rs 300.

Mail only Connection

This is the simplest way to get Internet E-mail link through UUCP (Unix-to-Unix Copy) connectivity to any NICNET nodes on dial-up. The main-only connections are links that enable one to send and receive E-mail and bulletin-board services (BBS).

Shell Account Dial-up Connection

With the dial-up terminal connection, one links to an Internet node of NICNET as a terminal on the NICNET computer and set up a shell account which uses a Unix a command line. The Internet access software e.g. Telnet, FTP, etc., are run on the NICNET node.

WEB

Centre for World Wide Web (C-Web) service over NICNET becomes the first Web server in the country to navigate through Internet for exchanging multimedia documents between computer users internationally. NICNET has now woven the entire country into one single communication entity for reaching out to the world at large without technical barriers.

SLIP/PPP on Demand Direct Connection

A variant of TCP/IP designed for telephone lines is called Serial Time Interface Protocol or the Point-to-Point Protocol (PPP). With one of these and a modem connection to an Internet site of Nicnet mode, we can have a link that makes one's computer a full Internet participant.

Basis WEB Server

NICNET brings the most advanced WWW server technology in the world through Basis Web Server installed on its National Information Highway. Basis Web allows users to access Internet Features given below.

Searching, Display, Publishing Data Management, Data Validation Basis Plus Accessibility.

Applications of Internet

Internet being a network of networks spread world-wide is capable of offering the following major services.

(a) E-mail
(b) Mailing Lists
(c) Usenet News Groups
(d) WWW (World Wide Web)
(e) Miscellaneous Tools

E-mail

E-mail is the most popular activity on the Internet. There are about 4.62 million E-mail boxes world wide almost a quantum growth of 84 per cent in E-mail sites during 1991-93. Service providers deliver E-mail connectivity by linking together all those who wish to send or exchange messages. By using a system that can generate millions of unique addresses, Internet's addressing scheme is called the Domain name System which creates addresses including name, geographical location and other conceptual information.

An Internet address would be read as nsg @ gillcompany.com where "nsg" stands for the name of the user, "gillcompany" would represent the name of the organization and com symbolize that the user is a commercial user. The last entry would vary depending on the user classifications. The domain extension mentioned below signify the corresponding description:

com : Commercial user for business organization
net : Network sites e.g. VSNL, USNET
gov : Government e.g. Parliament House
edu : Educational e.g. universities colleges
mil : Military e.g. Ministry of Defence
org : Non-commercial organization

In case of geographical location of the server the address would carry an extension, for example, in for India uk for United Kingdom hk for Hong Kong and so on.

Mailing Lists

The activities of the Internet mailing-lists communities are managed world-wide by List-servers. The server acts like a grant message particular for a group. Any message posted by any member is automatically broadcasted to the E-mail box of every person on the mailing list. To join the mailing-list one can send an E-mail message that includes one's own E-mail address to the list server.

Usenet NewsGroups

Network News Transport Protocol (NNTP) servers around the globe, host NewsGroups that share information and commentary on defined topics. The basic building block of the Usenet is the NewsGroup, which is a collection of messages with related theme. Each group takes the form of a large bulletin board where members post and reply messages, creating messages threads. Nearly 10,000 groups are replicated to all the servers so that the group members may tap the discussion from any server.

World Wide Web (WWW)

WWW offers facilities to the users to share information with others. The WWW servers can publish text and graphics including sound and video. This is the fastest growing part of the Internet. The Web is a vast network of documents and it also gives access to every Internet service, including FTP and News. One of the best way to let the world know about what you have to offer is to advertise and in this age of the Internet, advertising means putting up WWW pages. The WWW servers are designed to handle documents created using HTML (Hyper Text Markup Language) format. What makes the HTML documents unique is their ability to include hypertext links that facilitates rapid access to: other locations within the same document (other documents on the same site) and documents at another site. This capability makes the Web so powerful. HTML also supports internal references to external objects, such as image files. The Web is based on HTTP (Hyper Text Transmission Protocol) which supports a client server model. The protocol covers operations ranging from simple get commands, to complex authentication mechanisms. HTTP is currently specified to run on top of TCPIP. To connect a WWW, a Web address is required. URLs (Universal Resource Locations) are the equivalent to E-mail address. URLs come in many forms and can represent a hypertext page, mailservers, gopher server, FTP server or Telnet connection.

Miscellaneous Tools

Various types of operations may be desired by the information seeker on the Internet. There are numerous tools to perform the specified task on Internet, which facilitate the user. Prominent tools are briefly discussed below :

File Transfer Protocol (FTP)

FTP is a tool to copy files from remote host to one's host and vice-versa. It has made it possible to set up public accessible archives on Internet with all links documents and software. Its access is granted to everyone under the user name anonymous using the E-mail address as the password.

Gopher

Gopher was developed at the University of Minnesota and is menu-driven application that allows one to move around the globe looking for information in various information centres or libraries or servers. Gopher actually goes out, gets the information desired and puts the information on the screen.

Archie

This system enables locating files on the anonymous FTP servers on the Internet. It is actually a collection of servers on the Internet. All of the Archie servers talk to each other and they pool the information into a huge, global database that is periodically updated.

Veronica

It is a search tool that allows one to quickly scan Gopher space for particular files and directories. It is a program that one can access through Gopher.

Mosaic

A Web browser like Mosaic brings the way Internet is used into a new era. It provides an easy way to reach audio, video, text and graphics.

WAIS (Wide Area Information Server)

It was developed by a company called Thinking Machines. It allows users to search indexed text on a number of servers. With WAIS, one uses a computer to search in natural language among all the servers and indexed documents.

Internet in India

Internet was available for some time through ERNET and it was made available for commercial use by VSNL since August 1995. Presently VSNL operates in the following six metros: New Delhi, Chennai, Calcutta, Mumbai, Bangalore, Pune. The membership and networking rules are controlled by VSNL. VSNL has its own leased lines to USA where the Indian network is connected to the main Internet network. VSNL is India's international telecom carrier, has the high speed Internet back bone. VSNL offers three types of membership to any user to be connected to Internet. The three types of Internet accounts are:

(a) Shell account
(b) TCP/IP account
(c) Website or Homepage

Shell Account

It is usually subscribed by students and other members who want to access technical information in any branch of knowledge. The information is available only in text mode and no graphics and pictures are available. One can send E-mail to others on Internet, obtain information about latest research papers of various universities, search for product information, having on-line discussion, float questions to be answered by others, find out the latest news on any topic. Shell account is more useful and cheaper. It requires very small hardware set up and the membership is economical. The membership fee are Rs 500 for students and Rs 5000 for a professional per year and Rs 25,000 for an installation.

TCP/IP account

TCP/IP account provides the same advantages as that of shell account plus it provides unlimited access to Internet. It requires UNIX-Based machine. 1.2 GB of Hard-disc, 16-32 MB of RAM and SVGA-VGA monitors and TCP/IP software for better results. It provides an access to graphics, games, movies and other multimedia products along with text and chapters. The membership fee for this account to an educational institution is Rs 15,000 and Rs 500 for registration.

Website or Homepage

Website makes a user as a node of Internet. This means that if a university decides to float its own Website, then all information regarding admissions, scholarships, rules and regulations, courses it offers, departments, staff and their profiles, workshops, conferences, seminar and symposia to be conducted, etc., can be kept at University's Internet centre. This computer can be accessed by any member on Internet for any particular course. It will be automatically listed with all its details. The Website is important to a university and its libraries to offer 24-hours service and on-line help to international clients.

Developing a Website on Internet is a costly affair as far as hardware and other costs are concerned. There are no set of rules and regulations for granting Website by VSNL. Homepages can have text, graphics, pictures and animation. Some homepages can add sound and give multimedia capabilities. Any access to a homepage is called a "hit". The more popular the homepage, the more hits it will receive Homepages can be grouped together in any order and be hyperlinked.

Problems

Lack of required information infrastructure is the biggest problem for academic libraries. The libraries are not treated as sacred cows in academic institutions. The tools such as gopher, WWW and Archie, etc., are designed by computer scientists who are seldom accustomed with collection, organization, processing and dissemination of knowledge. As yet multimedia elements are not fully integrated. To create electronic home page is very expensive compared to traditional printed material. Internet information system is of distributed nature. Every resource has its own information retrieval system. Staff resistance to change, lack of training is also creating hurdles in accessing Internet benefits.

Conclusions

Internet is a cooperative effort with decentralized structure. It is a global network through which one computer can talk to any other computer. Internet is the need of the hour specially in the large information centres such as academic libraries so as to extend the best possible services to its readers. Universities should go for Internet for providing exhaustive, accurate and uptodate services to academic community instantly. Keeping in view the utilities of Internet, special connections and permission should be given to academic libraries for developing information infrastructure. INFLIBNET, in spite of its limited resources is making sincere efforts in this direction.

REFERENCES

1. Fazzuludm. S.I. and Chikkamallaiah. Services for Indian libraries In Meeting the Information Challenge of Development and Self Sufficiency Papers 17th National Seminar of IASLIC, 10-13 Dec, 1996, Calcutta 1996, pp. 63-65.
2. "Internet opens new avenues," *Contemporary Academician* 7 (17) Dec, 1-15, 1997.

3. Kamaiah. P., "Internet and university libraries in developing educatio and research", In A.L. Moorthy & P. B. Mangla (Eds.): *Information Technology Applications in Academic Libraries in India* Papers 4th National conversation CALIBER, R-97, Patiala Mar. 6-8, 1997, 159-162.
4. Rajashekhar, T.B. "Internet Services: An introduction" *DESIDOC Bulietin of Information Technology* 16(3) 1996 : 20.
5. Rajashekar, T.B. "Internet and libraries" In A.L. Moorthy and P.B. Mangla (Eds.), *Information Technology Applications in Academic Libraries in India*. Papers 4th National Convention CALIBER-97, Patiala, Mar. 6-8 1997, pp. 118-23.
6. Stewart, Barbare, "Internet Advantages for the Technical Services Librarian" *DESIDOC Bulletin of Information Technology* 16(3) 1996.
7. Tewari R.K. & Gupta G.S. "Internet : An Introduction", *CSI Communications* Oct. 1996: 8-11.
8. Tewari R.K. & Gupta G.S. "The Wonders of Internet", *Employment News* XXI(33) Nov. 1996: 16-22.
9. Venugopal, S., "Internetising the academic research library system; Need of the hour for hour of need" In A.L. Moorthy and P.B. Mangla (Eds.), *Information Technology Applications in Academic Libraries in India*. Papers 4th National Convention CALIBER-97, Patiala, Mar. 6-8 1997, pp. 137-41.
10. Wolinksy, Judi, "Internet Sites of Librarian's Interest", *DESIDOC Bulletin of Information Technology* 16(3) 1996 : 21-28.

Twenty Seven

Statistical Methodologies in Library and Information Science Research

PADMA V. UPADHYAY

Introduction

Research is defined as a systematic self critical enquiry. Research methodologies contain body of scientific strategies and methods which are useful in the research process. Statistics is a tool in the research methodology to obtain the result from the data obtained through different types of data collection process. Since 1940's statistics has been applied in the library and information science discipline which is now being studied as bibliometrics/ informetrics. It can be said that the application of statistical methodologies and techniques in the library and information science research is very recent. Very few studies can be found until 1980's where the statistical methodologies have been applied in our country.

Statistical techniques can be applied to study both quantitative data and qualitative data obtained during research process. Few common statistical terms which are used are population, variable, mean, median, mode, geometric mean, harmonic mean, mean deviation, standard deviation, probability, probability distribution, correlation, rank correlation, sampling, hypothesis, etc.

Basically statistical methodologies are used in the library and information science research as a tool in designing the research project, analysis of data and drawing conclusions therefrom. Analysis of the data is one of the crucial processes to obtain the result and also to test the hypothesis formulated during the study. These methodologies can also be applied to study the routine library activities and the quality of library and information services provided to the users, in order to improve the quality of service and library activity. Therefore, one can not neglect or ignore the study and understanding of basic statistical techniques and methodologies even though he/she may not have the occasion to use statistical methods in all their activities.

In this paper an attempt has been made to describe few important non parametric statistical tests which can be applied and used in the library and information science research which mainly include data collection process through survey, interviewing, field study, case study and experimental methods.

Qualities of Data Obtained to Adopt Statistical Methodologies

To apply the statistical methodologies in Library and Information Science research, in order to draw conclusion from the data obtained, it is necessary that the data obtained must have the following qualities.

(a) Appropriateness
(b) Clarity
(c) Measurability
(d) Compatibility

Appropriateness is determined by the purpose of a study. Clarity implies precision and simplicity. The data must be able to express the objectives and quantitative form, since they are used for counting and measuring. The data must be defined in such a way as to make them comparable with units of similar studies.

Why Statistics in Library and Information Science Research

As mentioned, statistical methodologies enable the researcher to draw authentic conclusions from the data obtained. Though tabulation and clarification of data enables one to get some idea about the objectives to be achieved to some extent, it fails to draw conclusion where a sample of data is studied. One may not be able to generalize the results obtained. Statistical methodologies allow librarians to obtain maximum amount of information from their research. Here statistical methodologies help one to generalise the process. The application of statistical methodologies also enables one to measure the statistical average or central tendency, measure of dispersion (i.e. variance and its square root, standard deviation, etc.), measure of skewness or asymmetry, and measure of relationship.

Types of Statistical Tests

The statistical methodologies or tests are grouped into two types:

(a) Parametric tests

(b) Non parametric tests

In parametric tests, we assume certain properties of the parent population from where we draw samples. Assumptions like observations from a normal population, sample size, assumptions about the population parameters like mean, variance, etc., must hold good before parametric tests. In parametric tests it is assumed that the source of data is to be normally distributed. The important parametric tests are z test, t test, F test, and Chi square test (Chi square test is also used as a test of independence and as a test of goodness of fit in which case it is a non parametric test). As a parametric test, Chi square test is based on the parameters like mean and standard deviation.

In a non parametric test, assumptions are not made, about the parameters of the population and about the parameter of distribution. Therefore, non parametric tests are also called 'Distribution free test'. Few important parametric tests are: Chi square test, rank correlation test, Kendall's co-efficient of concordance test ANOVA etc. These statistical tests/methodologies can be used in library/information science research. Apart from these tests, sign test, Fisher Irwin test, Rank sum test, are also grouped under non Parametric tests. In this article the Chi square test, rank correlation test and Kendall's coefficient of concordance test are described with illustrations.

Chi Square Test

Test (Chi square) pronounced as Ki square is an important non parametric test used to test the independence of the variables and also test the goodness of fit. This test enables us to see how well the assumed theoretical distribution of it to the observed data. If the calculated value of Chi Square is less than the table value of Chi square at a certain level of significance, the fit is considered to be good one and if the calculated value is greater than the table value the fit is not considered to be good one.

As a test of independence, of the Chi square test enables one to see whether or not the two attributes of the data are associated. In the Chi square test it is essential that the observed and theoretical frequencies must be grouped and the Chi square is calculated using the formula:

$$X^2 = \Sigma \frac{(O_{ij} - E_{ij})^2}{E_{ij}}$$

Where, O_{ij} = Observed frequency of the cell in the ith row and j^{th} column.

E_{ij} = Expected frequency of the cell in the ith row and j^{th} column.

To see the significance of the Chi square value, the significance of Chi square is ascertained with the Tabulated value of Chi square for a given degree of freedom at a certain level of significance. The degree of freedom is worked out as

$$d.f = (c - 1)\,(r - 1)$$

where, c means the number of columns in the table

r means the number of rows in the table.

For a 2 × 2 contingency Table the degree of freedom is 1.

To apply Chi square test in the data analysis process one must see that

(a) The observations recorded must be on a random basis.
(b) All the items in the sample must be independent.
(c) The group must contain more than 10 frequencies. If the frequencies are less than 10, then regrouping must be done.
(d) The overall number of items must also be reasonably large.

The Chi square test is illustrated here with simple example. The steps involved are described in the following paragraphs.

Illustration 1

About 200 patients suffering form a disease were treated with conventional and new methods of treatment. Of them 60 patients showed favourable response to the new method of treatment and 70 patients to the conventional method of treatment. 20 patients showed no response to the new method of treatment and 50 patients showed no response to the conventional method of treatment. State whether the new treatment is comparatively superior to the conventional treatment.

The data given in the illustration can be tabulated as in Table 1.

TABLE 1
CHI SQUARE TEST COMPUTATION

Treatment	*Number of Patients*				*Total*
	Favourable		*No response*		
	O_{ij}	E_{ij}	O_{ij}	E_{ij}	
New	60	(52)	20	(28)	80
Conventional	70	(78)	50	(42)	120
Total	130		70		200

(Chi - square value for 1 d.f at 5% level of significance is 3.84)

In the process of chi square test computation, the basic and primary procedure is to formulate null and alternate hypothesis in order to justify the results obtained. Here the null and alternate hypothesis on the basis of the illustration 1 are :

H_o = New treatment is comparatively not superior to the conventional method of treatment.

H_i = New treatment is comparatively superior to the conventional method of treatment.

First one has to calculate the expected frequencies on the basis of given observed frequency provided in the Table 1. In case of 2*2 contingency Table or in ant contingency Table the Expected frequency is calculated as below:

$$\text{Expected frequency } E_{ij} = \frac{\text{Row total for the row of that cell} \times \text{column total for the column of that cell}}{\text{Grand Total}}$$

For the above Table 1 $E_{ij} = 80 \times 130/200 = 52$
$= 120 \times 130/200 = 78$
$= 80 \times 70/200 = 28$
$= 120 \times 70/200 = 42$

The computed Expected frequency is given along with the related observed frequency in the Table 1.

Secondly obtain the difference between the observed and expected frequency and find out the square root of the difference i.e. $(O_{ij} - E_{ij})^2$.

Then divide the value obtained therefrom i.e. $(O_{ij}-E_{ij})^2$ by corresponding expected frequency (E_{ij}) i.e. $(O_{ij} - E_{ij})^2/E_{ij}$.

This process must be done for all the cell frequencies. Lastly find the summation of $(O_{ij} - E_{ij})^2/E_{ij}$, i.e. (Equation No. 1)

$$X^2 = \Sigma \frac{(O_{ij} - E_{ij})^2}{E_{ij}}$$

The value obtained after the summation is the Chi square value. This value of Chi square then should be compared with the relevant Table value of Chi square and on the basis of that one can draw inference. In case of the above illustration, the Chi square value is 5.85. Since the computed value is greater than the Table value i.e. 3.84 for 1 d.f at 5% level of significance we can infer that the new method of treatment is comparatively superior to the conventional method of treatment. We may reject the null hypothesis and accept the alternate hypothesis.

Illustration 2

Let us see another illustration. Determine whether or not the variables (the sex and the reading habit) are independent or not.

Sex	*Reading habit*		
	Poor	*Good*	*Excellent*
Male	38	39	21
Female	26	49	38

By computing the expected frequency for the variable and also calculating the row and column total, the data obtained can be represented as in the Table No.2 (Here also the same steps should be followed to compute the expected frequency of the variable). (The figures in brackets represents the expected frequency).

TABLE 2
READING HABIT VS. SEX

Sex	*Reading habit*			*Total*
	Poor	*Good*	*Excellent*	
Male	38 (29.7)	39 (40.8)	21 (27.4)	98
Female	26 (34.3)	49 (47.1)	38 (31.6)	113
Total	64	88	59	211

Here the hypothesis formulated are:

H_o = There is no difference in the reading habit of men and women.

H_i = There is difference in the reading habit of men and women.

The Chi square is computed using the formula 1 and the computed value is 7.26 and the Table value for 2 d.f at 5% level of significance is 5.991. [Note : Here d.f is (3 – 1) (2 – 1) = 2]

Since the computed value is greater than the Table value, we may say that the sex and reading habit variables are not independent, i.e., reading habit of male and female differ. Reading habit vary among men and women.

The Chi square test is an important non parametric test and can be applied to study the various factors related to the routine activities of the library and user need and there satisfaction and many other facts related with the users in order to improve the quality of library and information services.

Spearman's Rank Correlation Test (r)

This test is generally known as rank correlation test. Since it was first developed by Charles Spearman as early as 1990, it is known as Spearman's rank correlation Coefficient test. This test can be used when the information is sufficient to rank the data as first, second, third, etc, and so on. The rank correlation test enables us to measure the correlation that exists between two sets of ranks.

In order to calculate the rank correlation coefficient, first of all the observations must be replaced by their ranks i.e. by giving rank 1 to the highest value and so on. In case of tied ranks i.e. if two or more values happen to be equal, then the average of the rank should be assigned to such values. Once the ranking is over, then the second step is to record the difference between ranks (d) for each pair of observations. In the third step, the square of the difference between the rank i.e. 'd' for each pair of observation is computed and the sum of such difference which is denoted as E_{ij}^2 is calculated. The spearman's rank correlation coefficient test r is computed as below. (Equation No. 2)

$$r = 1 - \frac{6\,\Sigma_{di}^{2}}{n(n^2 - 1)}$$

where Σ_{di}^2 = Sum of square of difference between two sets of ranks.

n = number of paired observations.

If the number of paired observations i.e. 'n' is less than 30, the distribution of 'r' is not normal. It varies from + to - value. Suppose if the number of paired observation n is greater than 30, then the distribution of r is considered to be normal with a mean of zero and a standard deviation of

Thus $\sigma_r = 1/\sqrt{n-1}$

The above factors are described here with an illustration.

Illustration 3

In the following Table 3, data relating to the use of 8 books during a five year period is given in a library. Find out whether the distribution of X and Y are identical. (The data gives the number of times each book issued out and the number of times used within the library).

The figures in the brackets represents the ranks of the books according to the number of times each book is issued and used within the library. 'd' represents the rank difference and 'di^2 represents the square of the difference between the two sets of ranks. For this purpose the following hypothesis were formulated.

H_o = The ranks X and Y are independent.

H_1 = The ranks X and Y are not independent.

TABLE 3
USE OF BOOKS BY THE USER

Book	*Number of Times Borrowed (X)*	*Number of Times Used in the Library (YY)*	*d*	*di²*
1	25(6)	32(7)	–1	1
2	34(3)	42(3)	0	0
3	19(7)	33(6)	1	1
4	42(1)	50(1)	0	0
5	17(8)	31(8)	0	0
6	28(5)	46(2)	3	9
7	30(4)	35(5)	–1	1
8	35(2)	40(4)	–2	4
				16

Here n = 8

$$\Sigma_{di}^{2} = 16$$

Hence, r is calculated using the Equation No. 2. By substituting the values, the computed value of r = 0.81. The Table value of r for n=8 at 5% level of significance is 0.643. Since the computed value is greater than the Table value, we may reject the null hypothesis. We can infer that the use of books when borrowed and used within the library vary.

The Spearman's rank correlation test is applicable only when two sets of rankings are possible. When several sets of rankings are available, then this test can not be applicable. In such cases another important non parametric test called Kendall's coefficient concordance test can be applied.

Kendall's Coefficient of Concordance Test

As mentioned, this test is applicable where we get multiple sets of rankings. Kendall's coefficient of concordance is represented by the symbol 'w'. This test is also an important non parametric test. This test is used for determining the degree of association with several sets of rankings of N objects. This can be well understood with the following example. Say 4 teachers are assessing 10 students. Let us assume that the first teacher is ranking a student as first 2nd as second and so on. The second teacher also ranks in the same order and third and fourth also in the same order. If this is so, then there is perfect agreement between the four teachers as they have ranked each student with the similar agreement. When all the teachers agree the sum of ranks is maximum. In case if the ranking of the students by the four teachers differ, then there is no perfect agreement between the teachers. Say, if the first teacher is assigning the first student as first, second as second and so on, then the second teacher may assign first rank to the third student second to sixth student, etc., similarly the third teacher may assign the first student as fifth, etc., and so on. Here in this case the sum of ranking is not maximum. The W is calculated using the equation 3 as given below:

$$W = \frac{S}{{}^{1}/_{12}\, K^2 \,(N^3 - N)}$$

Where,

N = number of objects ranked

k = Number of sets of rankings

$1/12 \times k^2 \,(N^3 - N)$ = maximum possible sum of the squared deviation

This can be well understood by the following illustration:

Illustration 4

The different library users have ranked different library resources which is given in the following Table.

TABLE 4
DIFFERENT LIBRARY RESOURCES

Books	*Journals/ Periodicals*	*Reference Sources*	*A/V*	*CD ROM*
UG 1	2	3	4	5
PG 1	2	4	5	3
Staff 1	2	5	3	4

Find out if there is any association between different types of users and their preference to the different information sources.

For this purpose let us formulate the following hypothesis.

H_0 = There is no association between the types of users and their preference to the different sources.

H_i = There is association between the types of users and their preference to the different sources.

From Table 4 let us compute the required data to compute the W. In Table 5 the values obtained are given.

TABLE 5

RANKING OF DIFFERENT SOURCES OF THE LIBRARY BY THE USERS

Users	*Books*	*Journals and Periodicals*	*Reference Books*	*A/V*	*CD Roms*
UG	1	2	3	4	5
PG	1	2	4	5	3
Staff	1	2	5	3	4
Sum of ranks	3	6	12	12	12

ERj = 45

Rj = 45/5 = 9

$s = E(Rj - Rj)^2$

s=72

W is computed using the equation 3.

W = 0.8.

Since N = 5 and is less than 7, the Table Value of W is seen in correspondence with the computed value of 's'.

For k = 3 and N = 5 and s = 64.4. The computed value of s=72. Since the computed value is greater than the Table value, we may reject the null hypothesis, i.e., H_0. Thus, we may say that there is association between the type of users and their preference to different sources.

When N is greater than 7 we may use Chi square value to be worked out as X^2

$X^2 = k(N-1) \times W$ (Equation 4) with d.f = (N – 1) for judging the W's = significance at a given level of significance.

For Example, in a survey undertaken for the need of different media in library, the data computed was as follows.

W = 0.129

k = 15 (profession of the user) (Number of sets of rankings)

N = 15 (Media needed) (Number of objects)

Chi square value thus obtained using the above equation 4 is 27.1.

The Table value of Chi square for 14 d.f is 23.685. Since the computed value is greater than the Table value we may reject the null hypothesis. We may infer that people in different professions have preference to varied type of media in which they would like to have information for their information needs satisfaction.

Conclusion

These non parametric tests can be further explained with many examples if data is available and on the basis of different case studies. Thus we can say that statistical methodologies enable us to interpret the data obtained in a systematic way. The systematic way and interpretation of data leads to get the trend in the librarianship research as a whole over a period of time. In a library, the application of statistical methodologies helps to determine the performance and trend in the growth of library resources, quality of service provided, etc. This enables us to develop new strategies to meet the user needs. As more emphasis is given on the user component of the library and information centre, it may be essential to adopt the statistical methodologies in library and information science research. As research in library and information science becomes sophisticated, the application of statistical methodologies will improve the process in research and enable to get authentic results therefrom.

REFERENCES

1. Freedman, P. Principles of Scientific Research 2nd ed. New York: Pergamon Press, 1960.
2. Kothari, C.R. *Research Methodology: Methods and Techniques*. Delhi: Wiley Eastern, 1985.
3. Ravichandra Rao, I.K. *Quantitative Methods for Library and Information Science*. Delhi: Wiley Eastern, 1983.
4. Sidney, S. *Non parametric Statistics for the Behavioural Sciences*. New York: McGraw hill, 1956.
5. Young, P. *Scientific Social Surveys and Research*, 3rd ed. New York: Prentice-Hall, 1960.

Twenty Eight

Library and Information Science Research in India

DR S.R. IJARI

Introduction

It was more than 86 years ago in 1911 that the first formal training in Library Education was started in India by H.H. Sayajirao Gaekwad, Maharaja of princely and progressive State of Baroda. The Maharaja, a staunch believer in the importance of libraries, invited W.A.Borden, an American librarian to be the Director of the Department of Public Libraries, who was a disciple of Melvil Dewey. He initiated the teaching programme to train the persons, by the approval of the Maharaja. After four years a more systematic training course was started by another American by name Asa Don Dickenson at Punjab University in 1915. However, Andhra and Karnataka, States started the training courses during 1920 and 1921 respectively.

Teaching Programme

During 1931, Dr S.R. Ranganathan, the doyen and father of Library Science in India took the lead in furthering the cause of Library education by starting an under-graduate course in Library Science at the University of Madras. This course was upgraded and designated as Post-graduate Diploma (Dip.Lib.Sc.). In the mid sixties, the course was re-designated and upgraded into Bachelor's degree (B.Lib.Sc). At the instance of the UGC and in keeping with the developments in the field of Library Science, the course was renamed as Bachelor of Library and Information Science (B.L.I. Sc.) in most of the universities. During the 1980s the University of Calcutta, started the two-year M.L.I.Sc. degree course. At present, 75 universities are engaged in imparting LIS education for Bachelor's Degree. Out of these, 45 universities have facilities for offering Master's Degree and 45 Universities have introduced Ph.D. Programme.

Research Programme

The University is a centre for teaching and research. The status and importance of the University is generally measured by observing the encouragement it provides for the promotion of research in various disciplines.

Research is a process wherein a planned and structured investigation is made on specific segment of knowledge either at macro or micro level. It is a systematic quest for knowledge. New knowledge is created, investigations are made and added by systematic and scientific knowledge.

The need for research, especially at the Ph.D. level and particularly in LIS has been aptly observed by Krishna Kumar and J.L. Sardana ... research in LIS has an important role to play in the educational process towards creation of new knowledge and situation of problems faced by librarians, information scientists and documentalists. Incidentally, these programmes will also enable the library profession to achieve academic and professional respectivity, which it lacks to a certain extent at present. Thus, there is a need to set up research programmes in library schools.

It is essential that the research activities help to develop the subject and keep abstracts of current trends.

In India, research programme at the Ph.D. level in LIS was initiated by Dr S.R. Ranganathan, in 1948, at University of Delhi, with active support and encouragement of Sir Maurice Gwher, the then Vice Chancellor. The first candidate who completed his Ph.D. Degree in 1957, was the late Dr B.D. Krishna Rao. In late sixties, other universities also gradually started providing facilities for Ph.D. programme. However, a peculiar situation exists in the matter of awarding Ph. D. degrees. While some universities link the degree with their LIS Departments, some others link it with the Department of History, Economics, Education, etc. A few universities have made provision for registering candidates without the LIS Department in the University. Some others have made provision for registering candidates independently without being required to work under the guidance of a recognised teacher.

Research Progress

As far as research progress is concerned in India, some of the Universities are actively involved in research programmes. It is needless to say that Department of LIS, Karnataka University has already awarded forty Ph.D. degrees since 1980.

Research Trend

The topic chosen by different candidates for research is quite interesting to note, covering major and active areas in the field, ranging from traditional to contemporary aspects.

It is observed that the researchers are concentrating more on computer application, bibliometric studies, user studies, information network and system, information sources and services, classification. Some researchers are engaged in academic, public and special library systems.

The trend shows that many persons are actively engaged in new technological development in the field of information networking and systems.

Problems in Research in Library and Information Science

Since librarianship is a problem oriented field the focus is on practical problems in the real world. Hence, research may be conducted both in universities and in the libraries which are supposed to be laboratories of library science. It may be done voluntarily, or may be commissioned by an employed or professional association. No matter where and how research is undertaken, it has problems. These problems may be broadly grouped into the following four categories.

1. Administrative Problems
2. Financial Problems
3. Thematic Problems and
4. Problems concerning facilities of literature

Administrative Problems

Administrative problems are those caused by sticking to the letter of the law or rules and regulations. Rigidity is at the root of all such problems.

There is lack of uniformity regarding recognition of guides, jurisdiction of students, duration of the programmes and appointment of experts for evaluation. These dissimilarities are hinderances in the development of the research programmes.

Financial Problems

Finance is the fulcrum on which the intensity of research rests. A researcher may not be able to get the basic information on the problem of research, if he does not have proper financial assistance. In such circumstances he may conduct a superficial inquiry for want of funds, instead of conducting an indepth study.

In LIS education, scholarships and fellowships are limited as compared to other faculties - Science and Technology, Humanities and Social Sciences.

Thematic Problems

We often hear comments about the quality and content of research. We hear people say that 'X' has counted a few citations and produced a thesis on bibliometric studies, or what is the use of a particular research. Also there are people who say, it is all good in theory but it is not practiced one. The fact is that such people, in most of the cases, neither know theory nor practice. Till now, the completed studies in librarianship have been of applied nature. Like any developing discipline, the study of Library Science is characterized by a weak body of theory and research findings are often irreconcilable with previously acquired knowledge.

Thus, choosing a topic for research is like a tight-rope-walk.

In absence of information on ongoing research programmes, there is every possibility of duplication of topics.

Problems Concerning Facilities of Literature

Literature is linked in almost all the instructions where the research programme is in operation. No library is self sufficient to cater to the needs of the users. Some of the libraries, do not subscribe to the secondary sources like LISA or Library Literature.

To collect the literature from the available libraries is also a problem. Now we are having LISA on CD-ROM Disc, it costs more, and if it is available, it is difficult to get the printouts because the library people may not oblige.

These are the selected categories of problems. There are several other difficulties regarding statistical assistance, or access to a micro-computer, etc. These problems are interdependent.

Suggestions

The above are only a few of the many problems which one finds in the discipline of LIS. As every one will agree that LIS is a new discipline and has to establish its foothold firmly in the academic world. Some of the suggestions are made here to improve the research programme in LIS. They are as under:

1. There should be a national body to bring out the common set of rules and regulations for LIS research programme.
2. The Universities and the UGC and other allied bodies should provide sufficient funds to develop LIS research activities.
3. Information about ongoing research programmes should be made available for avoiding duplication.
4. The professional persons should help the researchers in providing required information to them without much loss of time and money.
5. The UGC should appoint an expert committee to examine these and many other problems the LIS is facing, and to suggest ways and means to overcome them.
6. Professional bodies - the ILA, IASLIC, IATLIS and such other bodies must also take up these issues raised here and try to solve them.

Concentrated efforts by the intelligentia in the profession can promote a high standard research in the field of Library and Information Science.

REFERENCES

1. Baxfer, Paul. *Role of British Library R & D Department in supporting Library and Information research in the UK.* American Society for Information Science, 36 (14), 1985.

2. Bush, Charles, H. Research methods. In *Encyclopaedia of Library and Information Science*, V. 25. p. 254, 1978.
3. Busha, C.H. and Harter, S.P. *Research Methods in Librarianship: Techniques and Interpretation*. New York, Academic. p. 4, 1980.
4. *Ibid.*, p. 8.
5. Ijari, S.R. Research in LIS : A Case Study. Timeless Fellowship, 15, 1993.
6. Ijari, S.R. Whither Research in LIS: Problems and prospects, In S.R. Ijari, et. al., (ed.) *Human Spirit: An Anthology Library Systems*, Dharwad, Deptt. of LIS, 1988.
7. Ijari, S.R. and Savanur, S.K. Research LIS: Some problems. In H.A. Khan and S.R. Ijari (eds.), *Current Problems and Trends in Library and Information Services*, Varanasi, IBC, 1990.
8. Krishan Kumar and Sardana, J.L. Research in LIS. In P.B. Mangla (ed.) *LIS Education in India*. pp. 122-24, Delhi: MacMillan, 1981.
9. Mangala, P.B. Ed. *Library and Information Science Education in India*. Delhi: Macmillan, 1981.
10. Pathak, V. and Ramaiah, I.S. *Comp. Bibliography of Research in LIS in India*. Gurgaon: IDS. 1986.

Twenty Nine

Marketing of Library and Information Services: Concepts, Issues and Strategies

C.V. HIREMATH *and* DR C.R. KARISIDDAPPA

Introduction

Over the past few years, enormous progress has been made in the acceptance of marketing approach in the information sector. The recent years have witnessed the recognition that marketing is an integral part of the library and information centre management. The benefits associated with the marketing approach have now been well acknowledged by the professionals. The surviving and prospering business in information handling is a big question before the professionals as they are facing stiff competition by other competitors in the market. Further, there is a tremendous amount of increase in number of users and sophistication in information seeking behaviour, due to the availability of technology as compared to earlier days. Gradual transformation is taking place in converting libraries and information centres from administrative and cost centres to marketing and profit making centres, thanks to the information technology and marketing tools.

The advent of information superhighways has made the libraries and information centres more competitive and alert. The challenges faced by the professionals towards budget cuts, increased users base, competition by the private vendors, outflow of information, and complexity in the information requirements are forcing the professionals to adopt the marketing tools for the betterment of the management of library and information centres. Despite the fact that calculating the returns on investments in libraries and information services is difficult, it has been accepted all over that libraries and information centres play a key role in socio-economic upliftment of a country.

Marketing

The majority belief is that the marketing concept was "profit, sales, and advertising" and it was confined to business firms involved in production activity for profit. The above concept of marketing prevailed until recently and it was seen as a relatively low status activity. Philip Kotler and Sidney J. Levy[1] broadened the concept of 'services' from 'physical products' and to 'customer satisfaction engineering' from 'pushing products'. Marketing is the process of planning and executing the conception, pricing, promotion and distribution of ideas, goods, and services to create exchanges that satisfy individual or organizational objectives.[2] Marketing is a management process that involves identifying, anticipating, and monitoring the needs of the customers, designing the products, services, and ideas to satisfy the requirements of the customers, communicating to the customers about the services that structured, and measuring the customer satisfaction within the framework of the objectives of the organization.

Characteristics of Products and Services

It is important to know the difference between products and services before understanding the marketing process. A physical product is anything that is produced to satisfy the needs of consumers which can be acquired, stored and consumed, whereas, services are not stored and used. A service according to Philip Kotler[3], is any act or performance that one party can offer to another that is essentially intangible and does not result in the ownership of anything. Its production may or may not be tied to a physical product. Table 1 shows the differences between physical goods and services.[4]

TABLE 1
DIFFERENCE BETWEEN PHYSICAL GOODS AND SERVICES

S.No.	*Physical Goods*	*Services*
1.	Tangible	Intangible
2.	Homogeneous	Heterogeneous
3.	Production and distribution are separated from consumption	Production, distribution and consumption are simultaneous processes
4.	A thing	An activity or process
5.	Core value produced in factory	Core value produced in buyer-seller interactions
6.	Customers do not participate in production	Customers participate in production.
7.	Can be kept in stock	Cannot be kept in stock
8.	Transfer of ownership	No transfer of ownership

Libraries and information centres are essentially engaged in offering services. The attributes of services are discussed below.

Intangible

Services are intangible in nature compared to physical products. This is due to the very fact that services cannot be put to test before they are used. It cannot be stored, displayed, demonstrated, possessed, tasted, seen, heard and smelled. A reference query answered, a referral service, user orientation, help extended in on-line searching, etc., are few services which are of this kind.

Inseparable

In general, services are produced and consumed at the same time as compared to the physical goods. In most of the cases a service is generated and supplied against a demand. A literature search made upon the receipt of demand will not affect the original source. Even after consulting the books and journals several times by several users, they are still available for use.

Perishable

As said earlier, a service is offered and consumed at the same time. The life span of the service is very short. It cannot be inventoried. As a result, a library service is generated only when it is required by a user.

Simultaneous

Services are produced and utilised simultaneously. Services cannot be produced in advance and stored. It is a need-based activity. Physical products are produced, sold, and consumed, whereas services are generally sold first, and then produced and consumed simultaneously.

Less Standardised

The services offered by any organization or individual are not usually standardised. A specific query answered over different point of time may vary. It has no consistency in nature. The services offered by the library or information centre are highly personalised. Hence, they vary from one person to another depending on their expertise, level, and knowledge.

The characteristics described above present a number of problems for the marketing of services in general. However, it is not more difficult than marketing of physical goods. More importance should be given to understanding the distinctive features clearly so that efficiency and cost effectiveness in service can be achieved.

Application of Marketing Concept to Library and Information Services

Libraries and information centres are in the business of acquiring, storing, and retrieving various information sources. All this has been done to satisfy the needs of the users. User has been the core of the information services. Libraries and information centres have been positive in responding to the changes like new technologies and others. Similarly, the recent days have seen the libraries employing the principles and tools of marketing. The two reasons why the marketing is important as D.J. Stone[5] points out: "The most obvious is that with so may technological changes, libraries must work harder than ever to let their patrons know what libraries and librarians can do. Secondly, because marketing is an integral part of management and advocates the involvement of all staff members in product or service development, promotion, and distribution, a market-oriented staff is far more successful in responding to technological change and in seeing that new services reflect the needs of the library's users". Application of marketing strategies help libraries market their information products and services successfully. Information professionals should be clear in their mind about the underlying principle of marketing that it is user oriented and not profit or product oriented.

Marketing Plan

Most important aspect in the marketing process is marketing plan. Successful marketing must begin with the formulation of a marketing plan, and the marketing plan should begin with the formulation of specific objectives.[6] It is a framework on the basis of which decisions can be taken and implemented. A written marketing plan gives directions to achieve desired results. The plan helps to forecast and compare the results. The basic elements of the marketing plan are explained in the following paragraphs.

Market and Situation Analysis

Market analysis is an activity of identifying the market, selecting and positioning it, and assessing the competition. It presents the current scenario of the size, growth potential, market segments and the prevailing competition. The market in the context of library and information services means target clientele to be served. This element of the marketing plan provides detailed account of data on current and potential users and their needs, wants and demands, users behaviour patterns, library products and services, competition, and communication strategy followed.

Mission Analysis

Marketing plan calls for a well defined mission statement. All the activities of the library are planned in the light of this mission. It is a complex activity as the libraries and information centres are, in most of the cases, not independent as they are attached to a parent body. Its mission statement is derived from the mission statement of its parent organization. The mission statement should present the purpose, objectives, and goals of the organization clearly. Most of the libraries are obligatory in nature. It is not an easy task for the libraries to have the mission statement as they are dependent on the parent body. The objectives should be workable, specific, measurable, and attainable.

Resource Analysis

Achieving the set objectives largely depends on the availability of resources. Information resources, support of information technology, and competent professionals are essential. Library professionals therefore should analyse their strengths, and weaknesses. It is also essential to identify the opportunities that are available before them and the threats facing their products and services.

Marketing Strategy

Marketing strategies focus on the broad marketing approach to be used towards meeting the objectives of the marketing. It provides means to apply the library resources to attain the goals. Marketing strategy statement encompass all the aspects of marketing mix and the target markets.

Marketing Programme

Programmes provide game plan for each strategy. It draws responsibilities for people. Action programmes indicate who should do what, how, and when. The marketing program also contains other factors like budgeting, staffing, and schedule of responsibilities. The programmes should be communicated properly.

Monitoring and Evaluation

The last element in the plan is to monitor and evaluate the performance. An appropriate mechanism for feedback and control of programme helps in knowing whether the objectives are being met. Revisions and updates are made with the results shown by the evaluation of the plan.

Marketing Mix

One of the strategies involved in the marketing task is development of a marketing mix for each selected segment. The essential elements of marketing mix are known popularly as the four P's are: product, place, price and promotion. The library and information professionals should understand the basic concepts of these elements as E. E. de. Saez says "marketing mix need more properly to be marketing mixes, to encourage librarians and information managers to perceive the value of different marketing mixes for specific market segments or group of users."[7]

Product

A product is anything that can be offered to someone to satisfy a need or want.[8] In the context of libraries and information centres, products or services which are not tangible in nature as said earlier, are to be designed in satisfying the information users needs. The service design takes help of market research and market segmentation as these important tools provide detailed account of users needs, their seeking patterns, their distribution, their value definition, cost implications and the benefits expected. Product design requires knowledge of users, subjects, and communication skills. The issues to be considered while designing the product are quality, differentiation, quantity, design, packaging, branding and competition. The product development is a continuous process as the products are user-intensive, hence subject to fluctuations in their information needs and the advance of information technology. In the case of library services the products mean books, periodicals, bibliographies, indexes, CAS bulletins, photocopying, reference service, referral service, information searches, inter library loans, and so on.

Place

The second element of the marketing mix is 'distribution'. It specifies how the information products are made available to users. The place refers to when, where, and how the products are distributed to the users. Working hours, accessibility, availability of library and information managers, and the channels are the key factors to be addressed to ensure Document delivery, loan facilities, on-line access, telephonic information queries, local area networks, faxing the CAS bulletin, mail, etc.

The above issues which are important in preparing an action plan for distribution are not an easy task for the library managers. In order to reach the clientele, it is advisable that establishment of branch libraries, participating in the networks, extending the working hours, and appointing distributors are done carefully after accurate segmentation and targeting.

Price

One of the most difficult tasks before the library and information managers is how to price their products and services. Pricing as an element of marketing mix draws special attention of the libraries. There is a big debate going on among the library professionals whether to charge for their services. Some are against pricing while others feel that pricing can be a political and promotional tool for boosting the image of library and information centres.

The basic purpose of the marketing is user satisfaction and promotion of exchange of values. It is therefore pricing not necessarily in terms of money. Setting the right price towards marketing the products and services is significant. Varieties of considerations are to be taken into account while pricing the services. Economic models towards pricing the services should be developed and applied. A policy for pricing should be devised keeping in mind the objectives and missions of the organization.

Libraries and information centres involve expenditure in acquiring information sources, appointing competent staff, maintenance, electricity, stationery and equipment, communication, and so on. The other factors that affect the pricing are: competition, quality, quantity, distribution, promotion and differentiation. Among the alternative options available, a suitable one may be selected and adopted. Varieties of pricing techniques such as cost-based pricing, average cost pricing, marginal cost pricing, demand based pricing, price discrimination, competition based pricing, and premium pricing are available.

Promotion

The fourth element of marketing mix is promotion. It underlines the strategies for marketing communication. Once the products or services are designed and priced, then the issue as to how to communicate users about their services comes before the professionals. Market research must provide the user database, and the market segmentation must define the target segment. It is up to the promotional alternatives to communicate to the targeted users. Large amount of money spent in advertising indicates the importance of promotion activity.

Ample promotional avenues are available for library professionals to communicate to their clientele. Wide varieties of tools that are available are: advertisement, direct mailings, speeches, sale representatives, demonstrations, samples, coupons, posters, sales literature, packaging, public relations, trade literature, films, catalogues, sales conference, and personal interaction.

Marketing Research

Marketing research is the function which links the consumer, customer, and public to the producer or marketing agency through information which is used to identify and define marketing opportunities and problems; generate, refine, and evaluate marketing actions; monitor marketing performance, and improve the understanding of marketing as a process.[9]

The basics of a market research are:

(a) Analysing the market
(b) Analysing the market's response to the product or service
(c) Analysing the effectiveness of advertising or promotion and
(d) Strategic planning.

The steps, according to Vincent P Barabba[10] involved are:

(i) Assess market information needs;
(ii) Measure the market place;
(iii) Store, retrieve, and display the data;
(iv) Describe and analyse market information; and
(v) Evaluate the research and assess its usefulness.

The market research is done before getting into marketing business; at the time of introducing a new product or service, to maintain the existing service. The following elements are involved in the process of marketing research.[11]

(a) Purpose of research - why is information to be gathered?
(b) Statement of research objectives - what information is needed?
(c) Review existing data to discover - what is already known?
(d) Value analysis - is the research worth the cost?
(e) Research design - How are the data to be collected?
    (i) exploratory

(ii) descriptive
(iii) casuals

(f) Methods of primary data collection
(i) communication
(ii) observation

(g) Research tactics - sampling procedures and instrument design
(i) universe
(ii) sample selection
(iii) sample size
(iv) instrument design
(v) pre-setting

(h) Field operations - collection of the data

(i) Data analysis

(j) Completing the project
(i) interpreting the data
(ii) recommendations
(iii) report writing

The results of a systematically conducted research give a good insight in defining the users market accurately, undertaking a new market approach, market segmentation and determining the marketing mix. A thorough understanding of the information seekers and their needs and information seeking behaviour patterns is made possible by the market research. It is an effective tool in gathering data about the market which will be used in designing the product or service to suit the requirements of the information seekers.

Market Segmentation

In the customer-driven marketing, segmentation occupies a key role in the overall marketing success. The concept of marketing segmentation was recognised in 1956 by Wendell R. Smith. A segment is a group which is distinguishable, accessible, measurable, substantial and responds to a tailored approach. Segmentation is basically an process of identification of the universe of users (market) and partitioning them into various groups based on the characteristics of information needs and information seeking behaviour. The segmentation - driven marketing strategy helps companies design responsive products, develop effective promotional tactics and campaigns, gauge competitive positions, and fine-tune current marketing initiatives.[12]

Factors Determining Market Segmentation

The market segmentation process is done based on several factors mentioned below:

- *Demographic Segmentation*: population, age, sex, ethnic group, individuals, marital status, race, religion, family size, language, culture, and life-stages.
- *Socio-economic Segmentation*: occupation, firms, organizations, income, purchasing capacity, and educational level.
- *Geographic Segmentation*: local, regional, national, multi-national, global, TV regions, courier regions, neighbourhoods, urban, rural and remote areas.
- *Psychographic Segmentation*: aggression, anxiety, community involvement, leisure activity, and attitudes, values, beliefs, and benefits expected from a specific service/product.
- *Product usage Segmentation*: purpose of use, occasion of use, situation of use, usage rate, and method of use.
- *Benefit Segmentation*: quality, speciality, career changes, knowledge, status, degree, professional, avoiders, and convenience seekers.

Market segmentation is, thus, a useful technique in identifying the user and their needs, dividing them into homogeneous sections, and providing basic ingredients for marketing mix.

Conclusion

There is considerable difference between the marketing of physical goods and marketing of services. The prevailing conditions force libraries to adopt the marketing techniques for their advantage. Technological innovations facilitate tools for enhancing the effectiveness of such services. The information marketing concept in its totality is at the nascent stage in India where many library and information centres have not fully understood its implications. There have been some efforts in some of the organizations where the marketing concept is being implemented with benefits. The culture created by the marketing approach gives a competitive edge to the professionals in competing with others and delivering the best. Innovation is the key aspect of marketing which pays substantial dividends when it is effectively planned and implemented. There should be a continuous process of innovation and technological upgradation. The impact of the information technology and the adoption of the marketing approach will go a long way in improving the facilities for information users and enhance the reputation of library and information services and professionals.

REFERENCES

1. Kotler, Philips and Levy, S.J. Broadening the Concept of Marketing. *Journal of Marketing*. 33 (1). p. 10, 1969.
2. American management Association. In *Marketing News* dated March 1, 1985.
3. Kotler, Philips, *Marketing Management*. New Delhi: Prentice-Hall of India, p. 455, 1991.
4. Gronross, Chaistian. Service Management and Marketing. Massachusetts, Lexington Books. p. 28, 1990.
5. Stone, Dennis J. Marketing as an Integral part of Law Library Management. *Law Library Journal*. 79(1). p. 105, 1987.
6. Schewe, Charles D. *Callier's Encyclopaedia*, Vol. 15. New York: MacMillan, p. 424, 1991.
7. Eileen Elliot de Saez. Marketing Concepts for Libraries and Information Services. London: Library Association, p. 38, 1993.
8. Kotler, Philips, *Marketing Management*. New Delhi: Prentice-Hall of India, p. 5, 1991.
9. AMA. *Definition of Marketing Research*. Chicago: American Marketing Association.
10. Barabba, V.P. The Market Research Encyclopaedia. *Harvael Business Review* 90(1), p. 105, 1990.
11. Lovelock, Christopher H. and Weinberg, Charles B. *Marketing for Public and Non Profit Managers*. New York: John Wiley & Sons., p. 129.
12. Art Einstein. *Market Segmentation: Using Niche Marketing to Exploit New Markets*. Chicago: Probus, p. 14, 1974.

Thirty

Client/Server Management

Yet another Strategic Survival Tool for the Academic Librarianship in the Internet Era

S. VENUGOPAL

> To start out with the consumer's or client's need for a significant change is often the most direct way to define new science, new knowledge, and new technology, and to organize purposeful and systematically work on fundamental discovery.
>
> Peter F. Drucker

Introduction

Management is the critical determinant factor of the character and destiny of any organization, whether profit or non-profit, in the competitive world. As rightly pointed out by Hammer and Champy (1993),

> Creating a corporate value statement alone is useless and just another faddish exercise. Without supporting management systems, most corporate value statements are collection of empty platitudes that only increase organizational cynicism.. The statement articulates values; the management systems give those values life and reality within the company.

It should naturally have clear vision of its mission, and commitment to fulfil it through optimum use of its resources.

Lack of vision and commitment would lead to nowhere but utter chaos. Personnel at the helm of affairs must possess leadership qualities, which have an overriding influence, inspiration and enabling vision rather than the technical and professional skills. Investing a person with power and authority alone would not make him a good leader, for leadership is personal rather than positional. A leader is more to lead, than to command. To quote Warren Bennis,

> A leader is not just born; he can be self made. The crucial characteristics: He must be a person of character. He must know the business. He must have a track record of success. He must be able to think creatively, and inventively. He must be capable of quick judgement even with imperfect data. He must be capable of picking people who compensate for his deficiencies. He must be able to motivate people.

A leader cannot inevitably be omniscient or omnipotent. His acumen lies in how he compensates for his deficiencies. Next he has to motivate people. Motivation is really about treating people with dignity, to think creatively, and inventively. He is not supposed to be wedded to the status quo. An organization is nothing but its people, who are the real asset. Managing people is not the same as managing machines. While the former requires leadership, the latter needs scholarship — both technical and professional. According to Stephen R. Covey's, Principle-Centered Leadership, "People are not just resources or assets, not just economic, social, and psychological beings. They are also spiritual beings, they want meaning. There must be purposes that lift them, ennoble them, and bring them to their highest selves." Dynamism is the vital force of any organization. Life time learning should be a part of the game plan.

If there is one aspect that is very much lacking in the academic librarianship, it is management. For several decades, almost every school of library and information science has been devoted giving thrust more on proficiency in classification and cataloguing. Some front line members would be quick on their feet to reject the statement, citing management as being included in the syllabus. Teaching theory to the students is one thing, and preparing them to become competent leaders is another. No school could foresee and teach them all. But what is needed is to make the students realize the potential benefits/imperative on engaging themselves on the lifetime learning. The dismal look of many academic libraries in India could be attributed to lack of leadership, competent, staff and team work. 'The information high waves in the 'white water' environment have not visibly rocked the library boat got mired or anchored in the 'still water'.' Good opportunities should be given to the senior library professionals to equip themselves with information technology, to play new character roles in the Internet theatre, failing which a golden hand shake seems to be the only solution to get rid of dead woods blocking the way for the young trucks to jump on to the bandwagon of Information Superhighways. Valid reasons may be there to justify the status quo. But status quo is tyranny that could no longer be tolerated. It is better to make an earnest attempt at redesigning/reorganizing the library in response to the Internet call, and fail, than to make no attempt at all. Failure locks within itself the seed of success. To quote corporate Mogul, Bill Gates (1996):

> Corporate reorganizations may be prompted by failures now and then, but more often they are essential elements of success. Done properly, a "reorg" can move people into new areas where they can be more creative and effective. People often hit plateaus, get too comfortable in their jobs and no longer come up with new approaches. A realignment presents them with fresh challenges.

Management becomes crucial in the technology-driven society. Let us address ourselves to this aspect from an irreducible perspective of Client/Server Management.

Tuning and Pruning in Academic Libraries

Shaughnessy has keenly observed that, concerted efforts in research libraries to attract the best recruits, improve the competencies of existing staff, establish teams, restructure and recognize, and improve staff recognition and reward systems - have resulted in very positive outcomes in many instances, but no library has yet been able to achieve the kind of radical transformation that is needed to bring it to peak performance. Are we to blame the system or the individuals? Divided opinions cannot be ruled out but I find myself an ardent supporter of Deming's statement that 85 to 90 per cent of the variations within organizations are due to their systems or processes and only the remaining 10 to 15 per cent are attributed to individual staff performance. TQM (Total Quality Management) strongly underscores this statement. We have to overcome the intertia imposed by smugness, or by library traditions and cultures which can inhibit our "being all that we can be." We should take cognizance of the changes in the environments, the so called "white water" in which libraries now operate. It is an uphill task to bring the professional staff to appreciate that they more than anyone or anything else — collections, buildings, equipment, systems — are the library? Just as teaching faculty in the last analysis are the university, so it is that librarians define what the library is and determine its character. It is this group of staff, more than any other which must assume responsibility for leadership and understand that leadership is first and foremost personal, not positional, that it is rooted in ethical behaviour, and that it is engaged and action oriented. Each member of the staff must take responsibility for becoming informed about what is going on. Administrators, in turn, must work to make the organization a safe place in which to work, a place where fear has no foot hold, where risk is encouraged, team work applauded, goodwill is contagious, and staff are recognized and rewarded. The roles and functions of librarians are undergoing such dramatic change.

The Internet Landscape

The Information Age is causing many of the changes happening in our economies and governments. Businesses will have to change from merely accumulating and processing information to acquiring and applying the knowledge contained therein; in other words, they must move from the information age to the knowledge age. Every sphere of human activity has begun to weigh the impact of Information Technology. Take for instance the IT invasion in the Olympic games of 1996: "Over three billion people from 185 countries were watching the Olympics in 1996, multimedia technology being a major part of it." Some 100 million multimedia personal computers were used at the 1998 Winter Olympics in Nagano, Japan, according to Richard K. Snelling (President of Video Conferencing Systems, USA).

Network Information System

Innovation in libraries today is often synonymous with changes in library computer information systems, which are "the primary links between patrons and items.. [and] offer the only alternative (or at least the primary alternative) to browsing the shelves" (Crawford 1987). Librarians and automation staff are taking a proactive role in developing computer information systems to meet the needs of today's library users and anticipate their needs of tomorrow. These systems promise the library will continue to be a dynamic environment and library staff an important facilitator to accessing information.

Home on the Net

In the Internet era, Home Page and Web Sites are no longer buzz jargons, but household words. Building a home online means setting up some sort of private space for yourself within the public space of the network. The Web is technically only a part of the Internet (the Web is a graphics-intensive application running on top of the Net's operating system), but it seems to be rapidly taking over the Net. The space is cheap and, theoretically, infinite. We are moving from E-mail to Web site: A virtual home where millions can "visit" you. What exactly is a home page? In the simplest terms, it is like an E-mail address, a place on the Net where people can find you; but whereas an E-mail address is just a mail box, a home page is a reception area. Building home pages or Web sites (a collection of pages of which the home page is the natural starting point) is a way to meet people. If you want people to visit your home page, it helps to have appealing content to offer. In an information society such as the Web, all the members have their chunks of information. In a way, setting up a home page is an exercise in self-promotion, like writing a personal ad.

Desktop Digital Library

Clair in her beautiful article, "The Future of Scholarship," pinpoints the changing roles of the libraries and the librarians. As the library presents itself on each scholar's desktop, its need for a central geographical place on campus vanishes. Ross Atkinson, associate university librarian at Cornell University, reconceptualizes the library as an institution that identifies materials along a source/needs continuum. The library will ensure access to all materials, but the speed of delivery to the patron will vary. The library will add value to certain materials by creating a control zone in which some materials are available locally, some are quickly produced for less frequent use, and others take even longer to access. Chodorow believes that librarians will be recognized as information specialists; they will be jointly trained in information retrieval and in a subject discipline to navigate through the broad electronic information landscape.

Libraries and librarians are part of a system designed to serve a lifelong learning model for higher education. The ideal behind that model was a democratization of learning; knowledge was a public good that should be made freely available to all. Now that the whole system and its underlying ideals are being challenged, librarians must make a stronger commitment to their role in the creation of scholarship — as scholarly publishers, organizers, indexers, and information specialists. As the scholars begin to use resources on the Internet and to work with multiple versions rather than with a fixed text, the library's instructional responsibilities intensify and proliferate. Information Desk is the liaison between the library and the clientele to serve; reference librarians can provide (or fail to provide) patrons with access to the information they expect to find. There is a consensus among experts that there needs to be more emphasis on references service as a whole, not just how accurately patrons' questions are answered (Clair, 1995). The libraries could not equip themselves well without transforming themselves into learning organizations.

What is a Learning Organization?

According to Garvin, it is "an organization skilled at creating, acquiring, and transferring knowledge, and at modifying its behaviour to reflect new knowledge and insights" (Garvin, 1993). System thinking, based on general systems theory, is the cornerstone of Senge's ideas about learning organizations. Systems thinking enables managers to see holistically the organization, its environment, and the interrelatedness of events affecting the organization. Putting the learning organization theories into practice, according to Kramlinger, requires that the organization incorporates the following eight basic assumptions into its policies, procedures, strategies, value statements, and personnel practices:

- Everyone can be a source of useful ideas.
- The people closest to the problem usually have the best ideas about solutions. This involves decision making at the lowest possible hierarchical level.
- Learning flows up as well as down in the organization.
- Nothing is sacred except the governing vision and values.
- The process of open dialogue improves ideas. Open dialogue is defined as the sharing of information and ideas, unencumbered by fears, insecurities, or concerns over turf and status.
- The more information people can access, the better.
- New ideas are valuable and can be generated by activities such as brainstorming at retreats.
- A mistake is simply an opportunity to learn new ideas are encouraged; and mistakes are accepted as an inevitable part of the innovation process.

Academic Libraries as Learning Organizations

Library literature contains little discussion about learning organizations. Philips summarizes the ideas of The Fifth Discipline and suggests that the theory of learning organizations may be useful in transforming academic research libraries in the face of technological change.

The learning organization concept is not a miracle cure or a quick fix, and it may not be workable in all libraries. Resistance to change is inevitable, especially among longstanding employees. Critics and malcontents must be made an integral part of the planning and implementation process, so that their complaints are dealt with openly. Clear communication and education about proposed changes are essential, and managers must ensure that employees have adequate emotional support and the necessary training to adjust to new work arrangements. English fluency is rapidly becoming critical to success in the global economy. One reason, notes *Look Japan* magazine, is that computer operating systems and communication technologies developed in the United States have become the international standards - and you need to know English to use them. Surfing the internet virtually requires English fluency, and as the internet becomes a growing economic force in the world, so will English

Innovative Problem Solving

As part of his management improving programme, the librarian should think of innovative problem solving. It may be of immense use if he remembers the eight steps of Basadur's problem - solving process summarized below:

Step 1

Problem finding means sensing, anticipating, and seeking out problems, changes, trends, needs, and opportunities for improvement. A skilled problem finder takes the initiative and welcomes change and imperfection as a chance to improve.

Step 2

Fact finding involves gathering information about a fuzzy situation without prematurely judging its relevance. A skilled fact finder avoids unwarranted assumptions, examines a situation from a wide variety of viewpoints, listens to and accepts others' versions of the facts, extends effort to dig out hidden information, and shows no reluctance to ask simple questions.

Step 3

Problem defining means composing clear, insightful challenges from a few key facts. These challenges reveal directions for solutions. An individual skilled in defining problems can create unusual ways to view them through broadening the problem's scope by asking why it needs to be solved (the intent) and through narrowing its scope by asking what stands in the way (stumbling block).

Step 4

Idea finding means creating a variety of ways to solve a defined problem. A skilled idea finder is never content with a single good idea but continues to hunt for more.

Step 5

Evaluating and selecting involves converting selected ideas into practical solutions. An individual skilled in evaluation and selection considers many criteria and avoids leaping to conclusions based on a single criterion or on unrelated hidden motives.

Step 6

Action planning means creating specific action steps that will lead to successful implementation of a solution. An individual skilled in action planning can see the end result in a specific, concrete way that motivates people to act on the plan. Moving toward action means developing ideas as to what will be done, how it will be done, by whom, when, and where, and also anticipating difficulties by answering such questions as "what new problems might this idea create?" and "Who will this idea affect?"

Step 7

Gaining acceptance means understanding that even the best ideas and plans can be scuttled by resistance to change. Someone skilled in gaining acceptance creates ways to show people how a particular solution benefits them and how possible problems with the solution can be minimized.

Step 8

Taking action means "doing" the steps in the action plan. It also means continually revising and adapting the plan as things change in order to ensure that the solution is successfully implemented. An individual skilled in taking action avoids getting mired in unimportant details and minor road blocks on the way to implementing the solution.

Creativity is important in overcoming our own procrastination and fear of failure.

Client/Server Management

The concept of client/server in the computer network environment is well understood. A new theory of Client/Server Management has evolved quite recently in the Japanese organizations. An organization may be viewed as bipartite client and server. This may be quite true in any service organization. Though I have not come across any article applying this concept to library organization, I cannot foresee the exclusion of it. Library is the server and users are its client. The librarian's role is just the human interface. Client and server are only roles, that is, client will act sometimes as server, and server may become client. Imagine hundreds of hosts (servers) and thousands of nodes attached to the Internet. In the internet world, all academic libraries are simply nodes. Libraries could exchange information via internet.

Clients in the traditional sense (within local boundaries) have no meaning. Even an unknown or remote user becomes a client. The resources and value-added information services attract the client across the world. The population of clients is wider in scope and variety. Server may have myriad database created in different environments. The client need not know the intricacies involved in the accessing process.

The server's primary task is to process the requests from the users and try to answer their questions. It is immaterial whether the server he is addressing has the information or not. It is the responsibility of the server to get from other servers, hosts. The library may follow whatever strategies found to be convenient, the delivery of service has to be ensured. In the context of client/server management, the librarian has to develop the core competencies demanded in the technology-driven organization. As we talk about high-value manager, we can also envision high-value librarian. The words "high value" are emphasized for reason. Today's right-sized restructured organizations cannot tolerate mediocrity. We have to maximize the contribution of their human assets. But in putting the spotlight on quality and customer service, high-value librarians do not allow themselves to be blinded by an aspect of quality alone. 'Quality' and 'value' are not synonymous. We have to determine client needs, then develop action plans designed to achieve those needs. How could the librarians remain ever prepared to take up the challenging task, if they do not have faith in lifetime learning?

Lifetime Learning

The world of the early twenty-first century will be one in which learning must go on, out of necessity, throughout working life. "Grow or Die" would be the new maxim in the global competitive market.

Unless we can improve early education, significant numbers of people over the next few decades are going to find it very difficult to achieve even a modest degree of success at work. Unless we can help schools to increase students' competitive drive and desire for lifelong learning, we are all going to suffer the consequences.

In a fast-moving and competitive world, past success does not ensure future success. Just the opposite: Past success often makes it more difficult to succeed in the future (Katter, 1995).

Doomsayers within the profession predict that academic libraries will one day become dinosaurs as students and faculty turn more to commercial and other alternative electronic sources of information. Academic librarians should not imitate Senge's parable of the boiled frog. If one puts a frog into a pot of boiling water, it will immediately try to scramble out. If, however, one puts the frog into a pot of room temperature water and slowly heats the water to boiling, the frog will do nothing. It will enjoy itself and become groggy until it is unable to climb out of the pot. This is because, like man, the frog's internal mechanism for sensing threats is geared toward sudden changes in the environment, not slow gradual changes.

The technological imperative forces the re-design of jobs, the acquisition of new sets of skills, and changes in our visions both at the personal and corporate domains. But the purpose of learning is not to solve all our problems but to create a future. It is in the process of meeting and solving problems that life has its meaning. "Problems call forth our courage and our wisdom; indeed, they create our courage and our wisdom" (Peck, 1978).

REFERENCES

1. Clair, Gloriana st. Editorial, *College & Research Libraries*. 473, Nov. 1995.
2. Cornish, Edward. Review of Simplex (R) : A Flight to creativity by Min Basadur. *The Futurist*, 49, Nov-Dec 1995.
3. Crawford, Walt. *Patron Access Issues for On-line Catalogs*, Boston: G.K. Hall, p. 2, 1987.
4. Garvin David A. Building a Learning Organization. *Harvard Business Reviews* 71. p. 78, July-Aug, 1993.
5. Gates, Bill, Reorganization: A Necessary Art in a Fast-Changing World. *The Telegraph*. p. 2, 15 April, 1956.
6. Hammer, Michael and Champy, James. *Reengineering the Corporation*. New York: Harper Collines, p. 75, 1993.
7. Katter, John P. Lifetime Learning. *The Futurist* 27 Nov.-Dec. 1995.
8. Katter, John P. and Leonard S. Schlesinger. Choosing strategies for change. *Harvard Business Review*. 106-114 March-April, 1979.
9. Peck, M. Scott. *The Roadless Travelled*. New York: Simon & Schuster, p. 192, 1978.
10. Philips, Shelley E. Transforming Libraries into learning organization: The challenge for leadership. In Catalysts for Change : Managing Libraries in the 1990s. Edited by Gisela M. Von Dran and Jennifer Cargill. New York: Haworth Press, pp. 19-37. 1993.
11. Roecker. Fred. Basic Foundations for Creating an Effective Computer Information System. *The Journal of Academic Librarianship*. pp. 167-74, May, 1995.
12. Seabrook, John. Home on the Net. *Span*. 3-7, Feb./March, 1996.
13. Senge, Peter M. The Fifth Discipline: The Art & Practice of the learning organization, New York: Doubleday/Currency, 1990.
14. Shaughnessy, Thomas W. Key Issue; Achieving Peak Performance in Academic Libraries. *The Journal of Academic Librarianship*, 155-56, May, 1995.
15. Worrel, Diane. The learning organization: Management theory for the Information Age or New Age Fad? *The Journal of Academic Librarianship*. 351-57, May, 1995.

Thirty One

Computerisation of Libraries: A CDS/ISIS Package

SUDESH KUMAR SOOD

Introduction

Ranganathan recognised an objective relating to the internal efficiency of the library in his fourth law which says: "Save the time of the readers". In a corollary to this law, he further argued that while a library has objectives to maximise users satisfactions and to minimise time loss to the user, the library management has even an objective to save the time of the librarian. Perhaps, it can only be done by increasing the internal efficiency of the day-to-day work within the library. The use of computers in almost all fields of life is gaining more and more importance gradually and library can not remain aloof to this. A number of libraries especially special and research libraries have been automated to handle the huge amounts of information and data they have for providing effective, accurate and quick information services to their clientele. Kaul provides a brief account of automation in Indian libraries and states that the number of libraries turning to automation has increased at reasonably good pace.

Computerisation in the field of library and information work in India started in 1964 by INSDOC. Even though India started using computer in its early stage, it is lagging behind many other countries. It is unfortunate that not much has been done in developing the facilities of computerisation in academic and public libraries due to various reasons. According to a survey done by PSG Kumar in 1987, there are many problems and hinderances in the field of library automation in India. But in spite of all the problems and many more with the passage of time, there has been a growing awareness among the library personnel about the potentiality of computers and their use in library and information work. Among the various functions performed in a library, those which appear to the reading are amenable for computerisation Ambia enlists seven aspects of library and information service which can be computerised. These aspects include; 1. Acquisition, 2. Cataloguing, 3. Maintenance, 4. Circulation Control, 5. Serials Control, 6. Documentation and information retrieval and 7. Stock Verification.

Since the information technology of tomorrow is based on computers, it will get more sophisticated when computers become more powerful and more intelligent. The new computer system will be knowledge information processing system, having problem solving capabilities of a very high level. Therefore, instead of the present online search, where only, the source of information is located, it will be possible to answer a user's question directly.

Need for Automation

Our profession today faces mightly challenges from the information explosion on the one hand and increasingly sophisticated hardware on the other. The explosion of information keeps the budget of the library in a critical position. Librarians feel more difficult to acquire relevant documents for their readers. These conditions have led to the creation of data bases on various subjects for providing pinpointed information services to the users. Hence the objective has now been changed to comprehensive selection and acquisition of documents in libraries to satisfy the readers requirement by providing nascent and relevant information within a short span of time. Now computers are widely used in the library's housekeeping operations which are of a repetitive nature. Following factors emphasize the need for automation:

1. Capacity to handle any amount of data/information.
2. Participation in networking programmes and resource sharing.

3. Flexibility in information search.
4. Standardization.
5. Complexity and scattering information.
6. Literature explosion or information load.
7. Speedy processing of information and its retrieval.
8. Better bibliographic control at local/regional/national/international/informational level.
9. Interdisciplinary nature of research and information.
10. Economic implication of new information technology.
11. Geographical and other barriers to communicate.
12. Increase in the number of users.
13. Literature searching is cumbersome and time consuming.
14. Non-availability of documents/information in the library.
15. Access to the information/data generated, but not published.

Strategy for Automation

There are basically three strategies that can be followed for introduction of computer techniques into a library:

- It can adopt a piecemeal approach, converting individual operations one at time.
- It can go directly for a full integrated system.
- It can work towards progressively using a planned instalments approach.

The Piecemeal Approach

The piecemeal approach has several advantages :

1. Effort is concentrated into the most urgent and cost effective areas.
2. Greater availability of existing software.
3. Ease of implementation.
4. Greater efficiency in each application.
5. Unnecessary mechanization of satisfactory manual system is avoided.

There are also dangers in this approach, the chief one being lack of compatibility between systems for different applications.

The Integral System

The essential characteristics of an integral system is that data files are interlinked in such a way that deletions, additions or changes to one file automatically activate changes in related files. Thus, keyboarding effort is kept to a minimum and better control over the files maintained. The important advantages of an integral system are:

1. Increased overall efficiency, especially by reducing duplication of input and output.
2. Assured compatibility between various parts of system.
3. Improved service to users.
4. Greater scope for the provision of management information.

The main disadvantage is the size and complexity of the task of designing and implementing an integrated system.

Factors Affecting Success of Computerisation

To computerise any library function there are three main factors affecting the degree of success of the project. These factors are hardware, software and peopleware.

Almost all brands of hardware are now reliable as long as they are produced by reputed factories. To be successful, the selected hardware must have sufficient capabilities for immediate application and must be expandible to cope with increasing demand for the next several years, without having to replace the whole unit.

Software must be fully tested and should be user friendly. Several software packages or pre-written programs are available, but they may or may not fit to the requirement.

Most important factor for successful computerisation is peopleware. If sufficient amount of money is available, we can buy best hardware and the best software, but not the best peopleware, because they are in short supply.

Micro CDS/ISIS

Computerised Documentation Series (CDS)/Integrated set of interchanged system (ISIS) is a Data Base Management System (DBMS) developed and distributed by (UNESCO). In India it is being distributed through NISSAT (New Delhi) since September, 86. The ISIS version currently supplied is 3.2 release. The 4.0 version has just been released and has an upper limit of 999,999 records. It is a simple, menu driven and user friendly software which can handle up to 16 million records. It is best suited for creating, maintaining, searching and retrieving records by their generalised system i.e. the same set of program preforms all the required functions on different database, managed through this system. There is no need to develop and modify any program. However, in case any further specified manipulation is desired, CDS/ISIS is also supported by an advanced programming facility through PASCAL computer program language.

Why ISIS Programme?

The roots of CDS/ISIS are found in ISIS, i.e., Integrated Set of Information System, a generalised information management and retrieval software package developed in the late 1960's by the international labour office in Geneva. This software offered powerful capabilities for managing text, including bibliographical records on the IBM 360/370 series of computers. Demand by member countries for access to the software, brought the package into the semi-public domain by 1970's and developing country institutions approached the ILO, UNESCO and other agencies for assistance in the installation and implementation of ISIS software, in most cases, for automation of specialised information services. ISIS is more efficient for management of database in the IR activities, indexing and abstracting features demanded by special libraries than in the acquisition, circulation and other library administrative functions needed by many libraries.

CDS/ISIS and Management of Database

This software has a special advantage for IR activities as this package can run on macros. Libraries even with a small budget can now think of using microprocessors for bibliographic data processing, particularly for management of database activities. It is updated continuously to improve its user friendliness and to make it less error prone. Besides this, no expertise or exposure to computer programming is required in using this software.

CDS/ISIS not only takes care of the management of database, but can also be used for the production of union catalogues running current awareness services, compilation of subject bibliographies. It was a generalised information storage and retrieval system (ISRS) designed specifically for the computerised management of structured non-numerical databases, whose major constituent is text. One of the major advantages offered by this generalised design of CDS/ISIS is that the same set of computer programmes are able to manipulate an unlimited number of databases each of which may consist of completely different data elements. This is also available for PDP-II and Microvax-II systems and adopts the popular inverted organization for storing information in their databases.

System Environment

The minimum hardware required for running CDS/ISIS consists of an IBM PC/XT/AT or compatible computer with 512 KB RAM 1640 KB or higher recommended for better performance, a 5¼" floppy drive, a hard disk (CD/ISIS requires only 10 MB), a monochrome of colour monitor running on MS-DOS operating system and a printer to take hard copy print out. CDS/ISIS software package can be obtained from UNESCO or organization designated by UNESCO like NISSAT in India.

CDS/ISIS : Capabilities and Services

It is a completely menu driven generalized information storage and retrieval system and allows one to build and manage structured non-numerical databases, i.e. database whose major constituent is text. In most general terms, CDS/ISIS database is a file related data, collected to satisfy the information requirements of a given user community. The unique characteristic of CDS/ISIS is that it is specially designed to handle fields (and consequently records) of varying length, thus allowing on the one hand an optimal utilization of your disk storage and on the other hand, a complete freedom in defining the maximum length of each field.

A group of eight major services of the system classified in two broad categories, user services, operating on existing databases and system services, designed for the database administrator to create new databases and perform various system tasks. The major tasks operable in CDS/ISIS are:

1. Define database containing the required data elements.
2. Enter new records into a given database.
3. Modify, correct or delete existing records.
4. Automatically build and maintain fast access files for each database in order to maximize retrieval speed.
5. Retrieve records by their contents, through a sophisticated search language.
6. Display the records or portions thereof according to your requirements.
7. Sort the records in any sequence desired.
8. Print partial or full catalogues and indexes.
9. Develop specialized application using the CDS/ISIS integrated programming facility.

CDS/ISIS consists of a set of programs performing the various system functions. The manual describes the 'user' programs, which operate an existing database and the system programs designed for the database administrator to create new database and perform various system tasks.

The three user programs are:

1. ISIS, which performs all the tasks related to the database maintenance and retrieval.
2. ISIS PRT, which reduces printouts such as catalogue and indexes, and
3. ISIS INV, which provides for defining file maintenance and utility functions.

The three system programs are:

1. ISIS DEF, which provides for defining new databases and modify existing databases definitions.
2. ISIS TL, providing miscellaneous system utility functions.
3. ISIS XCH, providing facilities for interchanging data with other systems as well as master file utility functions.

File System

All files in a data base have the standard names. Arrangement of data base file names is as under:

nnnnnn.eee
Primary file name (6 characters)
Secondary file name (3 characters)

Master File

A master file contains all the records of a given database, each records consists of a set of variable length fields. Individual records are identified by a unique number known as master file number (MFN) The MFN is automatically assigned by CDS/ ISIS when a record is created. To allow fast access to each master file record, CDS/ISIS creates another file which is a cross reference file.

File structure

The foregoing is possible because ISIS is made up of a number of files which are used together to process data. The information in a database is distributed among these physically separate but logically related files, allowing for online batch mode data entry and retrieval. This integrated system, facilitates updating of records; searching and retrieval of records using Boolean logic operators (AND, OR, NOT) and other search terms and special outputs according to customer preferred formats.

The FDT file (Field Definition Table) and the Transaction file are issued for data entry and modification. Online search is processed by the inverted files (Search index terms); the transit files (Search formulations saved for batch execution, overnight, after the online system is closed down); and the ANY file (Synonym tables). The Look-up file (Full text for coded data) is used for code look up. The Master file (Primary records) is used for all operations.

The Master file contains the full set of records stored. One of the most interesting features in ISIS is that the Master file record can not be modified from a terminal, thus reinforcing data integrity. It offers an additional degree of protection from inadvertent modification and deletions. A 'scratched' file, viz. The Transaction file, is used for inputing new data and storing modified and updated record. In this procedure, existing records from the Master file must first be copied into the Transaction file before any modification can take place. Likewise, a whole new record is initially stored in the Transaction file. It is only after the newly entered records or modified data have been certified, error-free (Usually an over night process) that they can be passed into the Master file for storage.

In summary, the system has three operational components for each database.

1. File Maintenance: Date preparation, entry, modification, deletions and updating. This is done through the entry processor.
2. Retrieval: Through the search processor.
3. Sorting and Printing: Production of catalogues, indexes, printing forms and special outputs.

Confidential or restricted data may be protected from unauthorized users through the use of passwords. A whole new record or part of record may be displayed depending on which part of the record can be made available to the user. For instance, a general user may access the bibliographic information but not the financial data in the Acquisition data base. Similarly, only the Acquisition staff is permitted to modify, add or delete data in the same data base.

Prototype Database

The ISIS database is offered as a prototype. If a system is set up for supporting the activities of an organization, it would, of course, be necessary to study the needs of the user groups. So you select the most appropriate data element for the database. Some of the fields are divided into sub-fields: for example the 'imprint' field is divided into three sub-fields; 'place of publications', 'name of publisher' and date of publication. For indexing purpose one may choose one or more or all of the sub-fields if necessary. In using CDS/ISIS, subfield delimiters are to be prefixed to the corresponding data entry.

Creating a Database

In creation of a database the following main steps are involved:

1. Setting up a Field Definition Table (FDT).

2. Preparing a default worksheet for online data entry or input (FMT).
3. Specifying the parameters for at least one display format for database (PFT).
4. Establishing a Field Select Table (FST) specifying the indexing parameters of the inverted files.
5. Specifying print out parameter.

In creating a new database, the task of establishing the Field Definition Table, the online work sheet, the default display format and the Field Select Table are to be completed one after other at one string, as the system moves automatically from one task to an other. You complete the FDT, FMT and FST for one or two fields or data elements; each of them can be updated later on.

Accessing the Database

Make sure that your PC/XT/AT is switched on

Type: CD/ISIS <Return>

Type: ISIS <Return>

Following main menu will be displayed :

Micro CDS/ISIS

L - Change dialogue language.
C - Change data base.
E - Data entry services.
S - Information retrieval services.
P - Sorting and printing services.
I - Inverted file system
D - Data base definition services.
M - Master file services
U - System utility services
A - Advance programming services.
X - Exit.

From main menu, try first to select an invalid option. *Type 'Q'*. The bell sounds, because 'Q' is not a valid option.

Type 'C'

CDS/ISIS will relay with the line prompt:

Database name:

On keying in the selected option (no return), the system may respond asking for further input, i.e., Database name, or display another menu from which another option may have to be selected, or executes the desired function.

Type 'D'

On typing 'D' the following menu will be displayed

Data Base Definition Utilities

L - Change dialogue language
C - Define a new data base
U - Modify data base definition
I - Re-Initialize master file
X - Exit

Select Option C

The data base name should not be more than six letters.

Type HSLIS <Return>

Field Definition Table (FDT) *Data base : HSLIS*

? : Tag :	*Field Name*	*: Len:*	*Type*	*:Rep:*	*Subfield/*
1.	Subject Heading	50	X	R	
2.	Author	200	X	R	
3.	Title	200	X	R	
4.	Publication	150	X		
5.	Imprint	150	X		bcde
6.	Imprint (book)	200	X		bedef
7.	Series	70	X		
8.	Type of Document	50	X		
9	Keywords	200	X		
10.	AccCiColl	100	X		bcd
11.	Microform Available	50	X		
12.	Recommended by	50	X	R	
13.	Priority	50	X		

Second component is worksheet. After completing FDT, default worksheet is to be created. The screen will look like this:

Enter Filed Tag ?

HSLIS/1

The last line of the screen contains the worksheet name and the page number. A series of various prompts are displayed for each field you want to define in the worksheet. Eight times the option will come one by one. The eight options are:

1 : Enter Field Tax
2 : Enter L/C position of the field name
3 : The name of the field is displayed on the screen. We can change it.
4 : Enter L/C position of field value.
5 : Screen Attribute
6 : Field Length
7 : Enter help messages the field
8 : Enter default

Enter the following option:

I	II	III	IV	V	VI	VII	VIII	IX	X	XI	XII	XIII
1	2	3	4	5	6	7	8	9	10	11	12	13
2/1	3/1	4/1	5/1	6/1	7/1	8/1	9/1	10/1	11/1	12/1	13/1	14/1
<CR>	<CR>	<CR>	<CR>	<CR>	<CR>	<CR>	<CR>	<CR>	<CR>	<CR>	<CR>	<CR>
/17	/17	/17	/17	/17	/17	/17	/17	/17	/17	/17	/17	/17
2	2	2	2	2	2	2	2	2	2	2	2	2
50	S1	S1	S1	S1	S1	S1	50	S1	S1	50	40	51

3 Message option
1 Ex. Indian Economic Development
2 Ex. M.C. Johar
3
4 Business India (Name of the Journal)
5 ^bYear ^cVol No. ^dIssue No ^epage No
6 ^b
7
8 Working paper/ pattern/ monograph
9 <Economic development>
10 ^bAccNo ^cClass No. ^dCollection No.
11
12 Library section
13

<CR> <CR> <CR> <CR> <CR> <CR> <CR> <CR> <CR> <CR> <CR> <CR> <CR> <CR>
<CR> <CR> <CR> <CR> <CR> <CR> <CR> <CR> <CR> <CR> <CR> <CR> <CR> <CR>

The moment FDT is completed, the system will ask Display formats specification. One or more display formats may be specified for each data base. Simple format is entered in the screen below:

Database Name: HSLIS	Format Name: HSLIS
MHL,V2(5,5)+I, I/V3(5,5)/, C6, D4, "IN:", V4, XI, D5, V5^B, XI, V5^C, XI. V5 ^E/, C6, D6, V6 ^B, XI, V6 ^C, XI, V6 ^D, XI, V6 ^E, V6 ^F/	

After completing display format we will be in the FST for inverted file where we have to define indexing techniques parameters FST (Field Select Table) for Inverted file. Let us create FST for the database "HSLIS".

Type as follows:

Database Name: HSLIS	*FST for Inverted File*	*FST Name: HSLIS*
ID	*IT*	*Format*
1	2	V1
2	0	(V2/)
3	4	V3
4	0	V4
5	1	MPL, V5
6	1	MPL, V6
9	2	V9
10	0	MPL, V10

Now use 'X' to come to main menu from where we can get data entry service by typing 'E' and to search by typing 'S'.

By typing 'E' the worksheet designed for data entry will be displayed and the data could be filled in accordingly.

The Data Entry Worksheet

Subject Heading	: <Capital Market> ....
Author	: Baliga, A ....
Title	: Zero-interest bounds V\S Convertible
Publication	: Fortune India ....
Imprint	: ^B1989 ^COct 1-15 ^ep 13-14
Imprint (book)	: ....
Series	: ....
Type of Document	: ....
Keywords	: ....
AcceCiColl	: ....
Microform available	: ....
Recommended by	: ....
Priority	: ....

By Typing 'T' we can see a list of terms by which we can search. We must type the three letter string to start the display of search terms. Screen pointer will now be pointing to the micro form available first term displayed.

Type 'S' select the search term

Or

Return to move the pointer to the next search terms. Select by typing 'S' as many search terms as are required.

Type 'D' <Return>

The Screen will now display the statistics as to the number of times selected search terms in the data base.

To formulate a new search, type Return.

Or

To view retrieved records : 'D'

Type return to see more retrieval records.

To save the search results press 'P' in the search and data entry menu

For getting a print of the data saved, call print and sort programme by typing '(P)' in the main menu.

Now to produce the printed output:

- Call ISIS program
- Select C to select data base
- Select P from the main menu

Print and sort programme

L - Change dialogue language
S - Print with your specification
P - Print with standard specification
X - Exit

- A sub-menu is displayed; select 'P'
- A system worksheet is displayed.

CDS/ISIS displays the following system worksheet

Data base name: SLIS. MFN limits 1/20 .... save file name .... First Title. Sample Listing ....
Second Title. (HSLIS) ....
Third Title ....
Print Format.@ HSLIS ....

Line width	50	Number of Columns	1	Column	50
Lines/Page	60	First page n	1	EDC tolerance	3
Data indention	0	Sort ?	Y	Sort worksheet name print file-name lpt.	1
Edit: Replace		Last page			

Print file assume that printer is attached. For sorting the data in a particular format type 'Y' in format 'Sort'. CDS/ISIS will ask you to define the sorting requirements through the following system worksheet:

Number of Heading 2 Stopword file name ....
Heading formet .... MHL, " " # Vo1. (10,10)/ " "# Vo2. (5,5)/...

Length of first sort key. 50 .... Single (0) Multiple (1) 1 .... FST for first sort key. 1 2 MPU, (VI/) ....

Length of second sort key..200 Single (D) Multiple (1) 1
FST for second sort key..2 2MPU, V9/) ....

Length of third sort key..... Single (0) Multiple (1) 0
FST for second sort key ....

Length of fourth sort key...........Single (0) Multiple (1) 0
FST for second sort key ....

Edit: Replace Last page

To get sorted output as per the requirement, this worksheet is filled by putting length of the field and serial number and indexing techniques actually used in FDT and FST.

Limitations of CDS/ISIS

Micro CDS/ ISIS is still a developing software which requires to be enriched with many facilities. With brief experience with the software, it is suggested that the following facilities be incorpo rated in the software:

1 Renumbering the HIT file.
2 Perform simple arithmetic functions.

3 Store the search expression as a file.
4 'Any term' to 'Any term' facility in 'Any file'.
5 Provision for exchange of data from data bases of other DBMS software.
6 Print different fields in different letter qualities.

Conclusion

The basic idea in the use of computer technology in libraries is to free librarians and information officers from routine jobs, which can be automated. More importantly a computer retrieval system, if implemented, can serve user needs better than manual library help can hope to do. Library computerization will result in better utilization of the library facilities. Computerization is of utmost importance at the present juncture. As far as software is concerned, the interactive, menu driven and user friendly CDS/ISIS software package provides to the users, an efficient, effective storage and retrieval system. Creating a data base using CDS/ISIS will not only save time and money, but also provide an efficient and effective way for searching and retrieving records, thus meeting users specific information need from varied information sources pin-pointedly, expeditiously and exhaustively.

REFERENCES

1. Ambia, Golam. Application of computers in different areas of university libraries. In Library and Information technology: In Pursuit of Excellence. Seminar papers, Thirty Eighth All India Conference, Utkal University, Bhubaneswar, November 21-24, 1992. C.P. Vashishth (et. al.), (eds.), Delhi Indian Library Association, pp. 73-75, 1922.
2. Arora, A.M. Computer based compilation of directory. DST Seminar on application of computers: Some developments in India. Bangalore, 10-13 July, 1978
3. CDS/ISIS general description documents and reference.
4. Chen, C.C, Ed. *Micro Computers in Libraries*. New York: Neal Schaman, p. 127, 1982
5. Devarajan, G. and Rehelam, A.V. *Library Computerisation in India*. New Delhi: Ess Ess; 1990.
6. Gupta, B.S.S. Program Package for a System for Document Finding, *Library Science* 7, 1970; Paper H.

7. Heillger, Edward M. and Henderson, Paul B. *Library Automation Experience, Methodology and Technology of the Library as an Information System*. New York: MacGrow Hill, 1971.
8. Kaul, H.K. *Library Networks - An Indian Experience*. New Delhi: Virgo Publications. p. 49, 1992
9. Kunnur, M.B. and Rajendra, A.R. Automated Libraries Some Experiences. *Herald of Library Science*, V. 33, Ni-2, Jan-April, 1994
10. Kumar, P.S.G., *Computerisation of Indian Libraries*. Delhi: B.R. Publication, pp. 211-19, 275-306, 1978.
11. Lundeen, Cerold W. and Davis, Charles, H. *Library Automation*. Annual Review of Information Science and Technology, pp. 161-86, 17 1982.
12. Parthasarthy, S. Area of library automation. Papers presented at Seminar on library automation, Madras. Madras, Library Association. p. 9-15, 1986
13. Rajasekar, T.B. Library software for library and information work. IASLIC Bulletin, 31(4), 1986.
14. Salmon, Stephen R. Library Automation. In Allen Kent, Harold Lancous and Vay E Daily, (edds.), *Encyclopaedia of Library and Information Science*, Vol. 14, pp. 338-445. New York: Marcel Dekkar, 1975.
15. Veneziano, Velma. Library automation, Data for processing and processing for data. Annual review of information science and technology, 15, pp. 109-45. 1980.

Index